Edited by Roger Smith
with a foreword by W. H. Murray

Spurbooks
In association with The Ramblers' Association (Scottish Area)

Published by
Spurbooks
(a division of Holmes McDougall Ltd.)
Allander House
137-141 Leith Walk
Edinburgh EH6 8NS

ISBN 0 7157 2094 5

CONTENTS

The poems are by *Sydney Scroggie*

List of Plates

FOREWORD

My hope is that you, the reader, will enjoy walking in Scotland as much as the authors of this book, and as much as I have too. It has brought us lifelong delight, which we would like you to share. The only way to know and fully enjoy a country is to get off the main roads on foot, and to walk far in its countryside. I welcome this book. Roger Smith has brought together several of Scotland's most far-travelled walkers; they have pooled their experience to help you — to help you discover what their land offers, to choose well at the outset from an endless variety of scene, and in exploring that to find exercise in the art of living.

W. H. MURRAY
President, Ramblers' Association
Scottish Area

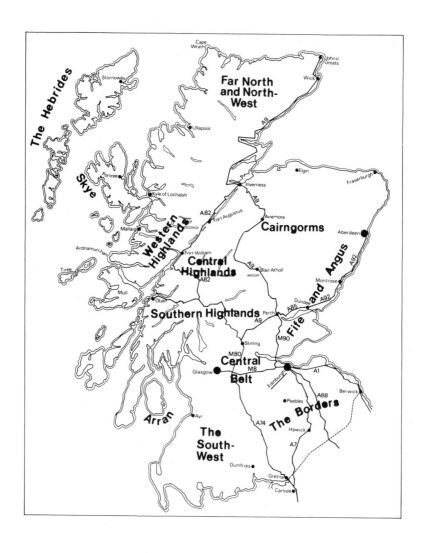

The Hebrides

Skye

Western Highlands

Ardnamurchan

Tiree

Coll

Mull

Arran

Stornoway

Portree

Kyle of Lochalsh

Mallaig

Oban

Ayr

Cape Wrath

Ullapool

Fort Augustus

A82

Fort William

Central Highlands

A82

Southern Highlands

A9

Stirling

M80

Central Belt

M8

Glasgow

Edinburgh

The South-West

Dumfries

Far North and North-West

A9

John o' Groats

Wick

Inverness

Elgin

Aviemore

Cairngorms

A9

Blair Atholl

Perth

M90

Fife

A85

Dundee

Montrose

A92

Fraserburgh

Aberdeen

Fife and Angus

A92

A1

Peebles

A68

Berwick

The Borders

Hawick

A7

A74

Gretna

Carlisle

INTRODUCTION
Roger Smith

For all its vast land area, Scotland has only ten per cent of the population of Britain, and as most of those are crowded into the Central Belt between Edinburgh, Glasgow and Stirling, it takes little imagination to realize the extent of the empty hill and loch country beyond.

One lifetime is scarcely sufficient even to scratch at the surface of what Scotland has to offer the walker. One can spend many years exploring the same range of hills, climbing them from different directions, at different seasons and in different weather conditions, and still find a different pleasure and a different satisfaction on every walk.

Our aim in producing this book has been to introduce the best of Scotland's walking country to the visitor. Each chapter has been written by an enthusiast with a deep personal knowledge of the country he describes, and in each there are walks for every level from easy to strenuous. The result is an immensely enjoyable mixture of personal styles with an underlying pride in Scotland and what she has to offer, and a genuine desire to share this with the inquiring reader. Each chapter is decorated with a poem by Syd Scroggie, the blind poet whose mountain verse has such immediate appeal.

Each chapter includes one or more sketch maps, but neither these nor the walk descriptions are intended to do more than give the reader an outline of the possibilities. You should *always* take the relevant Ordnance Survey or Bartholomew's maps. Knowing how to read a map and use a compass are vital skills and will add immeasurably to your scope and your pleasure.

There are bibliographies with the chapters and at the end of this Introduction. Many of these books are by walkers, and I think it is true to say that the more you read, the more you will know about the land you are visiting and the greater your enjoyment will be.

Please note that the walks in this book are described for *summer conditions*—winter walking in Scotland is a different matter, to be undertaken only by those with a fair level of experience.

Wherever you are in Scotland, you are not far from good walking country, and whether your taste is for coast, lochs, glens or the high tops, you will find something to interest you here.

It is not my purpose to pre-empt the contributors' own descriptions, but some background notes, both historical and practical, will serve to set the scene before the main players take over.

Hill Walking in Scotland— The Long Tradition

People have always walked long distances in Scotland. Most of the roads we take for granted nowadays were laid down less than 200 years ago. Before that, it was tracks or nothing; shepherds, drovers and lairds alike walked if they needed to travel, or at best rode hardy ponies.

The remembrance of this long tradition of foot travel persists strongly today, and is one reason perhaps why the parallel tradition of free access to the hills is so jealously guarded, and why many Scottish mountaineers feel that the waymarked path and the cairned trail are out of keeping.

After the roads came the surveyors and scientists, and among them we can number the first great hill walkers—men such as James Robertson, an Edinburgh botanist who covered many of the major hill ranges in the 1770s.

Despite the efforts of Robertson and his ilk—and of the early ordnance surveyors, no mean walkers themselves—the topography of Scotland was a mystery to most people, and up to the end of the nineteenth century the general belief was that there were at most 50 mountains over 3000 feet (914 metres). The man who put an end to that misconception was Sir Hugh Munro of Lindertis, founder member and third president of the Scottish Mountaineering Club.

In 1891 he brought out his *Tables of Heights Over 3000 Feet*, listing not 50, not 150, but nearer 300 mountains, 'some perhaps never ascended'. The list appeared in the second edition of the *Journal* of the SMC, and it has been available (and argued about) in some form ever since. The first fully revised metric version appeared in 1981.

The man gave his name to the hills he loved and listed, and the 276 3000-footers have been known as Munros ever since. He never succeeded in climbing them all himself; he left Carn Cloich Mhuillin above Deeside to the last, as it was an easy hill and the ponies could carry the champagne up, but the Inaccessible Pinnacle, a rock spire in the Skye Cuillin, defeated him several times.

The first Munroist was the Reverend A. E. Robertson in 1901. The list now numbers over 200 people, and in 1974 one of the contributors to this book, Hamish Brown, became the first person to visit all the Munro summits in a single expedition: 1639 miles (2638 km) with a total ascent of 449,000 feet (163,675 m).

Munro-bagging can be anything from a lifetime's incidental pastime to a fierce passion, but in its purest form it is a reflection of the joy of visiting unknown country and being granted the privilege of free access to magnificent hills. It is not necessary to ascend a single Munro to gain tremendous pleasure from walking in Scotland; it is, I suggest, necessary to appreciate how fortunate we are to have this splendour of 'the land of the mountain and the flood' to wander in, and to respect those few restrictions which may apply at certain times of the year and which are detailed later in this section.

All walkers are welcome in Scotland; those who respect the land, its traditions and those who gain their livelihood from it are most welcome of all.

Rights of Way and Access

The situation regarding rights of way is not the same in Scotland as in England and Wales. For most practical purposes I believe it is better, but the visiting walker should at least be aware of the differences.

A right of way in Scotland is defined as a route between 'places of public resort' for which use over a continuous period of 20 years can be proved. After that the right stays until disuse over a similar period can be shown, when the right is deemed to have lapsed. Partly because there is less purely agricultural land, there are no definitive maps showing rights of way for each county or administrative district as there are in England and Wales. The nearest to such maps is the set kept in the offices of the Scottish Rights of Way Society, a body which has kept a close eye on rights of way and defended them for well over 100 years. You are almost bound to come across their distinctive metal signposts if you walk in Scotland for any period of time. Some District Councils also keep sets of maps showing rights of way.

The society has published maps showing rights of way in some areas, and the two-volume work by D. G. Moir, *Scottish Hill Tracks* (Bartholomew) is also useful. Basically, if a clear track exists going from one place to another, it can be taken to be a right of way, though there has been some dispute as to whether mountain summits can be defined as places of public resort. On fine summer weekends, some of them certainly are!

There have been battles over classic rights of way in Scotland just as there have been elsewhere. One of the most famous was the Battle of Glen Tilt in 1847, when the Duke of Atholl tried to prevent Professor John Balfour and a party from Edinburgh using this great through route. After a considerable scandal the duke lost the court case, and this superb route from Blair Atholl remains open to this day.

You will find many walks along rights of way described here; others are easy to work out by studying the OS or Bartholomew's maps and following the line of the tracks marked on them.

Off the rights of way in open country, there is, generally speaking, little restriction as to access. As I have said, there is a great tradition of free wandering or stravaiging in Scotland and this is maintained today. In the lambing season (March-May) and while stalking is in progress (August-October) some areas may be closed to general access. Information should always be sought locally at those times, and the restrictions respected, particularly for stalking, which is a prime source of income for many Highland areas. The police and estate factors will always be able to recommend alternative areas or routes that you can take.

Quite large areas of Scotland are under the aegis of the National Trust, Nature Conservancy Council, and the Forestry Commission (e.g. much of Glen Coe, Ben Lomond, a large part of the Cairngorm massif, the Arrochar Alps, Ben Lawers). Access is again freely given, and added interest can be gained from calling at the visitor or information centres to be found at some of these places, and indeed from taking part in guided walks led by rangers who love the hills themselves and are expert in the geology, wildlife or botany of the area. Addresses for further information are given at the end of the Introduction.

I could not close this section without mention of military roads and drove roads. In the second half of the eighteenth century English ordnance surveyors, notably General Wade and his successor Caulfeild, planned and had made the first great network of roads in the Highlands—primarily to ease the task of the army in keeping the rebellious clans in order.

Many of these old roads are now hill tracks and offer splendid walking on good surfaces, and you can find them marked as 'Old Military Road' or 'General Wade's Road' on maps. The Corrieyairack

Pass from Fort Augustus to Laggan and the track across Rannoch Moor from Bridge of Orchy to Glen Coe are just two examples.

Drove roads are less often marked as such but their route can be traced with the aid of books and some are described here, a notable example being the route from Peebles to Craig Douglas in the Borders. The Glen Tilt right of way was also a drovers' route.

The Seasons and the Climate

It has often been said that we in Britain don't have a climate, only weather. In Scotland the saying is if anything even more true. I have known still December days when it was possible to bask in the sun (albeit briefly) at summit cairns, and June days when I was only too glad to get off the hills before I froze.

Winter can come early and stay late, and summer can bring fierce heat. The one thing you can never do is predict what will happen next month, next week, or even tomorrow, so you must always be prepared for change.

The best, or at least the most settled, weather is often to be found in spring: April, May and June can bring long sunny periods and magnificent walking conditions with perhaps the last traces of winter snow on the tops and the trees bursting into new life in the glens. This is a great time for exploring, for wildlife, and simply for being out of doors —and what better way to enjoy it than by walking?

In some years spring is a very relative term, there seeming hardly any transitional period between winter and summer, but May is perhaps my favourite month in Scotland, another distinct advantage being that the midge has not yet made its appearance on the scene.

The summer months from June to August are blessed with very long hours of daylight, and in the far north it hardly gets dark at all at midsummer. This gives the walker the chance to capture two magic times of the day with a very early start or a late finish; sunrises and sunsets, perhaps especially on the west coast and among the islands, are unparalleled.

Around June the midge does emerge and this little pest bites happily away at anyone within range until the autumn chill sees the back of him. He can be, to say the least, a nuisance to the walker and the camper, but he is just something to be put up with—don't let him spoil your holiday. Insect repellent will help, though it isn't infallible, and a mosquito net is a distinct advantage if you are camping.

Overall, the summer months show a rather changeable pattern, with long settled periods the exception rather than the rule, but this very changeableness brings its own rewards in sunshine after rain, hills glimpsed through shower clouds, rainbows and the feeling of being granted something special when you do get a good spell.

Autumn is a magic time. The magic is different from the magic of spring, because the days are growing shorter rather than longer, but it is a season to make the most of: crisp clear days with perhaps a dusting of snow on the mountains and all the glory of the flaming bracken and autumn colouring on the trees lower down.

When you have the two together—snowy tops and golden glens—the effect is indescribably beautiful and makes all the effort of reaching your chosen viewpoint seem as nothing. I have been privileged to be granted this a few times, and the memories will stay with me always. Even if you don't aim high, the vistas are still there, and in the glens you may hear the thrilling sound of stags roaring.

Autumn days end differently from spring ones: they close down with a suddenness and a finality that makes the homecoming to a fire and a dram all the more welcome. This is a time when most of the visitors have gone, a time ideally suited to the walker.

Right up to November there can be days when the warmth lingers, when the air is clear and the views enormous. Eventually—in recent years sooner rather than later—the last vestige of the warmer season goes and, perhaps with the ending of summer time, we are into a different type of walking altogether.

For five months the days are short and ambitions have to be tempered accordingly. This is a time for only the most experienced to attempt long treks or camping out; for most of us the rule is short days and a readiness to adapt our plans according to the weather.

Winter has its own rewards, of course, and simply facing the elements and meeting their challenge is hugely satisfying. Those establishments that do remain open are usually wise to the ways of the winter walker, and know how to deal with us, our appetites, and our wet gear!

Each season has its blessings and its drawbacks: know that and plan accordingly and you will get the most from your walking in Scotland.

Equipment and Safety

Comparison of the seasons and their delights leads us naturally to consider the equipment necessary for walking in Scotland, particularly in the hills, and the safety aspect.

I don't intend to lay down strictures or take a heavy-handed approach, but the climate in Scotland is fickle and severe conditions can be encountered at any time, especially at higher altitudes. For the reader intending only to attempt shorter day walks at a lower level, all that is needed is reliable footwear and reasonable protection against wind and rain.

Wear on your feet whatever you feel most comfortable in, accepting its limitations if necessary. In the summer months I generally go out in lightweight boots or even running shoes; a heretical approach to many, but I do it because that is the way I feel most comfortable and because I have, over the years, trained my ankles to accept the shocks of travelling over rough ground.

This approach would not do for many walkers, and if you are happy wearing proper leather walking boots, they will serve you well in Scotland. If it is your first visit and your ambitions are modest, however, don't feel you *have* to get a pair of 'pukka' boots before you come.

If you don't wear boots—or at least wellies—your feet will almost certainly get wet at some point. I find the type of super-wellies made in Scandinavia very good for mucky days—they keep your feet dry and are lighter than boots.

Socks are, if anything, more important than boots. Ill-fitting or worn socks can cause agony and ruin your holiday on the first day. Wool socks are excellent, as are the 'wick-dry' mix socks available from good outdoor shops. Make sure you bring spare pairs in case you cannot wash the ones that get dirty first!

A good walking jacket or cagoule can increase your comfort level enormously if the weather does turn against you. Naturally, the best are not cheap, but I believe the extra is well worth paying for the protection you get.

Better-quality waterproofs will also offer good wind resistance—a most important point in their favour, for still days, especially in the west, are the exception, and it is the wind more often than the rain that threatens to spoil your day.

Waterproofs often come as a set, with overtrousers to match the jacket, and if you can, do go to a good outdoor shop to make your choice. The staff will almost invariably be keen walkers or climbers themselves and will be able to offer sound advice. The magazines listed at the end of this Introduction give the names of such shops.

Remember too that the extremities—head and hands—lose heat more rapidly than other parts of the body. Even in summer I rarely go out without a woolly hat and mittens. They weigh virtually nothing and are a tremendous comfort if you start to feel chilly.

Mountain Safety

The safety aspect only really comes into consideration on higher-level excursions. If you are confining your walking to straths and glens and keep to the tracks you are most unlikely to get into serious difficulty.

So much well-meaning advice is thrown at us hill walkers in the name of safety that I sometimes wonder we go out at all! That's an exaggeration, of course—the hills are to be respected at all times, and it is as well to know the guidelines for safe walking, and what to do if things go wrong, before you venture on to the high ground.

What may seem a balmy day in the glen can turn out rather differently on the tops. Temperature decreases rapidly with height as a rule, and winds increase. Never be afraid to turn back if you don't feel happy. There's always another day, and the hills will still be there.

The item in the Mountain Code that perhaps causes most problems is the one that says 'never go alone'. Many people believe that solo wandering is the best kind, and the only way to gain real mountain experience, but for the less experienced walker it does make sense to go with a companion—perhaps someone a bit more experienced than yourself.

If you *are* going alone into the mountains, try to leave word of your route and likely time of return with someone—your family, your accommodation, or if necessary the police—so that if you are seriously overdue the alarm will be raised. This may sound rather dramatic, but it is surely better than getting into difficulties without anyone knowing where you might be.

There is a most efficient and willing mountain rescue service in Scotland, and they perform miracles every year. I hope you will never have cause to call them out, but if they are needed, simply ring 999 and ask for the police. Tell them you need the mountain rescue and give as many details as you can (you will of course be ringing on behalf of someone else) about the person in difficulty, where he or she is if you know that or where the most likely area is if you don't, and anything else that could conceivably be helpful—what colour clothes he or she is wearing and so on. By all means offer your services but don't be offended if your offer is refused—these teams know exactly what they are doing.

One of the most important aspects of safe travel in the mountains is the ability to use map and compass. Do practise this skill—it might save your life.

We hope that the possibilities outlined here will enable you to enjoy the best of walking in Scotland according to needs and experience, and to increase that experience by coming back time and again. Do it gradually and you will be more likely to do it safely.

Long-Distance Paths

Long-distance paths in Britain divide into two categories: those officially designated and grant-aided by the Countryside Commission, and those established by other bodies, who can include local authorities, clubs and individuals.

There are at least 100 such routes in England and Wales, of which only 11 are 'official'. The enthusiasm for such routes has not yet spread to Scotland, the tradition here being much more of the wanderer working out his route for himself and adapting it to circumstances and whim as he proceeds.

The Countryside Commission for Scotland (CCS) has, however, designated three long-distance paths, two of which should be open for walking by the time this book appears. A brief description of each follows.

The West Highland Way

The West Highland Way originated from an idea put forward by members of Glasgow rambling clubs in the 1960s and was adopted by the CCS some years later. The path was officially opened in October 1980 by Lord Mansfield, Secretary of State at the Scottish Office, at a ceremony at Balmaha notable mostly for the incessant rain.

The path runs from Milngavie, on the outskirts of Glasgow, to Fort William, using rights of way and old military roads. The route goes through Strathblane and along an old railway line to bypass Drymen into the Garabhan Forest. At Balmaha the first real hill, Conic Hill, is climbed. Although only 400 metres high it stands exactly on the Highland Fault line and gives impressive views of the hills to the north and west, and along Loch Lomond with its many islands.

From Balmaha the path works its way up the east side of Loch Lomond to Glen Falloch, Crianlarich and Tyndrum, to run parallel with the railway most of the way to Bridge of Orchy, with Ben Dorain looming above—a hard climb though not a difficult one if the diversion is fancied.

From Bridge of Orchy the Way uses the old military road across Rannoch Moor to Glen Coe, a splendid 13-mile (21-km) stretch with

fine views west into Corrie Ba and the Black Mount and north towards Buachaille Etive Mor and the other Glen Coe Hills.

After crossing the A82 in Glen Coe, the Way climbs from Alltnafeadh using the Devil's Staircase to cross the hills to Kinlochleven, and finally on to Fort William. The total length is about 95 miles (150 km).

Two guides are available: *The West Highland Way* by Robert Aitken, published by HMSO and including 1:50,000 OS strip maps of the route; and *A Guide to the West Highland Way* by Tom Hunter, published by Constable. A free leaflet on the Way is also available from the Countryside Commission for Scotland, Battleby House, Redgorton, Perth.

The Speyside Way

The Speyside Way is a mainly low-level walk from Spey Bay on the Moray coast to Glenmore, at the foot of the Cairngorms. The total length of 60 miles (95 km) includes about 25 miles (40 km) on old railway tracks. The path was due to be opened in summer 1981 and at the time of writing no guide was available, though again the CCS will supply a leaflet on request.

The Southern Upland Way

The third designated path is the Southern Upland Way, an ambitious 200-mile (320-km) route across the broadest part of southern Scotland from Portpatrick on the west coast (near Stranraer) to St Abb's Head in Berwickshire, passing over all the main hill ranges. Field officers are currently (summer 1981) engaged in finalizing the route on the ground, and it will be 1983-4 at least before the Way is complete. It should be a grand walk, though far from easy.

The Highland Regional Council is reported to be investigating the route of a Great Glen Way, from Fort William to Inverness, using tracks along the banks of the Caledonian Canal and through the forests of the east side of Loch Ness. Were it to be opened, it would be both a pleasant low-level walk in its own right and a logical extention of the West Highland Way for the long-distance enthusiast.

Each chapter contains descriptions of other long walks, and a few of the classic through routes using drove roads, passes and corpse roads are shown on the accompanying maps. The two Cairngorm Lairigs,

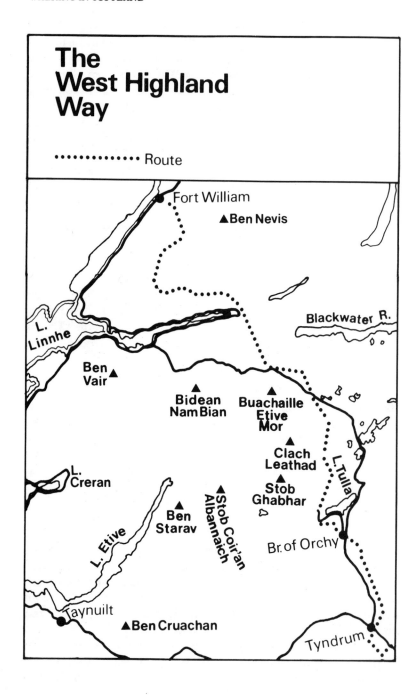

The West Highland Way

.... Route

Fort William

▲Ben Nevis

Blackwater R.

L. Linnhe

Ben Vair ▲

Bidean Nam Bian ▲

Buachaille Etive Mor ▲

Clach Leathad ▲

L. Tulla

L. Creran

Stob Ghabhar ▲

Ben Starav ▲

▲Stob Coir'an Albannaich

Br. of Orchy

L. Etive

Taynuilt

▲Ben Cruachan

Tyndrum

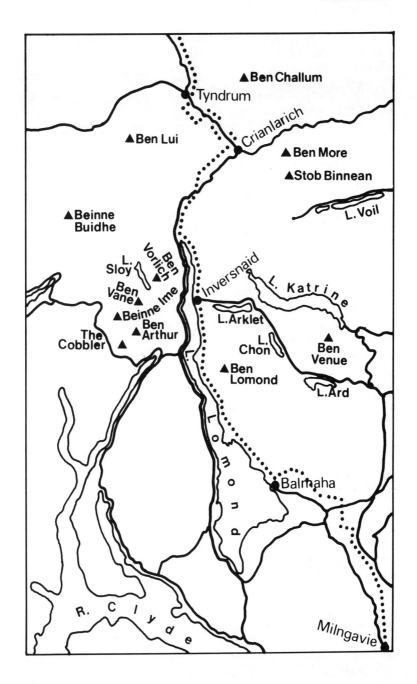

Fort Augustus to Laggan over the Corrieyairack Pass, Blair Atholl to Braemar through Glen Tilt and the upper Dee, and Jock's Road from Braemar to Glen Doll are all superb walks: study of the relevant maps will produce many others.

Maps

There are two principal sources of maps for the use of walkers in Scotland: Bartholomew's of Edinburgh, and the Ordnance Survey.

The Bartholomew's National 1:100,000 series, which has replaced the much-loved Half-Inch maps, are great for planning walks and tours of all kinds and with their tonal shading give a graphic impression of the shape of the land. Sheet numbers are given for all areas covered.

The OS 1:50,000 *Landranger* series is gradually extending its Scottish coverage; earlier 1:50,000 sheets derived from One-Inch maps are available for all areas, and these maps are ideal for the walker. Where special Tourist or Outdoor Leisure maps are available, as in Skye, Torridon, and the Cairngorms, these are detailed in the appropriate chapter.

Even the simplest walk is enlivened by carrying a map—it can show you so much about the surrounding countryside.

Measurements

Most walkers still think automatically in feet of ascent and miles of distance. To me, and to many others, there is something lacking about 914 metres—it just doesn't have the magic appeal of 3000 feet! However, we are at least partly a metricated country; the OS and Bartholomew's maps now show heights in metres, so that is the principle we have adopted throughout this book.

For those who wish to convert back, 1000 feet is 305 metres (actually a fraction under; hence 3000 feet is 914 metres, not 915). To convert metres into feet, multiplying by 3.1 will give you a near enough figure.

Horizontal distance poses more of a problem. The mile is still an officially accepted unit, and it is a lot easier for those of us past the first flush of youth to work out our map distance, and thus our likely journey time, in miles rather than in kilometres. So we have compromised and put both measurements in, hoping by so doing to avoid the wrath of both the traditionalists and the metric generation! The conversion from km to miles is achieved by multiplying by ⅝, and vice versa; a useful memory aid is that 5 miles is 8 kilometres, and 10 km is near enough 6 miles.

Transport and Accommodation

After all those figures it may come as a relief to get back to some facts. How easy is it to get around Scotland, and what types of accommodation are available?

Transport

Scotland is well supplied with public transport, except in the most remote areas, and with well-engineered roads. The roads have improved considerably in the past 20 years or so—surfaces are better, some of the worst bends and gradients have been eased, and the motorway network in Central Scotland is complete, allowing rapid passage from the south to Stirling or Perth.

Further north and west, even A-class roads may be single track with passing places, but they are generally well maintained and as long as you accept the slower pace they invite you to take, will open up the whole country to you.

For the non-motorist or those who prefer to leave their cars behind, there is still a good rail network. The best of both worlds can perhaps be obtained by travelling Motorail to Perth or Inverness before starting your driving, or by travelling by train or plane and hiring a car in Scotland for the duration of your holiday.

Rail lines penetrate to the west coast at Mallaig, Fort William and Kyle of Lochalsh—all rather special journeys well worth taking in their own right. The West Highland line has a long and proud tradition and taking the train to one of those small stations with magic names—Spean Bridge, Lochailort, Morar, Lairg—gets any walking holiday off to a great start. The journey up the east coast to Aberdeen is also very fine; that furthest north of all, to Wick, has a unique flavour.

Air travel is also well developed. There are regular flights from the south to Glasgow, Edinburgh, Aberdeen and Inverness, and a complex network within Scotland and to all the principal islands.

Most people going to the islands, however, prefer to use the more traditional means of travel, the ferry boats, and the name of Caledonian MacBrayne, the principal operators, is familiar everywhere. Ferries operate throughout the year on many routes, with extra services in the summer linking with the rail lines, so that you can travel by train to Oban or Mallaig and thence by steamer to the Hebrides. Many of the ferries—to Arran, Mull and Skye for example—take cars.

The bus network still survives in reasonably good shape, both locally and for longer distances. You can travel from Glasgow or Edinburgh to Inverness, Aberdeen or Fort William by bus, and at a very local level, the postbus has become an accepted part of the transport system.

Postbuses operate to the most unlikely places—Cape Wrath for one!—and are a friendly way to travel. A timetable is issued, and details of how to obtain it are given later in this section.

It is worth mentioning the *Travelpass* scheme, which provides you with an inclusive ticket allowing you to travel as far and as often as you like on trains, buses, postbuses and ferries within the period specified. This can obviously be a tremendous saving if you are planning a holiday using two or more centres.

The rates for 1981 were—March to May and October, for 8 days £43 and for 12 days £51; June to September, for 8 days £61 and for 12 days £74. *Travelpass* can be bought at principal stations of British Rail in Scotland, at most travel agents, or by post from Highlands and Islands Travelpass, c/o Pickfords Travel, 25 Queensgate, Inverness.

I hope this brief survey indicates that there should be no real difficulty in getting around Scotland. However, it will definitely pay to study the possibilities before coming, in order to make the most of what is on offer.

Accommodation

Much the same comment applies—you can find almost anything you need, from the five-star luxury of the Gleneagles Hotel to the basic shelter of mountain bothies. Prior study will again pay dividends.

The tradition of Scottish hospitality is, I am glad to say, very much alive, and all the Scottish hotels and guest houses that I have stayed in have really tried to look after their guests and anticipate their needs. This applies particularly in the more remote areas, where the hotels are used to caring for sportsmen whether their interest be shooting, fishing or walking.

Towns and larger villages offer a range of accommodation to suit all pockets, and the many Tourist Information Centres open through the summer operate a most useful bed-booking service; they know what is available and will do their best to find something to suit your needs.

Self-catering accommodation in cottages, chalets and caravans is also widespread, and the relevant Scottish Tourist Board publication (listed below) gives all the details you need. Information Centres can again help.

There are perhaps fewer well-equipped camp sites in Scotland than one would like, but it is not an ideal world, and if an organized site is not available, an informal pitch on a farm can often be found (and enjoyed). There is generally little restriction on wild camping except during the lambing and stalking seasons, which is only sensible.

The Scottish Youth Hostels Association has a chain of 80 hostels throughout Scotland and the islands, and for a modest membership fee you can avail yourself of their facilities. They make ideal bases for walking holidays.

The Ramblers' Association in Scotland

This book is being published in association with the Scottish Area of the Ramblers' Association, and a note about the RA and its activities is therefore in order.

The Ramblers' Association is a national body devoted to the cause of protecting the countryside and acting in the interests of walkers. In England and Wales it does this by preserving and maintaining the precious network of footpaths and bridleways open to walkers, and by campaigning against any developments in industrial or governmental areas which seem to threaten walkers' interests.

The RA in Scotland has largely the same aims but its approach is necessarily a little different. The rights of way network is generally under less threat from development than in England or Wales, and has a strong protector in the Scottish Rights of Way Society.

The Scottish Area of the RA seeks to bring walkers together by forming clubs and local groups, and hopes in the future to protect and expand local footpath networks through this medium. It is represented on amenity and countryside bodies and makes its views on environmental development known through the appropriate channels.

On a more personal level, walks are organized at weekends in various parts of the country, with experienced leaders taking groups out on both low- and high-level excursions.

The RA in Scotland is small in membership when compared with the national body, which has a membership of about 35,000 at the time of writing, but it has great ambitions and is actively seeking new members and more support.

If you are interested in joining the Ramblers' Association and you live in Scotland, write initially to the national office at 1/5 Wandsworth Road, London SW8 2LJ. They will put you in touch with the current Honorary Secretary for the Scottish Area.

Information Sources

General

Scottish Tourist Board, 23 Ravelston Terrace, Edinburgh EH4 3EU (031-332 2433). London office: 5/6 Pall Mall East, SW1 (01-930 8661/2/3).

The STB publish a wide range of extremely well-produced and helpful literature, including: *Where to Stay in Scotland* (two volumes— hotels and guest houses, and bed and breakfast); *Self-Catering Accommodation in Scotland*; *Camping and Caravan Sites in Scotland*; *Scotland: 1001 Things to See*; *Scotland for the Motorist*; *Scotland for Hillwalking*; and free pamphlets on car hire, bicycle hire, events in Scotland, tourist information centres, and many others. A publication list and order form will be sent on request.

Regional Tourist Bodies

These bodies are worth contacting in advance of your visit, as they can often supply more detailed information on a particular area:

Borders Regional Council, Tourism Department, Newtown St Boswells, Roxburghshire (083 52 3301).

Dumfries and Galloway Tourist Association, Douglas House, Newton Stewart, Kirkcudbrightshire (0671 2549).

Lothian Regional Council, Dept. of Recreation and Leisure, 40 Torphichen Street, Edinburgh EH3 8JJ (031-229 9292).

Strathclyde Regional Council, Dept. of Leisure and Recreation, Viceroy House, India Street, Glasgow (041-204 2900).

Fife Tourist Authority, Fife House, North Street, Glenrothes, Fife (0592 75441).

Central Regional Council, Tourism Department, Viewforth, Stirling (0786 3111).

Tayside Regional Council, Dept. of Recreation and Tourism, Tayside House, 26/28 Crichton Street, Dundee DD1 3RD (0382 23281).

Grampian Regional Council, Tourism Department, Woodmill House, Ashgrove Road West, Aberdeen AB9 2LU (0224 682222).

Highlands and Islands Development Board, Bridge House, 27 Bank Street, Inverness IV1 1QR (0463 34171).

Transport Enquiries

British Airways, 85 Buchanan Street, Glasgow G1 3HQ (041-332 9666).

British Caledonian Airways, 127 Buchanan Street, Glasgow G1 2JA (041-332 1681).

Loganair, St Andrews Drive, Glasgow Airport, Abbotsinch, Glasgow (041-889 3181).

British Rail, Buchanan House, 58 Port Dundas Road, Glasgow G4 0HG (041-221 3223)—or any main line station.

Scottish Omnibuses, Bus Station, St Andrew Square, Edinburgh (031-556 8231)—or through branches of the National Bus Company nationwide.

Scottish Postal Board, Operations Division (Postbuses), West Port House, 102 West Port, Edinburgh EH3 9HS—for the postbus timetable.

Getting Around the Highlands and Islands, published and updated annually by the Highlands and Islands Development Board (address above) is invaluable; it lists all routes by rail, sea, air and bus and is a great aid and companion to the traveller in the north and west.

Ferries

Caledonian MacBrayne, The Pier, Gourock, Renfrewshire PA19 1QP (0475 33755).

Western Ferries, Kennacraig, West Loch Tarbert, Argyll PA29 6XS (088 073 271/2).

P & O Ferries, Jamieson's Quay, Aberdeen (0224 572615) for services to the Orkney and Shetland Isles.

Countryside Bodies

Countryside Commission for Scotland, Battleby House, Redgorton, Perth (0738 27921). The Commission publishes a number of books and leaflets on Scotland's countryside, long-distance walking routes, etc. Publication list on request.

Forestry Commission, 231 Corstorphine Road, Edinburgh EH12 7AT
(031-334 0303). The Commission's Information Branch have produced a splendid free leaflet, 'See Your Forests—Scotland', which
shows all facilities available at their forests in Scotland, including
camp sites, picnic areas, and many miles of forest trails freely open to
the walker.

National Trust for Scotland, 5 Charlotte Square, Edinburgh 2 (031-226
5922). Literature available on the Trust's visitor centres, guided
walks, houses open to the public, etc.

Nature Conservancy Council, 12 Hope Terrace, Edinburgh 3.
Literature available on nature reserves open to the public.

Royal Society for the Protection of Birds, 17 Regent Terrace, Edinburgh 3. Literature on reserves and birdwatching in Scotland.

Scottish Rights of Way Society Ltd, 28 Rutland Square, Edinburgh
EH1 2BW. The Society was established as far back as 1845, and as its
title indicates, is set up to defend and preserve pedestrian rights of
way throughout Scotland. Advice is given to local authorities,
societies and individuals when difficulties are experienced in
resolving disputes, and inquiries regarding membership will be
welcomed.

Scottish Youth Hostels Association, 7 Glebe Crescent, Stirling (0786
2821). The SYHA maintains a network of over 80 hostels in Scotland, and celebrated its golden jubilee in 1981. Activity holidays are
run from a number of hostels—details on request.

Mountain Bothies Association, Tigh Beag, Macleod Homes, North
Connel, Oban, Argyll. The MBA works to restore and maintain
mountain shelters, members' own efforts playing a large part in this
vital work.

The Scottish Countryside Activities Council is an 'umbrella' body
representing the interests of about 30 voluntary bodies and organ-
isations. Policies formulated in discussion are pursued with the
relevant statutory bodies or authorities.

Holidays and Courses

A number of organizations and centres organize hill-walking holidays,
and courses in hillcraft are also available.

Scottish Sports Council, 1 St Colme Street, Edinburgh EH3 6AA—free
leaflet on courses at Glenmore Lodge outdoor centre in the
Cairngorms, including summer and winter hill-walking, rock and ice
climbing, skiing, etc.

Scottish Tourist Board (address above) publishes a free booklet entitled *Adventure and Special Interest Holidays in Scotland,* which lists walking holidays, field centres, etc.

Magazines

Three monthly magazines published by Holmes McDougall Ltd regularly carry articles on walking in Scotland: *The Great Outdoors* (for the general walker), *Climber and Rambler* (for the mountaineer), and *Scottish Field* (high-quality general outdoor/leisure magazine). All three can be obtained from newsagents or by subscription from 12 York Street, Glasgow G2 8LG.

Gaelic Names

Many of Scotland's mountains—and castles, villages and other sites—have very beautiful, descriptive and evocative Gaelic names. Gaelic is a difficult language to get to grips with, but the effort is worth making, at least to learn some of the basic root words, so that you know why there are so many Ben Mores about!

Many of the mountain names are given in the text of the book with their Gaelic name alongside, and the brief key listed here will help you to decipher others. I hope you will feel it worth doing—is it not much nicer, for instance, to be ascending The Butter Mountain rather than simply Beinn Ime?

Some Gaelic Words with generalized translations

Aber—river mouth
Abhain—river (pronounced aween)
Allt—stream (pron. alt!)
Aonach—ridge
Ard—height, promontory
Ban—white
Bealach—pass
Beg or beag—small (pron. veck)
Ben, beinn, bheinn—mountain, hill
Breac, vrackie—speckled (pron. vreck)
Cairn, carn—hill
Creag—crag, rock
Dearg—red (pron. jerack)

Druim, drum—high land
Dubh—dark or black (pron. doo)
Eilean—island (pron. ellan)
Fionne or fyne—white or shining (pron. feen)
Garbh—rough (pron. gar-v)
Inver—mouth
Knoc—knoll, hillock
Lairig—pass
Liath—grey (N.B. the mountain Liathach is pronounced Liach)
Linn or linnhe—pool
Meall or mheall—round hill (pron. mell)
Mor, more or mhor—big
Na, nam, an—the, of, of the
Ru or rua—point
Sgurr—peak (pron. as spelt)
Stob—peak
Strath—a broad valley
Tarbet, tarbert—isthmus, neck
Uaine—green (pron. *oo*ina)
Uamh—cave (pron. *oo*av)

Thus Carn Dearg is The Red Hill; Garbh Bheinn is The Rough Mountain; Ben More is simply The Big Hill!

The Mountain Code

1: Respect private property and keep to paths when going through estates and farmland. Avoid climbing walls or fences, and close any gates you have to open. Leave no litter.

2: In the lambing season (March-May) and the stalking season (mid-August to late October) inquire from local keepers, farmers or estate factors (or the police) before going on to the hills.

3: In forests, keep to paths, do not smoke or light fires. Avoid damaging young trees.

4: Plan your route with care, taking into account the experience and fitness of *all* members of the party, and both prevailing and likely weather conditions. Allow plenty of time.

5: Be properly equipped for the season, and take adequate food.

6: Leave a note with a responsible person of your route and likely time of return, names of the party, etc.

7: Don't be afraid to turn back if conditions deteriorate or you find your expedition overstretching you. There is always another day.

8: Be particularly careful on descents, especially if the route is unfamiliar to you. If it is easier to do so, go down by your route of ascent.

9: In the event of an accident requiring a rescue team, one person should stay with the injured walker or climber while one or two go for help. If there are only two in the party, the injured person should be left with all spare clothing and food while the other goes for help. To reach mountain rescue teams, dial 999 and ask for the police.

Bibliography

The District Guides published by the Scottish Mountaineering Trust give individual routes and are listed for each area covered, as are other books of local interest. Those books listed below may be found helpful and interesting.

Bennet, Donald: *Scottish Mountain Climbs*, Batsford

Borthwick, Alistair: *Always a Little Further*, John Smith & Son, Glasgow

Brown, Hamish M.: *Hamish's Mountain Walk*, Gollancz or Paladin paperback

Gilbert, Richard, and Wilson, Ken: *The Big Walks*, Diadem

Haldane, A. R. B.: *New Ways through the Glens*, David & Charles

Haldane, A. R. B.: *Drove Roads of Scotland*, David & Charles

MacInnes, Hamish: *West Highland Walks*, Hodder, 2 volumes

Moir, D. G.: *Scottish Hill Tracks*, Bartholomew, 2 volumes

Murray, W. H.: *Mountaineering in Scotland* and *Undiscovered Scotland*, Diadem (combined volume)

Poucher, W. A.: *The Scottish Peaks*, Constable

Poucher, W. A.: *Scotland*, Constable—a book of 101 colour photographs, many of mountain scenery

Prebble, John: *Glencoe* and *The Highland Clearances*, Penguin

Scottish Mountaineering Trust: *Munro's Tables*

Taylor, William: *The Military Roads in Scotland*, David & Charles

Wainwright, A.: *Scottish Mountain Drawings*, Westmorland Gazette (several volumes)

Weir, Tom: *The Scottish Lochs*, Constable, 2 volumes

Weir, Tom: *Tom Weir's Scotland*, Gordon Wright, Edinburgh

▌
THE BORDERS
Atholl Innes

here is a well-recorded story of an American tourist, in Edinburgh for the first time, who wanted to visit a woollen mill and was told to go down to Hawick. 'Gee, we passed there yesterday,' came the reply. Significantly, the Borders have just been a passing place.

But the region has much to offer the visitor—abbeys, salmon rivers, historic houses, and its hills . . . rolling, meandering ridges gazing down on narrow, steep-sided valleys far below.

The region stretches from the flat land of Berwickshire in the east across towards the Solway in the west. In between there are enough hills to satisfy the walker for all time, but they are apparently not the hills everyone wants.

The Border scene is of sheep rearing and forestry; the countryside is attractive and varied; its pleasing pastoral character belies its turbulent history, and in the valleys and on the hills explored by the walker love and legend still live. Every element of natural beauty is here—hills, valleys, lochs, burns—all the ingredients of untapped hill country.

Yet the fact remains that the Border hills are deserted! Not totally, of course, but in comparison to more popular areas such as the Cairngorms they are visited by few. You can expect to meet more people on Ben Lomond in one day than you would on White Coombe in a month. Paradoxically, it is this sense of loneliness that makes the Borders a mecca for the walker.

The southeast Borders, a mixture of hill land, afforestation, heathery slopes, slender ridges and narrow valleys, offer walking to suit everyone. From the less strenuous outings in the Lammermuirs to the much more difficult, but nevertheless attainable, heights of the Moffat Hills, the walker can choose a route to suit his capabilities. The sense of achievement can be accentuated by progressive promotion to the higher ranges.

Walking possibilities are extensive and wide-ranging, presenting a test of strength and character. Just because the hills are in the Lowlands does not mean that danger does not exist or that anyone can tackle them. The hills are to be respected and approached with care, and with the experience one might be tempted to reserve for the higher hills further north.

The Borders can be divided into hill ranges—the Lammermuirs, the Moorfoots, the Manor Hills, Ettrick, Moffat Hills, Cheviots, Hawick Hills—all different, all diversified in glowing colours and graceful contours.

The Lammermuirs, to the east, and with extensive views to the North Sea coast, could be classed as hills to learn on. They do not present the challenge of those mighty mountains further west, yet at the same time can be spectacular in their own way.

Without doubt the best time to explore the Lammermuirs is in August, when the heather is coming into full bloom.

Focal points for starting walks are Longformacus or Cranshaws, from where you can visit places with such enchanting names as Bermuda and Sebastopol. The land is often heather-clad, and the walking is not always easy, but it is worth the effort and circular routes can be followed in all seasons.

Moving westwards, the land falls ever so gently into the Tweed Basin, flat arable land dominated just outside Melrose by Scott's beloved Eildon Hills, the most dominant landmark of all and visible from almost every part of the Borders.

Here the walker reaches his Spaghetti Junction—either south to the Hawick Hills; west to Manor; northwest to the Moorfoots; or southwest to Megget and Moffat. Whichever route is chosen, the walker has to climb 600 metres before the sea is seen again.

Manor and Moffat Hills

Perhaps we could examine the Manor and Moffat Hills together. They are a natural continuation of each other and they are sometimes jointly known as the Tweedsmuir Hills (you may recall that the author John Buchan, who was raised in this area, took the title Lord Tweedsmuir). The main features are the high ridge running northwards from the Megget watershed along the west side of the Manor Water with a lower ridge running northeast to divide and form the valley of Glensax.

The right of way towards Megget leaves from the end of the public road at the head of the Manor Valley (OS 1:50,000 maps 72 and 73, GR

195278) and climbs gently, winding its way to the top, from where the walker must aim southeast on to Redsike Head and round the horseshoe at Water Head or Shielhope Head.

The walking is comparatively easy until you strike northwest to Notman Law and a long, but not difficult climb to Dollar Law, the third highest point in the Border hills at 817 metres. The views on a clear day stretch to Edinburgh, up the Firth of Forth to Grangemouth, and eastwards to the Berwickshire coast. From the summit a steep eastwards descent leads back to Manorhead. Four hours should be allowed for this moderate walk of about 7½ miles (12 km).

Some of the most shapely ridges are those which descend to the Upper Tweed valley—a constant invitation when seen from the road below. The hill names are magical, and the three highest—Broad Law (839 metres), Cramalt Craig (830 metres), and Dollar Law (817 metres) provide a relatively easy ridge walk, offering superb views.

Broad Law can be reached by various routes, none easier than from the Megget Stone (GR 151202), on the minor road leading to Talla Reservoir. Leaving the road, strike northwest for about 1 mile (1½ km) before going due north over Cairn Law and Porridge Cairn to Broad Law, where there is a weather station. Like many of the Border summits, Broad Law is a plateau and commands extensive views.

The walker can descend to Meggethead southeast by Wylie's Burn but this will entail a mile or so (1½ km) of road walking. If you can arrange to be picked up at Manorhead, you will be able to follow the splendid level ridge walk to Dollar Law via Cramalt Craig and Dun Law.

Those who want a long day in the hills should approach Broad Law from Hearthstane (GR 112261). Permission must be obtained in advance for this route.

From Hearthstane a track leads all the way to the summit, from where you should strike northeast and follow the route as described to Dollar Law. A spectacular ridge continues north to Long Grain Knowe and the Thief's Road to Pykestone Hill. Continue northwest on to the track at Den Knowes Head and follow this to Drumelzier. Map 72; distance 14 miles (23 km). Strenuous.

Of lesser height are the hills of Birkscairn, Drumelzier Law, Dun Rig and Glenrath Heights—interlinked, they give almost continuous ridge walking between Manor and Moffat.

The Moffat Hills are the first real hills encountered by northbound travellers from Carlisle, with Hart Fell being instantly recognizable. The continuing ridge to Swatte Fell is the southern extremity of a belt of high ground of a character unusual to Scotland. The hill tops are flat and offer excellent walking conditions mainly on grass; yet the eastern slopes are steep and broken, and there care has to be exercised in all weathers.

This is one area where the rock climber can find some satisfaction, particularly under the summit of Hart Fell. Its ascent can be made from Capplegill (GR 144098) or the Devil's Beef Tub (GR 055128). The walk described below starts at Capplegill (GR 144098) and the first part is the hardest, following as it does the long and strenuous northwest ridge over Saddle Yoke. The walker then passes along the top of the escarpment known as Raven Craig before hitting the boundary fence and striking west to Hart Fell summit. The surrounding hills form a massive plateau of tops unique in the Borders.

From Hart Fell, especially if you can be picked up at the other end, there are a number of alternatives open. You can continue westerly along the ridge over Barry Grain Rig, Spout Craig, Chalk Rig Edge, Great Hill and Annanhead Hill to the Devil's Beef Tub, a few miles north of Moffat on the A701—12 miles (20 km).

You can return to Capplegill by taking the ridge on the opposite side of Saddle Yoke, moving southeast and crossing Hart Fell Craig, Upper Coomb Craig and Swatte Fell before dropping steeply down to Capplegill. Map 78; distance 9 miles (14 km). Strenuous.

There is a challenging and invigorating ridge walk taking in White Coombe and Loch Skeen, with a starting point at Winterhopeburn in the Megget Valley (GR 185192 map 79).

The climb is steady and steep to Five Cairns Hill and Talla East Side to reach Lochcraig Head at over 730 metres. You must cross to the south side to catch a glimpse of Loch Skeen, hidden in its corrie as silent and eerie as the proverbial ghost. It is awesome even in summer, but very beautiful nonetheless.

From Lochcraig Head the walker moves southwest, dropping 60 metres before climbing to Firthybrig Head and then following the level ridge to Donald Cleuch Head and White Coombe.

Care is needed when descending, otherwise you may find yourself among some awkward rocky outcrops. Around Loch Skeen, favoured by fishermen, are many peat hags and you will have to find your own best course. It can be dangerous in misty weather, but there are still several options open.

You can descend the Tail Burn to the Grey Mare's Tail and the well-beaten path back to the valley; climb on to Watch Knowe and return via The Strypes to Muckle Knees; or just follow the burn back to

Winterhopeburn. From eight to ten hours should be allowed for the full round taking in all the tops. Map 72 or 79.

On the opposite (south) side of the valley is one of the best and most interesting ridges in the Borders, rising from the Potburn Pass beneath Bodesbeck Law and undulating, curving and switching over almost 12 miles (20 km) to the Loch of the Lowes, the drop to which from Herman Law is long and exciting. The road far below resembles a narrow ribbon with cars, apparently of Dinky Toy size, carving their way through while the hills stand sentinel above.

For the best views and a really good ridge walk, take the track leading from Potburn (GR 183088) to Capplegill, and at the foot of Bodesbeck Law strike up to the summit—a steep, sudden climb, and the hardest of the route. The ridge follows high above the road and gives superb views across the valley to White Coombe, Hart Fell, Loch Skeen and the Grey Mare's Tail while undulating its way over Bell Craig, Andrewhinney Hill, Mid Rig, Trowgrain Middle and Herman Law.

From here, diverge northwestwards over Mid Hill and Penistone Knowe before joining the track down Pikestone Rig to the Loch of the Lowes and so to St Mary's Loch, where the Tibbie Shiels Inn will be a welcome sight.

Five hours should be allowed for this 11-mile (18-km) walk, and transport will be needed to collect the walker. There is no public transport at either end.

The Moffat Hills are synonymous with steepness and deep-set valleys—Saddle Yoke, Blackhope Glen and Carrifran Glen all add much to the character of the area. The wild and impressive nature of the landscape is conducive to the walker with a camera, and is satisfying for any visitor. If I had to be selective, I would choose the ascent of Saddle Yoke, a perpetual invitation to any walker making his way along the road below.

Nor should you miss the circular route over Saddle Yoke to Hart Fell, which can be approached from the Devil's Beef Tub on the Moffat-Edinburgh road (A701).

You can leave the Tub and 4½ miles (7 km) later be on Hart Fell with only the final ascent to really stretch you. It is easy to return to Moffat, from where transport will be needed if you have left your car at the Tub.

Peebles—Dun-Rig—Hundleshope circular

This walk follows part of the old drove road from Peebles to Craig Douglas and offers splendid ridge walking with ideal underfoot conditions.

The climb from Peebles to Dun Rig is long but gradual, via the historic Gypsy Glen, Kailzie Hill, Kirkhope Law and Birkscairn Hill. There is a track for most of the way, although you will encounter heather and the last section over Stake Law can be wet going.

A rest by the trig point on Dun Rig gives time to take in the extensive views—southwest to Broad Law and Dollar Law, northwards to the Moorfoots, and with the Eildons just visible away to the east. From Dun Rig you can either descend to the valley at Glensax Lodge and

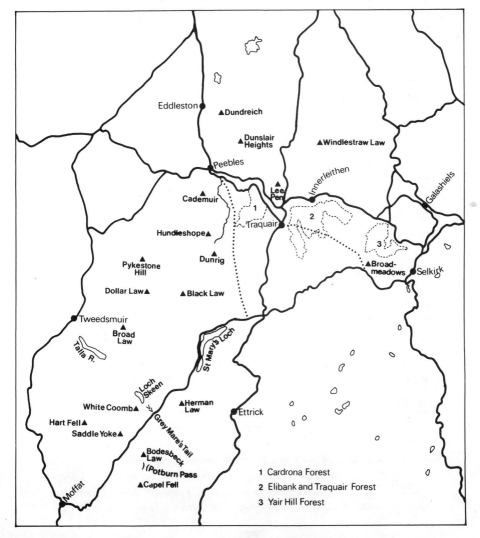

1 Cardrona Forest
2 Elibank and Traquair Forest
3 Yair Hill Forest

return along the easy track to Peebles or complete the circuit by contouring around to Glenrath Heights and following the path along the side of the hill to Hundleshope, where there is another trig point.

From Hundleshope a return to Peebles—clearly visible ahead—may be made via the east side of Preston Law and the Waddenshope Burn to join the Glensax track in the valley at Upper Newby, finishing the walk through the Haystoun Estate, home of Lt-Col Aidan Sprot, the current Lord Lieutenant of Tweedsdale and no mean walker himself.

The climbing is virtually completed by Dun Rig and this circuit is well trodden by walkers. The distance is about 11 miles (18 km).

As an alternative, instead of following the line of the fence up to Dun Rig, cross it at Birkscairn Hill and continue on the right of way to Craig Douglas in the Yarrow Valley. The path is somewhat obscure until it is picked up again over Whiteknowe Head for the descent to the Douglas Burn. This walk of about 14 miles (23 km) is popular in the reverse direction, and there is a Courier bus which runs daily from Peebles to the Gordon Arms Hotel (check times in Peebles). Map 73.

Ettrick Hills

If the walker could leap across the valley from Moffat he would be on the Ettrick Hills, which lie in a horseshoe formation round the head of Ettrick Water. Ettrick Pen, the highest point at 692 metres, lies on the east side of Ettrick Water, and despite its height has grassy slopes on all sides. The hills on the opposite shore are similar in character, but form much steeper slopes on their western sides.

Hills at the head of Ettrick form an impressive backdrop to the long, winding valley, from where the river begins its course to join the Tweed beyond Selkirk.

At the end of the valley road is Potburn, a lonely farm outpost from where the walker can approach the Ettrick horseshoe. Forestry has made its mark here as it has in other parts of the Borders but access to the head of the Ettrick basin is readily attainable. From there you can head in any direction, and if time allows can go off at a tangent to the trig point at Loch Fell. The hills are much gentler than those north of Moffat, and long, grassy ridges make for pleasant walking.

The Ettrick valley is steeped in history, snuggled as it is between Eskdale and Moffatdale, swallowed up in hill country that offers much easier walking than might be expected looking up from below. Ettrick

Pen, Loch Fell and Bodesbeck form the centre of no fewer than nine hills and six tops, all over 600 metres.

There is an easy walk from the Gordon Arms Hotel to Tushielaw. Starting from the hotel (GR 308249), follow the Ettrick road for a mile (1½ km) and beyond the Eldinhope Burn strike uphill, left, climbing steeply to the col south of Meg Hill. Then turn due south and after 1¼ miles (2 km) go southeast over Crosslee Rig and descend to Tushielaw. Maps 73/79; time two and a half to three hours.

From Ettrickbridge, another easy walk follows the track leading northwesterly to the old tower at Kirkhope (GR 390245). The walker should then turn north and follow the Tower Burn on to Black Knowe Head and cross the short ridge to Fauldshope Hill.

Return to Black Knowe and turn southeast past forestry plantations to Brockhill, where a swing bridge brings you back on to the road on the outskirts of the village. Turn right and follow the road back to Ettrickbridge.

The Moorfoots

Let us now return to the Tweed Valley. On its northern side are the Moorfoot Hills, five of which rise above 600 metres. These hills, between Leithen Water and the Tweed, form a narrow and winding ridge and offer the walker the most striking views to the north.

The dominating hill is Windlestraw Law, from where the city of Edinburgh can be seen in clear conditions, the view extending eastwards to take in North Berwick Law and the Bass Rock. Another striking hill is Lee Pen, guarding the neat mill town of Innerleithen, and the start of a perfect ridge walk to Dunslair Heights and the drop through the forest into Peebles. This walk can be continued all the way to Dundreich above Eddleston to give a long and very enjoyable day.

While Windlestraw is the highest point of the Moorfoots at 660 metres, it has only nine metres advantage over Blackhope Scar, reached either from Innerleithen or more easily from Dundreich.

The Moorfoots do not give the same terrain underfoot as can be found on the hills above Peebles. For example, the ridge walk from Thornielee to the top of Windlestraw is undulating, with peat hags, and it will be necessary to allow more time in wet conditions. To reach Windlestraw this way is a long and eventful journey compared with the easier approach from Glentress on the Peebles side, but the end justifies the means with views to match the best in the Borders.

Traquair to Yarrowford

Our next walk is an ideal introduction to hill walking. It follows another old drove road from Traquair to Yarrowford over Minchmoor. Start from the phone box in the village of Traquair, a mile (1½ km) or so south of Innerleithen. There is a long, steady climb through the forest and past the ancient Cheese Well (where you must stop to leave something for the fairies) on to the side of Minchmoor. The walker wishing to bag the trig point will have to climb a few extra feet, as the route bypasses the summit.

The track is easily followed to Hare Law, from where the traditional Minchmoor route goes southeast down a well-defined ridge to Yarrowford—distance 7 miles (11 km)—but a more popular variation is to keep on the drove road to Brown Knowe, from where you can see the striking triple cairn of the Three Brethren away ahead of you. You are just about in the centre of the Borders, and on reaching the Three Brethren can descend either to Selkirk (via the Long Philip Burn, a recommended route) or to Yair. The latter involves a turn-off left and a drop through extensive forestry, where it is easy to lose your bearings unless you know the way. Distance about 11 miles (17 km). Map 73.

On 2 May 1931 a walk over Minchmoor preceded the opening of the first SYHA youth hostel in Scotland, at Broadmeadows. This walk was repeated in May 1981 to mark the SYHA's golden jubilee.

Thornylee to Windlestraw

Windlestraw can be reached from various points, but the best for the hill walker is Thornylee on the Peebles-Galashiels road. A short walk along the road brings you to the start of the ridge leading up to Cauld Face and continuing over Southerley Nick and Stoney Knowe to the steeper slopes of Seathope Law. The ascent, although long, is generally easy and it will take most people two and a half to three hours to reach Windlestraw.

The hill commands a fine view of the Border landscape. A trig pillar marks the summit, from where you can descend rapidly in a southeast direction over Seathope Law to Seathope to follow the winding valley to Holylee and the main road. Unfortunately you then have about 2 miles (3 km) of road walking to get back to Thornylee. Total distance is about 12 miles (19 km). Map 73.

From the Moorfoot heights the Pentland Hills are readily seen, and this small range just south of Edinburgh is well worth a visit. The walking is easy almost everywhere and the traverse from the Hillend ski slope just outside Edinburgh to Baddingsgill near West Linton makes a comfortable day walk. (See *On the Pentlands* in Chapter 3.)

The Cheviots

Without doubt, and not least because of the Pennine Way, the Cheviots are the most popular hills in the Borders—even if we do have to share them with our English friends! These hills are renowned for their challenging ridges and unbroken contours, as well as their history and Roman encampments. Where better to begin than at Kirk Yetholm, scene of so many celebrations at the end of the 250-mile (400-km) tramp from Edale in Derbyshire?

The centre of attraction is 'Muckle' Cheviot, in the eyes of many walkers an attraction in name only. It is a rare day when the lonely trig pillar is not surrounded by a sea of mud and peat hags. I much prefer to come in winter when there is a good covering of snow.

Starting points for Cheviot are legion, but one of the best is Cocklawfoot (Map 80, GR 854186). One of the attractions is the spectacular walk through the Hen Hole; you can also follow sections of the Pennine Way.

Cheviot is the dominant hill, and there is a well-trodden path direct to the Border fence in a southeasterly direction. Apart from a break in the middle, the walker will be climbing all the way, until he reaches the fence midway between Windy Gyle and King's Seat.

Leave the fence at GR 896195 and head northwest for Cheviot (now on Map 74) and its trig pillar at 816 metres. From Cheviot, descend steeply in a westerly direction into the Hen Hole before dropping over Auchope Rig and down to Cocklawfoot.

This walk of about 14 miles (22 km) can take up to eight hours, though fit walkers will cover the ground more rapidly. The Cheviots are wild country where the weather can change more rapidly than in other parts of the Borders.

The Border fence stretches from Carter Bar on the A68 to Kirk Yetholm, and even to walk sections of it is very rewarding. Underfoot conditions, particularly in wet weather, can again be exasperating, but there are many fine walks away from the main ridge.

The Pennine Way offers easy access to the Border fence, and so many routes present themselves that for the first-time walker the choice seems endless. One must is the Hen Hole, a narrow gorge with its burn charging over rocky beds to create numerous waterfalls. Its beauty is breathtaking, and the winding burnside track is the ideal way to explore this famed route. Here peace and solitude reign supreme, crowning all that is best in the Borders.

Today much of the Cheviot range, once bare-backed, is mantled with trees, and the Kielder complex is the largest man-made forest in Europe. The trees do not really spoil the walker's enjoyment; a more serious threat is the possibility of test boring for nuclear waste dumping, under discussion at the time of writing. Let us hope these hills are not scarred with unsightly gravel roads and drilling equipment.

Walking in the Cheviot Hills gets the adrenalin going, but you should note the many steep slopes and narrow gullies on the map and take care accordingly.

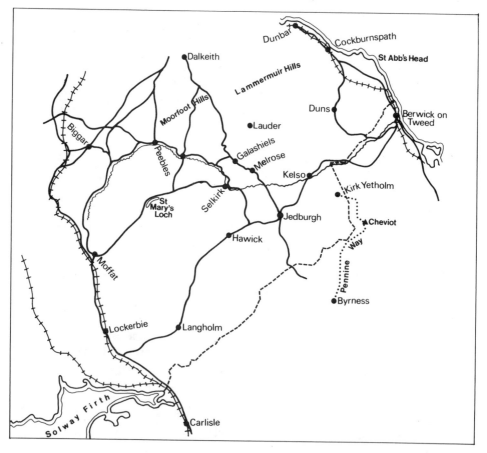

Hawick Hills

South of Hawick, following the channel of the A7 trunk road towards Carlisle, lie Teviotdale and Liddesdale. While the heights do not match those in other parts of the Borders, the enchanting scenery and the peacefulness will woo the visitor—and the local walker.

Passing through Mosspaul, the hills are so steep as to be almost unbearable, but their approaches from the hinterland are comparatively easy and bear no comparison to what the walker can see from the road.

Nowhere in the Borders, even on the Moffat Hills, will you discover steeper slopes, and for the person who stands on The Wisp there is just no knowing what lies below apart from the guidance given by the map.

Whether you are walking in the Craik area, with its heavy afforestation, or from west of the A7 at Teviothead, the ridges are clear and the conditions good. You can expect tremendous views down into Eskdale and out west towards the Solway Firth, while experiencing nothing that could be described as strenuous.

Even to the east, from Priesthaugh and Skelfhill, you can reach points over 600 metres on a ridge stretching over Cauldcleuch and Great Moor to the twin cones of The Maidens.

Narrow valleys wind through the hills, cutting off and dissecting them into sectional ridges, and you could spend a whole week puzzling over how to conquer all the tops in the Hawick Hills.

Cauldcleuch and Great Moor

One of the best walks encompasses Cauldcleuch and Great Moor, hills neglected by most walkers yet challenging and rewarding with exciting views stretching across the south of Scotland.

The starting point is Priesthaugh (Map 79, GR 467047) from where you follow the path to Priesthaugh Hill and a steep climb to Cauldcleuch. There follows a drop southeastwards and a climb over Windy Edge to Swire Knowe before swinging northeast on to Starcleuch Edge. You can then skirt around the forestry plantation to reach Great Moor. Because it stands on its own, there are no interruptions to the views to the east and west.

The strenuous part of the walk is now over, and heading northeast towards the Maiden Paps makes the circle almost complete. It can be rounded off by crossing The Catrail to The Pike and the track leading back to Dod Farm. A road walk of ½ mile (1 km) completes a full day of around 12 miles (20 km). The terrain is often uncertain and plenty of time should be allowed.

Short Walks

The Borders can also offer short hill walks which are ample compensation for the person unable or unwilling to achieve higher targets. The Eildons, Meigle Hill, Ruberslaw, Black Hill, all between 305 and 460 metres, provide pleasant and interesting half-day excursions.

One such walk leaves from the Tushielaw Inn (Map 79, GR 303178) and ascends steeply on to Tushielaw Hill before crossing the ridge northwestwards to Coom Law and Dead Side. A short walk would bring the enthusiast down the Captain's Road, but it is more satisfying to continue southwest via Cowan's Croft and Ramsay Knowe to Ward Law before descending to Ettrick Kirk, resting place of the poet known as the Ettrick Shepherd, James Hogg.

There are 2 miles (3 km) of road walking to complete the round, but such is the quietness of the road that it is not unpleasant; there is little traffic to spoil the fresh country air. Distance about 7 miles (11 km).

Although not attaining any great height, the Eildons are a must for any walker visiting the Borders. You can leave a car at the old railway station in Melrose and walk southwest up the Bowden road for a short distance before following the track marked Eildon Walk.

This brings you on to the foothills, and now the choice is wide open, but those wishing to cover all three tops should turn east and ascend North Eildon. A quick descent and equally sharp ascent bring you on to the Middle Eildon, where as well as a trig pillar there is an indicator board depicting the hills stretching into the distance.

A short, sharp descent on scree takes you into the Hollow and a path can just be discerned through the heather on to the third top. The round of all three makes a perfect afternoon or summer evening walk.

Access

In the Borders the walker's appetite is whetted by the variety—diversification of routes, of colour, of climbs and distances. Nature can transform the land—the barrenness of a wintry January; the eternal life of spring; the summer heats and haze; and the autumn tints, all unfolding to reveal a magical wonderland of opportunity. Time can stand still—so too should the walker, and reflect.

Access to open land is normally readily given. There are numerous rights of way, but in traversing open land the walker is always advised to contact the local farmer or landowner, if possible in advance. In most cases there will be no objection, but if walking in a group then please ask first. The question you should be asking yourself is 'Would I like someone walking through my back garden?'

A quick telephone call or a personal visit can ease many fears from the owner's or farmer's point of view and so erase potential problems. Of course, there are times when it is better to stick to recommended routes and rights of way—notably in lambing time (April-May) and when there may be stalking (mid-August to October). Local people will be glad to give advice.

Contact with local farmers and landowners earns walkers their respect. Remember that sheep farming is a major industry here, and the people are making their living from the land you will be crossing. In lambing time dogs must not be taken on the hills, even on leads. Gates must be closed and the Country Code observed to the letter. These points are particularly important for groups.

Despite these words of warning, all walkers are very welcome to the Borders, a beautiful area well worth spending time in. There is plenty of accommodation of all types, and tourist information centres, to be found in all major towns, will be glad to help.

Maps

The area is covered by OS 1:50,000 sheets 72, 73, 74, 75, 79 and 80, and Bartholomew's 1:100,000 sheets 41 and 46.

Bibliography

Andrew, K. M., and Thrippleton, A. A., *The Southern Uplands*, SMC District Guide, West Col Productions

Tranter, Nigel, *Portrait of the Border Country*, Hale

Sonnet

We are the kind that climb, and climbing know
What are the words the wastes have always sung;
There where the first, bright freshets twinkling flow
And, corrie-cradled, hinds bring forth their young.
High as the cloud-piled crags we upwards go,
Where in the balloch bare, frost-split, moss-hung,
Embed the ribs of dark and crusted snow
Cold boulders grey by tilting Titans flung.
Our summit looms; with deep-sunk, wrinkled eyes
He stares out Time, and we his subjects see
All ages imaged in each instant there.
As in the cloudburst night the lightning's glare
Finds for a flash that wind-wrenched rowan-tree
And, thunder crashing, truth triumphant cries.

2
THE SOUTHWEST
Ken Andrew

This region has something of the three main geographical zones of Scotland combined into one territory. It contains the highest and wildest countryside of the Southern Uplands; in Arran it has peaks, mountain ridges and seascapes which compare with the grandest scenery in the Highlands; and in Ayrshire, Wigtownshire and elsewhere it has farmlands and plains more in keeping with the lowlands of Central Scotland than with the Uplands. Arran is dealt with at the end of the chapter. First we shall concentrate on the mainland.

Mainland southwest Scotland comprises the old counties of Dumfries, Kirkcudbright, Wigtown and Ayr. The first three are now grouped into the local authority region of Dumfries and Galloway, while Ayrshire is part of Strathclyde. In the past, the shires of Wigtown and Kirkcudbright, with south Ayrshire and west Dumfriesshire, were known as Galloway, and this term is still used for that area by many people.

The roughest and least developed ground of the region lies along the chains of hills and ridges of the Southern Uplands. There, consequently, will be found the best walking routes and the most unspoiled countryside.

The boundaries of the southwest tended to be set historically on the highest, wildest horizons, which held little climatic comfort or economic value for man. They often followed the high ridges, which are today landmarked in many places with the remains or abiding monuments of dry stone dykes or wire fences. These can make excellent aids to route-finding in misty weather.

Around the coast and stretching well inland, there are large areas of lower ground which have been used for sheep, dairy and arable farming, and for extensive forestry plantations. The forests stretch to the 700 metres contour. The spread of farming throughout the region has given it an intricate network of field boundaries and minor roads. Many of these roads offer pleasant walking conditions in varied rural landscapes, but they limit the chances of walkers finding any important or lengthy footpaths in those areas which have not been made up for motorized transport. Generally, the further inland you travel the wilder it becomes as the roads and farms are left behind.

The roughness of the Uplands is a stunning revelation to many walkers deluded by their exploits among higher hills. Mere height is no criterion for judging the rigours of a walk. Some comparatively low areas in the southwest can offer walking conditions to match the toughest in Scotland. This is particularly so around areas of granite, where long coarse grasses and wiry heather abound on the exhausting crumpled landscape of exposed bedrock and glacial spoil heaps.

Moving eastwards across Dumfries and Galloway, the vegetation undergoes a gradual transformation to softer, gentler and drier tones of green and brown. Here, patches of cloudberry give warning of damp hollows and there is a noticeable scarcity of lochs with the decreased rainfall.

Paths in the southwest tend to be wet and muddy, and the ideal footwear for the region has still to be developed. Stout boots are the best compromise but feet still get wet and legs black in the prevailing conditions. I confess to preferring wellingtons for outings where steep ground, ice and deep snow are not expected. I have also adopted a stick which acts as a very useful third leg for levering myself out of bogs.

Adders are common and may cause alarm to some people. While they are probably widely distributed around Scotland and are reputed to be numerous in Arran, I have never seen one outside Galloway in all my wanderings. Sightings of them at Carsphairn, Rockcliffe, Glenapp (twice), and on numerous occasions between Glen Trool and Loch Doon suggest that this could be a favoured region for them.

While it may be wise to keep your fingers out of the undergrowth, adders do no harm if left alone, and invariably glide off for cover at the first vibration of advancing feet. Insects are much more of a nuisance and can bring misery to the finest camp sites and nights in the open. Repellents are useful (some would say essential) between May and September.

Many of the best walks in the southwest are hill walks and inexperienced walkers are advised to seek detailed directions for these from the bibliography at the end of the chapter. Along the border between Strathclyde and Dumfries and Galloway stretch several extensive ranges—the Galloway Hills, the hills around Glen Afton, and the

Lowthers. The eastern boundary of Dumfries and Galloway marches with that of the Borders Region over the high summits of the Moffat and Ettrick hills. All these areas possess excellent walking country with numerous circular routes possible using the various ridges—for those able to read a map.

The valley of the Moffat Water, northeast of Moffat, has high ridges rising steeply from the road along the valley floor. A lateral valley containing the Blackhope Burn is worth a visit from Capplegill (OS Map 78, GR 145099) for its views of Hart Fell and its coombs, and the twin-peaked Saddle Yoke. They can be combined in a round of the valley. On the other side of the road at Shortwoodend (OS Map 78 or 79, GR 137079) a track leads up the Selcoth Burn and round Capel Fell on a good through route to the Ettrick Water. This path takes on the character of a Highland route south of Capel Fell, crossing a steep scree slope high above an intimidating drop to a rocky gorge—quite

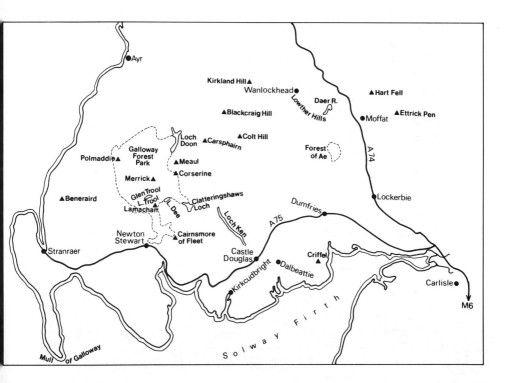

uncharacteristic of the Southern Uplands. The walk is worthwhile just to see this feature even if the return is by the same route.

Further along the A708 the fine waterfall known as the Grey Mare's Tail dashes down to the Moffat Water from Loch Skeen. Both features are worth seeing but great care is required on the very steep slopes above the gorge as a number of people have slipped to their deaths from the vicinity of the path. The waterfall can be seen from the road and a large car park has been constructed beside the stream where the low and high paths diverge.

The Lowthers offer good ridge walks and a number of through routes north and south of the A702 Carronbridge to Elvanfoot road. The most celebrated route is the Enterkin Pass south of Wanlockhead. The Well Path from Durisdeer to the A702 at GR 926085 passes between Well Hill and Durisdeer Hill on the Roman Road into Clydesdale; a well-preserved fortlet once guarded the pass on the south side. Southeast of Durisdeer a path up Glenaggart leads through to Ae Village with variations offering circular returns around Bellybought Hill. From Mitchellslacks on the Thornhill-Ae Village road, a longer walk of 7 miles (11 km) crosses the Lowther range to the Daer Valley. The ascent from the south is fairly stiff to the col at 500 metres between Gana Hill and Earncraig Hill but brings a reward as Clydesdale opens out to the north across the Daer Reservoir. The path descends by the Daer Water, which can make a strong claim to be the source of the River Clyde.

A number of tracks lead north and west from Wanlockhead towards the Snar Valley, the Crawick Water and Sanquhar. Long valleys south and west of Kirkconnel and Sanquhar and northwest of Thornhill provide through routes to Glen Afton and the Ken Valley near Carsphairn.

Galloway Forest Park

The Galloway Forest Park undoubtedly holds the most adventurous walking opportunities in this region. The triangle of country between Loch Doon, Loch Trool and Clatteringshaws Loch contains the most scenic and rugged of the granitic intrusions in the southwest. The scenes of wild isolation are enhanced by the surrounding higher ranges of metamorphic rock. The four ranges of hills dominated by the Merrick, Mullwharchar, Corserine and Lamachan hills offer numerous hill walks, through routes across the passes or along the ridges, or shorter scenic outings up the burns or forest roads among the foothills. The park extends south of the Newton Stewart to New Galloway road (A712) taking in the granite hill mass of Cairnsmore of Fleet with its satellites grouped around lonely Loch Grannoch. Here again there are many excursions possible, from the short and easy to the long and arduous. The ascent of the Cairnsmore is the most popular expedition. It is an easy walk by a good path from the Cairnsmore estate near Palnure on the A75.

The Dungeon Range in the centre of the Galloway Forest Park is the finest expedition on the mainland of the southwest, but is only for fit and experienced walkers. The range has been scalped and chiselled by the ice sheets of former ages and remains in fairly pristine condition despite the encroaching forests. Bare rocky summits, erratic boulders, morainic mounds and depressions, coarse heather and knee-high grasses make up a confusing wilderness stretching from Hoodens Hill over Mullwharchar, Dungeon Hill and Craignaw to Craiglee of Dee. Plans for research drilling on Hoodens Hill in connection with a nuclear waste disposal could have a drastic effect on the area's charms.

The traverse of the whole range is a great expedition but misses out many worthwhile corners—some at fairly low altitudes. Each hill and loch is worth its own expedition although walkers will mostly have to make their own paths.

Access to the range can be had from the public roads to the foot of Loch Doon, into Glen Trool and around the west side of Clatteringshaws Loch. These roads are also good ways on to the higher ranges to the east, south and west—the latter containing the highest ground in the Southern Uplands. These three ranges are smoother than the Dungeon but offer expeditions to suit all tastes, up to all-day traverses of the Merrick and Corserine ranges.

Walkers can move quickly once on the ridges but access to the high ground can be tedious because of the large forests and dense undergrowth. Ascents of the Merrick range or Awful Hand—so called after its five finger-like ridges—can be made from the hill road between Bargrennan and Straiton. The Kells Range, with Corserine as its central summit, can be tackled from the A713 and A762 Dalmellington to New Galloway roads and the side glens off these. Forest roads and firebreaks should be used from the ends of the public roads to get on to the hills in the park. It is unwise to trust to luck with short cuts or routes up burns as the forests are too vast—unless the route can be seen to be clear to the open hillside. The long ridge of the Kells stays above 550 metres for 9 miles (14 km) so that it is fairly easy to collect a number of summits on it once the initial climbing is done.

Transport is the big problem for routes in the park as there are no bus routes nearer than the A713 and A714. Walkers have to rely on their own transport unless pick-up cars can be arranged. Fortunately, numerous circular routes can be worked out and the following strategically placed bothies exist among the hills:

Shiel of Castlemaddy (GR 539901). Backhill of Bush (GR 481843). Tunskeen (GR 424905). Culsharg (GR 415821). Cross Burn Bothy (GR 392879). White Laggan (GR 467775).

Walkers are indebted to the Forestry Commission, the Mountain Bothies Association and others for the provision and maintenance of these unlocked shelters. They make possible all manner of great cross-over routes in this scenic wilderness, such as Glen Trool (or Barrhill) to Loch Doon, Carsphairn, Dalry or New Galloway; Newton Stewart to Loch Doon; New Galloway to Straiton; and many others. The possibilities are endless for competent walkers, and this area deserves to rank with the finest in Britain for its wilderness quality.

Wigtownshire

Wigtownshire is a low-lying area with relatively few trees. Its highest ground is to the north on 'The Moors' where large expanses of lonely, rolling, boggy, featureless countryside exist with very few objectives notable enough to tempt a walker. The most celebrated walking route is the right of way from New Luce to Ballantrae in Ayrshire across the side of Beneraird, passing only a contour beneath the 439 metre summit. The approaches to this route include long stretches of public roads as far as the Penwhirn Burn (GR 135696) on the New Luce side, and to the crossroads (GR 116810) on the Ballantrae side. A postbus service operates in the New Luce area.

While there is great satisfaction to be had from completing the Beneraird crossing, and the views from it to Ireland, Arran and Ailsa Craig are unusual, Wigtownshire has more to offer scenically around its coastline. The cliff tops at the Mull of Galloway (GR 155304), Fell of Carleton (GR 395374) and Burrow Head (GR 450341) are well worth visits for short walks. The latter can be combined with a visit to St Ninian's Cave (used by the fifth-century missionary, according to tradition) from a car park at Kidsdale (GR 431367), or in a longer round from the Isle of Whithorn.

Ayrshire

Ayrshire has a good coastal walk from Glen App to Ballantrae, starting at Finnarts Bay (GR 052723), with Ailsa Craig and the hills of Arran providing good interest on the horizon. Boats can be arranged for Ailsa Craig from Girvan harbour during the summer. The crossing takes just over an hour and is most economical for parties of 12 or so. The rocky granite dome of Ailsa Craig is nicknamed Paddy's Milestone because of its prominent midway position between Glasgow and Belfast—although most of the journey is done by rail or road now, save for the short sea-crossing between Stranraer and Larne.

Coast Walking

The coastline of the southwest mainland offers great scope. Many areas of coastal scenery can only be enjoyed on foot, but roads are never far away for those who like to explore in easy stages. Few recorded rights of way exist along the cliff tops and some shorelines are inaccessible or are covered by the sea permanently or at high tide. Coastal walkers should make local inquiries if in doubt concerning access or tides. The tides move in swiftly along the Solway Firth, sometimes parallel to the shore, and can easily catch out the unwary.

Forest Walks

A large number of forest walks are available in the southwest. The Forestry Commission has developed a network of walks for its visitors, and hundreds of miles of forest roads are available to walkers free from traffic. There are special forest walks at Bareagle (near Wigtown), Bennan (New Galloway), Fleet (Gatehouse), Mabie (Dumfries), Dalbeattie, Lauriston, Ae, Carrick (Straiton), Kirroughtree (Newton Stewart), and Glen Trool. Car parks, direction signs, marker posts or cairns, and in some cases booklets, are available to help users of the trails. Some of the better walks are detailed below.

Bennan Forest

Bennan Forest walks start from Stroan Loch car park (GR 649700). The two walks follow the same ground through evergreen forest but the long walk continues to the summit of Bennan Hill for a fine view along

Loch Ken. The round trip of 3 miles (5 km) and 200 metres ascent takes about two hours.

Mabie Forest

Mabie Forest is approached by the A710 from Dumfries. The walks start at GR 949712. There are four walks of 1, 2, 3 and 4 miles (1½, 3, 5 and 6½ km). A feature of this forest is its varied wildlife enjoying a variety of tree species—some of which were planted in the nineteenth century. High points on the walks look to the Solway Firth and Lake District.

Dalbeattie

The three Plantain Loch forest walks at Dalbeattie stretch for 1, 2 and 3 miles (2, 3 and 5 km). They start from a picnic place south of the town on the A710 at GR 836602.

Kirroughtree Forest

Kirroughtree Forest walk starts at GR 451646, southeast of Newton Stewart. The walk goes round Larg Hill and past the three Bruntis Lochs, a distance of over 4 miles (7 km).

In the Talnotry section of the same forest a very fine walk of 4 miles (6½ km) starts from the camp site near Murray's Monument on the A712 Newton Stewart to New Galloway road. Alexander Murray was a shepherd's son who became Professor of Oriental Languages at Edinburgh University. There is a short walk to his partially restored birthplace further east along the road. The Talnotry forest trail lies on the north side of the road and has views from above the forest, burn-side walks past spectacular waterfalls, and an enclosed glen containing the Black Loch. This walk is rather arduous and is not recommended to the unfit.

Carrick Forest

Carrick Forest has two walks starting from Stinchar Bridge (GR 396957) on the hill road between Bargrennan and Straiton. The Cornish Hill walk of 4 miles (6½ km)—or shorter if one section is left out—follows the infant River Stinchar upstream, climbs out of the forest and follows a cairned route to a grand view over Cornish Loch from the summit of the hill at 467 metres. The path then descends to the loch and follows the Water of Girvan from its outlet as it tumbles over a series of steps towards the distant sea. A short section through the forest rejoins the Stinchar again for the final part of the trail. This walk is highly recommended for its ever-changing scenery and its novel use of two rivers (which never meet). It is an easy walk of about three hours and is a very good introduction to hill walking. There are fine views from it to Loch Bradan and Loch Skelloch, and over the sea to Arran, as well as to the Galloway giant of Shalloch on Minnoch across the Cornish Loch. Ascent 150 metres.

Glen Trool

Glen Trool is the finest glen in the south of Scotland so it is not surprising that the Forestry Commission has developed a number of walks here. A short walk from Glentrool Village leads to the White Cairn—a chambered tomb. On the road into Glen Trool another walk starts from the car park at Stroan Bridge near the Black Linn of the Water of Minnoch. This 3-mile (5-km) walk is mainly through the forest or along the Minnoch.

Two walks which are well worth doing start from the Caldons camp site in Glen Trool. Jenny's Hill Walk is a circular walk of 2½ miles (4 km) with good views over Loch Trool. The longer Loch Trool forest trail is a moderately easy circuit of the loch of 5 miles (8 km) although a third of the journey can be cut if transport can be arranged for the section along the road north of the loch. The walk is superb and is well worth the effort even to those not accustomed to it. Again it has the advantage of constantly changing scenery to hold the interest.

The walk starts at the southeast corner of the camp site where the natural broadleafed woodlands lead into the state forest. Here graceful banks of larch and open stretches of mature pine contrast with dark alleys through the spruce plantations. Soon Loch Trool is seen below and the views open out to the Merrick beyond the valley of the Buchan Burn and the granite wilderness beyond the Gairland valley.

Traversing across the steep slopes of Mulldonach you will recall that in 1307, according to tradition, a band of Scots under Robert the Bruce trundled boulders down this slope to rout an English force. The path descends to the meadows at the east end of the loch, crosses the Glenhead Burn and takes the rough road west to Buchan through the natural woodlands of sessile oak. Beyond the Buchan Burn the track climbs steeply to join the public road at the Bruce's Stone, which commemorates the victory of the Scots across the loch. If transport has not been arranged, simply walk along the road back to the Caldons, or take a short cut along the loch from the gates of Glen Trool Lodge. Time three to four hours.

Transport

Kirkconnel and Barrhill are the only two railway stations which might be of direct use to walkers.

The Western SMT company operates most of the bus services on the southwest mainland.

In addition to the easier forest walks given special mention, the following walks are endorsed to give a good sample of what the area has to offer.

The Merrick (843 metres)

Every visiting walker wants to climb this hill for the same reason visitors to the Highlands want to climb Ben Nevis—it is the highest in the region. This is Scotland's highest mainland hill south of Ben Lomond, and its ascent is not difficult. It is usually climbed from the end of the public road into Glen Trool at the Bruce's Stone. The start is signposted and a good path follows the west bank of the Buchan Burn, with very fine views back across the tumbling stream. The slope eases off and a hanging valley is entered. The path leaves the burn and passes through the forest to Culsharg bothy by a very muddy route. It then strikes up the hill, crosses a forest road, and emerges from the young plantations on the open moor near a dyke which leads you up to the right to the summit of Benyellary.

The Merrick appears as a great whale-back hill across a col 65 metres lower. The dyke continues across the col and is a good guide in mist to the steep northern scree slopes of the Merrick, which can be kept on your left as you ascend in a dogleg to the cairn. Otherwise take the direct route across the slope which has no view to the north until you reach the summit. The return is by the same route for the inexperienced. Competent walkers may prefer the variation of coming along the Rig of Loch Enoch and over Buchan Hill, or down the Buchan Burn.

Map 77. Distance 8 miles (13 km). Ascent 840 m. Time four to five hours. Moderate.

Craiglee (531 metres)

This small hill is one of the best viewpoints in Galloway due to its isolated position and the eight or more lochs visible from it. It is a connoisseur's hill for the quality of its ever-changing scenery and the value offered for effort expended. The best route to it starts (as for the last) at the Bruce's Stone in Glen Trool. Descend to the bridge over the Buchan Burn and follow the road around Buchan towards Glenhead. Leave the road at the bridge over the Gairland Burn and ascend the east bank of the stream until the steep slope on your right eases and you can climb on to White Brae Top for one of the best views of Loch Trool. Now follow the Rig of the Jarkness with splendid views of the lochs to the north and the Merrick. Grassy slopes give way to granite outcrops as Craiglee is reached and an appreciation develops of how complicated this little hill really is. With its humps and lochans, stepped precipices and hidden corners, it can be a confusing place in mist, although no one with a map and compass should go seriously astray. The return can be made between the lonely lochs of Glenhead, or the Rig of the Jarkness can be retraced to the outlet of the Gairland Burn from Loch Valley. If the burn can be crossed safely, follow its west bank and take the path around Buchan Hill back to the Earl of Galloway's bridge over the Buchan Burn, or else return by the outward route.

Map 77. Distance 8 miles (13 km). Ascent 615 m. Time four to five hours. Fairly hard.

Parton to Creetown by the old railway

The walk starts at the Loch Ken Viaduct (GR 686704) on the bus route from Castle Douglas. The railway was closed in 1965 and there is no right of way across the bridge but walkers do use it. If preferred, the walk can be started further west at New Galloway station (Mossdale) on the A762 but this may raise problems for getting back since it is not a regular bus route. There are buses on Saturdays and a postbus during the week.

The track-bed of the railway is mostly intact and much of the journey is over Forestry Commission land. The scenery is splendid on the viaduct over the Dee at Stroan Loch. Then comes the desolate ruin of the halt at Loch Skerrow. Cairnsmore of Fleet and Cairnsmore of Dee lord it over the forests and there are big viaducts to enjoy over the Little and Big Waters of Fleet. We meet a road again at Gatehouse of Fleet Halt and the best of the journey is behind. A gradual descent leads to the River Cree and the Western SMT bus back to Castle Douglas and Parton (if your car is there).

Maps 77 and 83. Distance 17 miles (28 km). Ascent 260 m. Time seven hours. A hard walk.

Sandyhills Bay to Rockcliffe

A superb cliff-top walk which packs an amazing variety of scenery into a few hours. Start from the car park on the shore side of the A710 at Sandyhills (GR 891552). The Fairgirth Lane has to be crossed where it enters the bay. A footbridge was washed away here and has not yet been replaced. If the lane cannot be crossed easily, retrace your steps to the A710, walk west along it and take the first lane to the left. This leads onto higher ground where the path along the cliff top can be picked up. Bare legs are not advised here because of the whin and brambles.

The path descends to Portling, crossing several stone dykes by steps. Turn up the road at Fishers Croft to the T-junction and turn left to the sea again. The path goes off the road to the right beyond the houses and heads uphill to its highest point west of White Hill, which gives fine views. The descent to the southwest passes a monument to the schooner *Elbe* which went aground here in 1866. The route continues over Barcloy Hill to Castlehill Point and turns north along the shore to Rockcliffe. Continue past the Mote of Mark and over the hill to Kippford. Rejoin the A710 and walk back to Sandyhills or take the bus (Carruther's Bus Service).

Map 84. Distance 10 miles (16 km). Ascent 280 m. Time five hours. The walk can be shortened by leaving out Kippford. The stretch between Rockcliffe and Kippford is a good easy walk on its own.

The Enterkin Pass

This starts from Muiryhill (GR 875035), west of Durisdeer and climbs the enclosed glen of the Enterkin Burn to Wanlockhead across the col at 533 metres between East Mount Lowther and Lowther Hill. The route is famous for its associations with Bonnie Prince Charlie's army on its retreat from Derby in 1745 and with Covenanters ambushing a party of dragoons to free several of their compatriots. Wanlockhead is the highest village in Scotland and gives a high start to those doing the route southwards. It has no public transport though, so it is better to start from the south and return mainly downhill.

Map 78. Return distance 12 miles (19 km). Return ascent 585 m. Time six hours. A moderate walk.

Green Lowther (732 metres) and Lowther Hill (725 metres)

The ascent of these two highest hills of the Lowthers is an easy dry-shod walk on account of the tarred road which runs to the tele-communications stations on the summits from Wanlockhead, starting at GR 879132.

Map 78. Distance 6 miles (10 km). Ascent 400 m. Time four hours. An easy walk.

The Old Edinburgh Road

The modern road from Newton Stewart to New Galloway runs parallel to this ancient route and crosses its line east of Clatteringshaws Loch. This reservoir and forest to the east spoil the continuation of the route. To the west of the reservoir it has great character. It starts at GR 439683 near Risk, northeast of Newton Stewart, and runs uphill to become a forest road past the Loch of the Lowes. It crosses a forest walk at Talnotry, passes the Black Loch and climbs past Lilie's Loch to descend to Clatteringshaws. Walkers can continue to New Galloway by the main road, for a long roundabout bus journey back to Newton Stewart (Western SMT) or return to Newton Stewart by this road, which has no buses. There is a youth hostel at Minnigaff.

Maps 83 and 77. Distance 22 miles (35 km) returning to Newton Stewart; 18 miles (29 km) to New Galloway. Ascent 370-460 m. Time nine to eleven hours. A hard walk.

Ailsa Craig

There are two very popular walks on this island which can be reached by boat from Girvan in the summer (telephone 0465 3364/ 2631/2626/3776/2320/2760 for boatmen). The ascent to the summit at 338 metres is the first priority for most visitors. From the jetty a path passes the lighthouse and slants uphill to the ancient tower house. A short distance above this castle it comes to a pool on a burn which was the castle's water supply. The route now slants up to the right to turn a band of steep rock and then cuts back to the left to a little loch. The way to the summit is now easy.

The other popular excursion is to traverse the shoreline right round the Craig. This can only be done at low water (up to about one hour before or one hour after). Your boatman will keep you right. The only difficulty is at the southwest corner of the island at Stranny Point where the Water Cave and the foot of the cliffs for 150 feet (100 metres) are only passable at low tide. The rocks here are very slippery when uncovered.

Both walks are short and take about two to three hours. Map 76.

Arran

This magnificent island is easily reached in an hour's sailing time by Caledonian MacBrayne car ferry from Ardrossan to Brodick. There are daily services, frequent in summer and less so in winter, which allow day visits of up to 11 hours to be made—and many of Arran's greatest spectacles lie only three or four hours from the pier. Alternatively, accommodation can be found on the island at villages and hamlets around the coast or at the youth hostel at Whiting Bay.

Brodick is the largest village on the island and has hotels, guest houses, shops, post office, tourist information centre and cycle hire facilities. Buses meet the boats at Brodick pier (Arran Coaches, telephone 0770 2121). Accommodation can be difficult to find in the summer months and booking in advance is required for cars and some passenger sailings.

The island is very mountainous, rugged and picturesque north of Brodick, while to the south it is less dramatic with lower rolling hills and moors, forests and farmlands. The northeast contains the finest climbing and walking territory but the northwest also has some fairly high and shapely hill country. The majority of Arran's walkers will be found in the northeast where the hills are most convenient to the pier.

Numerous paths have been worn along or across the ridges of the higher hills in the northern half of the island, but the existence of a path should not delude inexperienced walkers into assuming that they will be safe following it. Some of the ridge walks stamped out by countless feet involve considerable hill craft. Although all the summits except A'Chir can be ascended without rock climbing, some of the ridge

traverses involve a certain amount of rock scrambling and route finding. The problems are straightforward and very enjoyable on a good day
but mist, rain, wind, frost or snow can greatly intensify the difficulties.
Hill walkers and climbers should seek detailed descriptions from the
books listed at the end of the chapter.

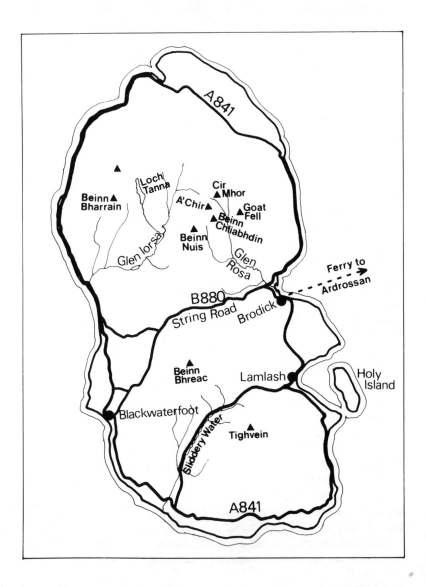

Walking Routes

A number of forest walks have been constructed on the island by the Forestry Commission. From the A841 2 miles (3 km) south of Brodick, start the Thomson Memorial Walks to Glen Cloy—4 miles (6 km)— and to Corrygills—3 miles (5 km). A 9-mile (14-km) walk across the island starts to the southwest of Lamlash from near the start of the hill road called The Ross and goes to Kilmory. From Whiting Bay a path of 1½ miles (2 km) leads up Glenashdale to an impressive waterfall. A branch from this path leads steeply uphill to the Giants' Graves—a mid-Neolithic chambered cairn. On the west side of the island a route of 4 miles (6 km) leads from Bridgend Cemetery near Shiskine on the B880 by the Clauchan Glen and south through the hill pass east of Tormusk to Glenree on The Ross. An easy walk of 1 mile (2 km) leads from North Sannox to the Fallen Rocks along the coast.

Those who prefer to organize their own walks can carry on along the coast from the Fallen Rocks to Laggan and take the track over the hill to Lochranza, 7 miles (11 km) from North Sannox. From Blackwaterfoot there is a very pleasant walk of 2 miles (3 km) around the coast to the King's Cave, which is associated with Robert the Bruce.

Goat Fell (874 metres)

This is the highest hill on the island and the first target for many walkers. The easiest route to it starts from the A841 at GR 012376 near Brodick Castle. A sign marks the start of the track which climbs through woodlands to emerge on the slopes of the hill on the east bank of the Cnocan Burn. The path leads into the corrie southeast of Goat Fell and up on to its east ridge. It then turns westwards up the steepening slope, zigzagging easily between the granite outcrops to the trig point on the boulder-embedded summit. The extensive view takes in Ireland, Ailsa Craig, the Galloway hills, Loch Ryan, the Ayrshire and Renfrewshire coast, the Cumbraes, Bute, Ben Lomond, Cowal, the Arrochar Alps, Loch Fyne, Ben Cruachan, and the Paps of Jura over Arran's own mighty attractions such as the Castles ridge with its tremendous cleft of the Witch's Leap, Cir Mhor, and Holy Island. The return to Brodick can be made by the south-southeast ridge to rejoin the path by the burn, but inexperienced walkers should return by the tourist path used for the ascent.

Distance, Brodick pier and back 10 miles (16 km). Ascent 900 m. Time five hours. Easy to moderate walk.

Glen Sannox to Glen Rosa

This is a very scenic route between the finest of Arran's hills. Leave the A841 at Sannox at GR 016454 for a lane running to the small cemetery. The scene opens out beyond here as the trees are left behind and the track leads past disused barytes mines at the entrance to Glen Sannox. Ahead lies the Castles ridge on the north side of the glen and the knife-edged ridge of Cioch na h-Oighe on the south side. Follow the burn up Glen Sannox and ascend to the col east of Cir Mhor at 416 metres—the lowest point on the ridge between Cir Mhor and Goat Fell. The ascent to the col is steep and rocky but the route is cairned and goes right to gain an easy gully, then left to the cairn at the col. All is downhill now by Glen Rosa, on easier slopes. If the route is done in the other direction the descent to Glen Sannox could be awkward in mist, while the ascent of Glen Rosa can seem unending. Its descent is long enough on a path which is generally very muddy. The views up the glen are very good but eventually the track turns the corner and leads out to the String road close to the A841.

Distance, Sannox to Brodick 10 miles (16 km). Ascent 416 m. Time five hours. A moderate to hard walk.

Maps

The following 1:50,000 Ordnance Survey maps cover southwest Scotland:
Sheet 69 Arran; 71 Lanark and Upper Nithsdale; 76 Girvan; 77 New Galloway and Glen Trool; 78 Nithsdale and Lowther Hills; 79 Hawick and Eskdale; 82 Stranraer and Glen Luce; 83 Kirkcudbright; 84 Dumfries. Maps are not necessary for the forest trails described.

Bibliography

Andrew, K. M. and Thrippleton, A. A., *The Southern Uplands*, SMC District Guide, West Col Productions
Hall, Tom, *Tramping in Arran*, Gall & Inglis
McBain, J., *The Merrick and the Neighbouring Hills*, Jackson & Sproat
Meek, Ronald, *Hill Walking in Arran*, Chambers
Moir, D. G., *Scottish Hill Tracks–South*, Bartholomew
Tennent, Norman, *The Islands of Scotland*, Scottish Mountaineering Trust

Walton, R. D., *Seventy Walks in Arran,* privately published
Walton, R. D., *Dumfries and Galloway Highways and Byways; Guide to 200 Walks and Climbs,* Dinwiddie, Dumfries

Conversion

A wheen of years I watched wet Summers by
Heard in crisp Autumn wild geese come again
Saw eerie Winter's dancers sweep the sky
And sniffed sharp Spring, a cold, damp butt and ben
Then rose no oil-burnt warmth to ease my lot
The wind that whistled from the grey dawn snell
As on the shoulders of some bygone Scot
Gaunt and unplaided in his old age fell.
Gone is that storm-scoured era stiff with rime
Which I from old acquaintance learned to thole
The bowed survivor of a harder land,
And I may yet get used to given time
Strange in their softness to my stubborn soul
Changes I half regret, half understand.

| **3** |
| **CENTRAL SCOTLAND** |
| **Bill Brodie** |

Milngavie Byways

Situated only eight miles from the centre of Glasgow, the village of Milngavie is a popular starting point for some fine walks. Outdoor types used to alight from tramcars at 'Mulguy' terminus, assemble into groups and tramp towards the Blane Valley—some to traverse the Campsie Fells, some to detour west to the Kilpatricks, and other hardy types to follow paths through Strathendrick.

The routes they trod are among the favourite rights of way in the west of Scotland. This ramble follows some of them. With the demise of the trams, the meeting place is now Milngavie Cross, opposite the War Memorial. The village has seen its share of change. Many can still recall walking from Garscube Bridge to Milngavie, passing only farms and an occasional house. Now trim bungalows line the route and the village is almost surrounded by housing schemes. Nevertheless, there's still a rural look about it, and the planners maintain that Milngavie is to be kept 'a leafy place'.

The walk begins at the first marker on the West Highland Way. You will find it tucked behind a shop frontage above the river. Go down the steps to follow the Allander Way, which traverses an old railway siding and the landscaped site of a former paper mill.

Passing the leisure centre, the path skirts the pond to bypass the footbridge. Follow the Allander Water and cross a stone bridge to continue upstream. The right of way enters the golf course at the car park, then follows the road. Where the road swings left, the path leads over a bank and descends obliquely towards the river, which it follows to Allander Bridge. A stile is at the far side near Craigallion Avenue, with its lodge house. The disused part of the avenue offers a short walk back if preferred.

To continue, follow the track by Craigallion Loch, with the sharp peak of Dumgoyne in front. Over another stile, then first right by the huts and the old swimming pool to join another track descending from the ridge above the loch. Follow this track to the road at another lodge. The 'Khyber Pass', where the road was hewn through rock, is downhill.

Uphill, and from the small wood we can see Craigend Castle, one-time residence of the Yarrow family, then a tearoom for a zoo and now, alas, partly demolished. Our way over the stile near the lodge leads to Mugdock Castle, ancient seat of the Grahams. The tower dates from the fourteenth century but the fine mansion house attached to it has recently been demolished. The estate has been gifted by Sir Hugh Fraser to Central Regional Council as the basis for a country park.

The track joins Mugdock Road below Smith's Folly, the little tower on the hill. A pleasant walk can be had through the waterworks, where aqueducts from Loch Katrine fill two large reservoirs for Glasgow's water supply.

For a slightly longer and more scenic route from Carbeth, join the Blanefield Road and walk downhill to the trough informing us of the 'McAllister Improvement'. A path climbs the ridge to join the farm road at Board's Farm. The road descends along the edge of a steep escarpment commanding fine views over the Blane Valley and beyond, with the rocky knoll of Dunglass prominent ahead. Have a slide and a wish on the Gowk Stane then walk across the moor, skirting Deil's Craig Dam, to join the road at an old quarry. Keep uphill at the crossroads to pass Mugdock village. At the end of the wood, a path descends to the bus stance and the waterworks gate.

Distances: back by Craigallion Avenue 5 miles (8 km); by Mugdock Castle 8 miles (13 km); and by the Gowk Stane 10 miles (16 km).

On the Campsies

This walk traverses the southern ridge of the Campsie Fells to Dumgoyne, a moderate walk with views ranging from Tinto Tap to the Arran peaks if conditions are favourable. Take the 175 Campsie Glen bus to Haughhead, the village at Campsie Road end, or if two cars are available park one at Blanefield and take the other to the starting point.

Follow the main road west through Haughhead for about ⅓ mile (600 metres) to a driveway on the right; the road immediately beyond goes into the hills. Over the stile, then beyond the abandoned farm of

Glenside, the path climbs steeply up a bank. Pause for breath at the cairn, as most of us do, then walk up the glen to the dyke. A path leads in a westerly direction towards a shoulder of the hills, giving easier walking.

Already the view commands most of the Clyde Valley, with the peculiar rock formation of Dunglass dominating the foreground. Passing a lone wood clinging to the hillside, follow the remains of a dyke towards the Ballagan Beds, a favourite haunt of geologists. Over millions of years, the burn has worn through layer after layer of soft rock, creating a spectacular gorge containing the Spout of Ballagan, a waterfall which is impressive in spate.

Climb well above the falls to a suitable crossing place, then follow traces of a drove road to the shoulder of the hill. The alternative is to take the path down the west side of the burn to another path which enters the rock gateway of the Strathblane Whangie, a hidden place

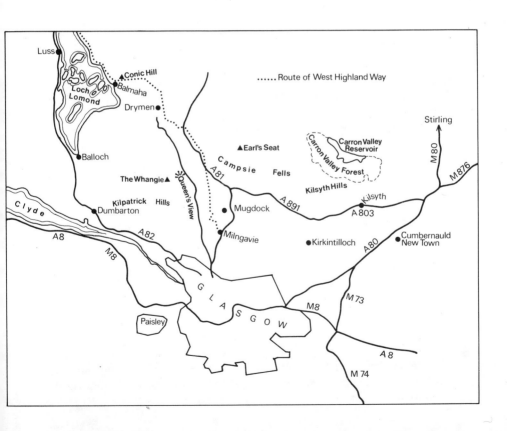

among the hills. Less well-known than the Auchineden Whangie, it is nonetheless worth a visit. The way through leads up to our original route. The drove road winds down a rocky ridge to Strathblane, but its terminus there is unclear at present due to the housing development lining the base of the hills.

Follow the shoulder to Jenny's Lum, a tiny waterfall dancing over the cliff. When the wind is in the right quarter, the fall is blown into a fine spray which from a distance resembles smoke. It is named after Jenny Brash, a local worthy who lived below the 'lum' at Netherton. A path follows the cliff edge, but take the one farther back, especially if a strong wind is blowing. We are now in the Strathblane Hills and a cairn on the flat top ahead indicates that we are on Slackdhu.

Descend to the burn between here and Dumfoyne, the twin peak of Dumgoyne. For those wishing to return earlier, a path on the west side of the burn drops steeply to the Pipe Track which follows the course of Glasgow's water supply to Blanefield. For Dumgoyne cross the next burn and contour round the southern base of Dumfoyne, then ascend Dumgoyne from its north side. It's a short, stiff climb, but the view from the summit is rewarding.

To return, retrace your steps to the pass between the two peaks. A path follows the burn then heads southeast through woods to emerge at Cantywherry on the Pipe Track, from where it is easy to reach Blanefield.

Distances: Slackdhu 6 miles (10 km). Dumgoyne 7½ miles (12 km).

The Falls of Clyde

> Where ancient Corehouse hangs above the stream,
> And far beneath the tumbling surges gleam,
> Engulfed in crags the fretting river raves,
> Chafed into foam resound his tortured waves,
> With giddy heads we view the dreadful deep,
> And cattle snort and tremble at the steep,
> Where down at once the foaming waters pour,
> And tottering rocks repel the deafening roar.

These lines from John Wilson's poem *The Clyde* describe Cora Linn in flood—a rare sight nowadays, but the area still has much to offer the visitor.

Embracing Corehouse Nature Reserve, the two upper falls and the village of New Lanark, most of this ramble is by estate drives and woodland paths on both sides of the Clyde. The distance is only 7 miles (11 km) but there is so much to see that a full day can be spent.

This stretch of the river tumbles through a deep, rocky gorge—tumbles or trickles according to the amount of rain that has fallen in its catchment area. The Clyde is harnessed to two power stations, and the upper falls and Stonebyres Linn downstream are usually only a glint of their former glory. To see them at their best, pick a suitable day after a very wet spell or wait until an 'open day'. On two days of the year, usually in June and September, the sluice gates are opened and the water surges over the falls as before. For a family outing or a quick visit to the falls, there is a car park at Corehouse South Lodge, 1¼ miles (2 km) from Kirkfieldbank.

The walk proper begins and ends at Lanark which is served by bus and train (no trains on Sundays). From the bus station walk down the main street to the first opening on the left. Follow this road to the Spinning Mill, walk across the small park and bear right at the end. The bowling green is on the site of Lanark Castle. Mentioned in Wallace's time, it fell into disuse and now no trace remains.

Enter Castlebank Park, where the drive branching right leads to the Mansion House. The gardens opposite are worth a visit. The drive continues to the road, which deteriorates into a path down to the river. Cross the old bridge to Kirkfieldbank, then walk uphill past the lodge and gates of Corehouse. Take the left fork for a smaller road to the south entrance, which is the public and car access to the falls. From the car park the route is clearly signposted. During an open day, or if you have a permit, enter the gates at Kirkfieldbank and follow the estate drive along the high bank of the river with occasional glimpses of New Lanark through the trees.

After about 1¾ miles (3 km) of pleasant walking we arrive at the policies of the Mansion House, which are private. The nature trail sign points to the beech hedge and the ramble is worthwhile if only to stroll down this leafy avenue flanked by giant beech trees. At the far end of the banking, a small path on the left winds down to the Clyde, and a few yards before the river's edge another path will be seen going upriver. Follow this uphill and bear left at the top to Cora Linn. Even in dry weather, the gorge is quite impressive.

Continue on the public path to Cora Castle, perched on a pinnacle high above the river. This was the stronghold of the Bannatyne family. The old castle is supposed to have shaken to its foundations when the

Clyde was in spate. Our path leads to a road and a choice of ways. We usually take the track which runs along the lip of the gorge, or the estate road can be followed. Both lead eventually to the sluice gates and give views of Bonnington Linn, with Tinto Hill in the background.

Cross the sluice for the path downriver, another delightful track which follows the edge of the gorge. Keep high if in doubt about the way, and when a concrete banking is reached descend to the power station. Follow the road alongside the river. On rounding a corner we are at New Lanark. Although expected, there is still an element of surprise at finding this unusual village nestling in the gorge of the river below Lanark. It was founded in 1784 by Richard Arkwright and David Dale on land belonging to Lord Braxfield, the Jeffreys of Scotland. From 1800, New Lanark was managed by Robert Owen, Dale's son-in-law, who introduced enlightened principles to work and education. Much has been written about New Lanark and attempts are being made to renovate and occupy the houses. Leaflets are available in Caithness Row, near the post office.

To return to Lanark, either follow the road for a long, easy climb, or take the path, which is shorter but steep. Turn right at the school and the steeples of Lanark dominate the skyline above a typical meadow.

Details of open days and permits for the Nature Reserve can be obtained from the Ranger, Scottish Wildlife Trust, New Lanark.

The Bathgate Hills

The Preceptory of Torphichen and the burial cairn of Cairnpapple are just two of the historic places on the West Lothian Heritage Trail. We visit them and other interesting features during this ramble over the uplands between Linlithgow and Bathgate, an area of volcanic outcrops, rich farmland and deep woods.

Alight from the train or bus at Linlithgow Station or leave your car in the car park behind the station. Walk uphill to the banks of the Union Canal. Learmounth doo-cot nearby is a relic of former days when local gentry kept pigeons for a tasty addition to the larder. Inside you can still see the hundreds of nesting recesses.

Following the towpath southwest, we pass two canal distance stones. Just before pipes bridge the canal, a path descends to a farm road which climbs by the golf course. Soon we glimpse the first objective—Cockleroy, a hill which dominates the area and provides a lofty viewpoint. The road passes through a walled gateway, then we leave it at a wooden gate for a path along the east side of the dyke. Climb up to the wood then bear right for the ridge leading to the top. The view includes the two Forth Bridges and Arthur's Seat, the southern Highlands and as far west as Misty Law. Below is a valley hemmed in by rocky outcrops, with Lochcote Reservoir at the far end. Cairnpapple is on the southern horizon.

A path descends the east shoulder, then we turn sharp right and walk below the cliffs to a field. Follow the wall down to the estate drive. The ruins of Kipps Castle are on our left, then we pass a remnant of Lochcote Castle, with the site of Lochcote House adjacent. The drive meanders above the reservoir and forks left at the gate to emerge on the road. Turn left then over the crossroads to Torphichen (pronounced Torfeeken), one-time headquarters in Scotland of the Knights Hospitaller of St John of Jerusalem. Their Preceptory still stands and is open to the public. In the kirkyard there is a Refuge stone, the centre of a group still standing.

At the village square, bear left then left again at the crossroads to pass some modern houses. At a bend in the road, an opening on the right leads to a gate on the Bathgate-Linlithgow road. Keep to the field edges for easier walking. The farm track across the road climbs the Bathgate Hills, the view improving all the while. Television masts guide us to a gate leading into the complex site of Cairnpapple, built and rebuilt over a period of 2000 years. During the summer months when the custodian is on duty, the cairn can be entered through a trap door. To the southeast we can see the Knock, a popular viewpoint for Bathgate folk.

Leaving Cairnpapple, make your way to the Linlithgow road, keeping Cockleroy ahead. To avoid some road walking, take the track which enters the wood on the right at a dip in the road. At the end of the straight section, turn left and follow a track until posts with direction arrows are seen. These indicate we have entered Beecraigs Country Park. Turn left at the posts and take the path leading north through the wood to a picnic area. At the park entrance, turn left to rejoin the main road. Look out for the path which avoids a V-section of road. On reaching the canal, follow the towpath back to the station.

If a shorter walk is preferred, you can drive up the Linlithgow-Bathgate road and park at the Cockleroy lay-by. After climbing the hill, the ramble can be followed as far as the picnic area, then take the track leading back to the lay-by.

Distances: Full ramble 10 miles (16 km); from Cockleroy 6½ miles (11 km).

Rough Castle and the Union Canal

Recent interest in the Antonine Wall and the proposed leisure uses of the Forth and Clyde and Union canals brought this rather unusual ramble to the fore. The route is lined with interest and provides a high-level walk with distant hills for a backcloth.

Alight from the bus at Bonnybridge or park the car there. At the foot of the hill bear right then first left to an enclosed walkway under the Forth and Clyde Canal. Follow the road and after crossing the main railway line the way becomes more rural. A few yards beyond Bonnyside House, the fort policies are entered.

The path runs alongside the Roman ditch, with the remains of the wall most impressive here. At a section close to the Ministry of Works hut you can stand on top of the wall with almost the same advantage a Roman sentry had. Crossing a burn, the path leads up to the remains of a typical Antonine period fort, square in plan with rounded corners and surrounded by a system of ditches. Of particular interest is the Lilia at the northern gateway across the ditch and near the dyke. This was a series of small pits, each with sharpened stakes, possibly intended to halt a charge of cavalry.

From Rough Castle a woodland path follows the north side of the ditch to emerge on a small plateau overlooking Camelon. The track winds round marshy ground, crosses a branch railway line and enters another wood. On a recent visit, two foxes ambled across the railway line a few yards from me. Trees partly screen the works of the Scottish Tar Distillers Company, scene of a spectacular fire in 1973. At the end of the track, bear right then left along the road for about ¼ mile (400 metres) to a wooden gate on the right. Steps lead up to the ditch at Watling Lodge and a path along the edge. This is the best section of the ditch on the Antonine Wall, looking almost as it did on the day the Roman engineers completed it.

The vallum ends abruptly for the time being, industry and modern housing having transformed the area. However, other items of interest have survived. On our left is the Forth and Clyde Canal at Camelon Lock. Nearby is the Union Inn, and between them the entrance to the Union Canal can still be seen. From here ships were raised by a series of locks to the working level of the canal, less than ½ mile (800 metres) away and 100 feet (30 metres) higher. Passengers on the leisurely journey from Glasgow could stop overnight in the hotel while their boat ascended the locks in readiness for the morning sail to Edinburgh.

The locks were filled in some years ago and are underneath our route to the new railway bridge. Just beyond the arch, a track leads to the towpath and a more extensive view. Falkirk is spread below, with the Ochil Hills and part of the Trossachs in the background. The Union Canal, or more properly the Edinburgh branch of the Forth and Clyde Canal, has emerged almost unscathed from modern development and some stretches of the towpath give pleasant walking.

Soon we reach the tunnel, for some the *pièce de résistance* of the ramble. At this section, the canal has been led through a hill rather than have a system of locks on each side, a practice more common on English waterways. You can either traverse the hill to the tunnel exit and walk down to Falkirk High Station or negotiate the ½-mile (700-metre) tunnel. I found the fence in the tunnel had been renewed so I went

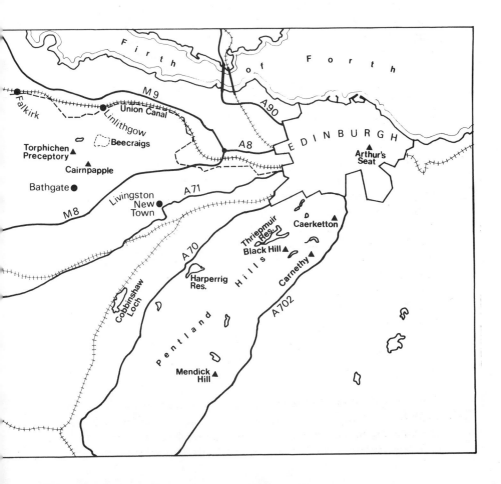

through, trailing my right hand lightly on the canal side of the wooden handrail.

On emerging, look for the carved stone faces on the next bridge, which is number 61 coming from Edinburgh. The two faces, one frowning and one smiling, are said to represent the builders of two canal sections. One had the tunnel to hew from solid rock, while the other had contracted for a comparatively easy stretch.

Beyond the bridge a track leads to the road. Skirt the edge of the football field to Falkirk High Station. For the bus route, follow the road to the town centre or take the path to the station and continue on the road from there.

To return to Bonnybridge, cross the bridge with the carved faces then turn sharp right at the end of the parapet to follow a stream, at first on the south bank and later on the north. Join the road near Seafield Farm and walk uphill to take the track on the right towards Craigieburn. Follow an old mine road west until it peters out then head north to the road, west of Greenrig Farm. Keep to the edge of Drum Wood to join a track below Bonnyhill Farm. This track leads to the road we left earlier for Rough Castle.

Distances: to Falkirk 8 miles (13 km). Bonnybridge circular 14 miles (23 km).

The Luss Hills

Situated between Loch Long and Loch Lomond, the Luss Hills are a popular range close to the Central Belt. They contain some fine walks with splendid views over Loch Lomond and the hills to the north, while to the south one can glimpse the steeples and tower blocks of Glasgow less than 25 miles (40 km) distant. In the north they curve towards the narrow isthmus between Arrochar and Tarbet where Viking raiders dragged their war galleys from the fjord-like Loch Long to the fresh waters of Loch Lomond, thence to embark on forays deep into the interior.

Southwards, the area is defined by the road to the Fruin Water, then northwest by Glen Fruin, where on a fateful day in 1603, Clan MacGregor massacred Clan Colquhoun in a running battle. This act led to the MacGregors being hunted like animals and their name proscribed. It was all triggered by hungry MacGregors helping themselves to a Colquhoun sheep, then being caught and hanged. Clan etiquette required these preliminaries in order to settle old scores.

In later, more peaceful times, cattle drovers led their herds towards the southern markets without mandatory protection money for the local clan chief. Slate quarriers were opened to provide roof coverings for the expanding towns. Drovers and quarries departed in the early years of this century and nature is gradually covering their roads and spoil. It's back to farming and forward to tourism nowadays.

Luss has been regularly voted one of the prettiest villages in Scotland. You can verify that with a walk to the pier, a visit to Saint Kessog's church nearby, then a stroll up the main street to begin the first walk.

Join the farm road which leaves the A82 south of the burn. Follow it to a slate quarry, then strike uphill towards Cruach Dubh, a wonderful view opening up as you climb. A more gentle path ascends Creachan Hill, then up to Beinn Ruisg to contour towards the fine ridge of Coille-eughain Hill. Descend by the Paps to Auchengavin and the quarry left earlier: an interesting round of 9 miles (15 km).

From Beinn Ruisg a longer walk can be enjoyed by following the ridge to Creag an Leinibh, a peak from which four walks radiate. Take the one to Beinn Tharsuinn, then on to Beinn Chaorach for a view of the Cowal Hills, the Arran peaks and the Firth of Clyde. Descend to Luss Water (there is a bridge downstream if required), then down the glen road to Luss to complete a round trip of 11 miles (18 km).

Beinn Eich (the horse hill) is a pyramid-shaped peak when viewed from the southeast. It dominates Glen Luss yet offers an easy climb. Walk up the glen road or park the car unobtrusively near Glen Mallochan. The farm track to Edentaggart leads to the ridge for a gradual climb. From the top there is another ridge walk to Beinn Lochain, then another to Doune Hill (734 metres), the highest in the Luss group.

If Inverbeg is your destination, make for Doune Farm in Glen Douglas. Otherwise descend into Glen Mallochan or, as most people prefer, retrace your steps for the pleasure of descending Beinn Eich with, hopefully, the sun behind you and a glorious view in front.

Beinn Dubh lies north of the glen road and is the most accessible of the Luss Hills. Walk up the road then on to the hill for the picture-postcard view of Luss village. From Beinn Dubh walk northwest to the cairn, then almost due south to Mid Hill for the descent to Glen Mallochan.

Conic Hill and Inchcailloch

Following a fairly straight line from Greenock to Stonehaven, the Highland Boundary Fault separates the Pre-Cambrian rocks of the north from the Old Red Sandstone of the Midland Valley. Conic Hill is an excellent viewpoint from which to identify the humps and ridges of the fault for several miles in each direction. Climbing Conic Hill and then spending the rest of the day on the island of Inchcailloch is a favourite outing of local rambling clubs.

The car park at Balmaha is a convenient meeting place. If a more leisurely day is planned, there are nature trails described in a booklet available from the village shop. If you have omitted to phone Balmaha 214, now is the time to visit the pier and establish the boat departure times.

From the north side of the car park, go through a gap in the fence and follow the forest track south then take the second track on the left. Climb steeply under a canopy of mature pine trees, then over a stile on to the open moor, to follow a path through the bracken. Climb Conic Hill by walking to its eastern end at the Burn of Mar, then ascend the ridge. Easier said than done when our path has other ideas, so abandon it later when it veers away from the hill. Climb gradually towards the ridge, then up to the top for a grand view of Loch Lomond and the Firth of Clyde with the hills of Arran in the distance. The Highland Fault is visible along the islands of the loch, looking towards the tall chimney of Inverkip Power Station. The Highlands are on your right, and the Lowlands on your left as you negotiate the knobbly ridge. A path to the right follows a rocky outcrop running parallel to Conic Hill.

Join the road, then climb Craigie Fort opposite Inchcailloch. The West Highland Way commemorative plaque is nearby. Take the path for Balmaha and the jetty, from where Macfarlane's boats have carried passengers and mail to the islands for many years.

Purchase a nature trail booklet from the box on the island pier then plunge into the interior. At post No. 2, fork left and make for the viewpoint to get your bearings in relation to Loch Lomondside. It is another fine view, this time looking up the loch. Inchcailloch is a quiet retreat just off the loch shore and it seems incredible that 20,000 people visit the island from Easter to September.

The trail layout and the foliage give an impression of solitude. Everyone has their favourite island place. For some it's the viewpoint, others favour Port Bann with its sandy beach, and still others prefer to potter around the remains of the farm. The old burial ground is a tranquil spot, shaded in parts by two massive oak trees. You might meet other visitors browsing among the stones while awaiting the boat to return them to Balmaha and modern times. A memorable day, given good weather.

Strathendrick

From the outskirts of Bearsden, the A809 Stockiemuir road climbs the eastern shoulders of the Kilpatrick Hills before beginning its long descent into Strathendrick and the Highland foothills. It's an old road, well known and liked by the outdoor fraternity. During the heady days of the 1930s rambling boom it was the walkers' Yellow Brick Road to favourite haunts with intriguing names such as Halfway, the Whangie, Devil's Pulpit, and the Pots of Gartness. The West Highland Way, Scotland's first official long-distance path, passes close to them as it traverses the Blane Valley.

Carbeth Inn at the Halfway has been altered in recent years but Rob Roy would still recognize it as the changing house on the coaching route from Glasgow Cross to Aberfoyle. At Auchengillan, where the Scouting movement has a permanent camp, take a last look back to the Clyde Valley, then on to the Queen's View where the northern vista always takes me by surprise.

The road crests a hill and—click—Loch Lomond and its attendant hills appear almost as suddenly as a slide on a screen. From the car park with its view indicator nearby, a path climbs towards the Whangie, that curious rock formation on the edge of Auchineden Hill. Long ago, Auld Nick was returning from a witches' and warlocks' convention, perhaps held at Back of the World above Inverkip. Recalling the night's revels he chuckled, flicked his tail, and a lang whang was sliced through the hill. That's the traditional version.

The solitude of the moor makes the scientific explanation only slightly more credible. Geologists describe a glacier grinding its course along the valley and pulling an entire rock face from the hillside by an action aptly called plucking. Walking through the cleft, one can visualize some sections matching the faces opposite. A list of graded climbs makes the Whangie a favourite practice area for rock climbers.

Another natural wonder is Finnich Glen, which literally begins under the Stockiemuir road about three miles (5 km) north of Queen's View. Look for the Hole in the Wall on the east side of the road, with two small parking places adjacent. Over the ages, the Carnock Burn has worn a deep gorge through a cliff of soft red sandstone to create a small-scale version of the Grand Canyon.

A path runs from the wall to a narrow opening where some large steps descend to the water's edge. They can be slippery and the odd one is missing, so go with care. The Devil's Pulpit is a moss-covered boulder in the river a few yards upstream, and can be viewed just as well from above.

The path ends at the far entrance to the glen, under a leafy canopy popular with artists and photographers. Like the Whangie visit, we are advised to return the way we came.

The small village of Gartness on the River Endrick is a peaceful haven for most of the year, but in late summer is thronged with visitors making their way to a ledge overlooking a waterfall. This annual pilgrimage (or ritual) enables them to view another more ancient ritual — that of the salmon leaping at the falls en route to their spawning beds upriver. Gartness is on the West Highland Way, but if preferred it can be approached from Croftamie, which was Drymen's station during the days of the Forth and Clyde Railway. A path on the track bed crosses the Endrick by a high-level bridge which doubles as an aqueduct.

Two miles (3 km) downriver are the roofless towers of Buchanan Castle. Formerly the seat of the Grahams of Montrose, it served as a military hospital during the 1939-45 war. Hitler's deputy, Rudolf Hess, was an inmate for some time.

From the bridge, follow the pipe track, then join the road to the village and the Pots of Gartness, where salmon can be seen in the 'pots' below the bridge. A farm track leads to the Salmon Leap, from where a chorus of 'oohs' and 'aahs' signifies that an exciting time is being had by all.

Students can also view, with mixed feelings, the site across the river where John Napier, the inventor of logarithms, once lived. Some of the stones from his former house are built into the house opposite. Retracing our steps to Upper Gartness, there is a choice of walks for Croftamie, Drymen or the Endrick ford to the south.

Duncryne Hill and the Loch Shore

The stump of an old volcano rises steeply behind the village of Gartocharn, near the south shore of Loch Lomond. It is a popular climb for locals, who maintain the finest view of the loch is from its modest 140 metre summit. Let's check this by joining a well-used path at a small lay-by southeast of the hotel.

Within minutes, the OS trig pillar is in sight and Loch Lomond, her islands, and the surrounding hills are spreading before you. Further afield you can recognize Ben Ledi, the Ochils, the Fintry Hills and the Campsie Fells. There's the gap of the Blane Valley then the Kilpatricks, Misty Law in Renfrewshire, and the Cowal Hills.

Most of these hills are lavas from a period of spectacular volcanic activity long ago in the earth's history. In one eruption during the Carboniferous period, a volcano pierced the Old Red Sandstone rocks to pour its lava on the surrounding area. Gradually the vent filled with hard rock, more resistant to erosion than the soft sandstone. So the crag later to be named Duncryne was formed. Dumgoyne and Dumbarton Rock are two more well-known examples.

A path circles the top then meets the one climbed earlier. Descent can be made from the steep north side, but it is easier to retrace your steps to the road and Gartocharn, where the next ramble begins.

From the road opposite the hotel, a lane (just beyond the church) leads to a path alongside the field hedgerows. A pleasant walk, made more so by railway sleepers placed at strategic points to keep us dry-shod. The ubiquitous railway sleepers—what will take their place if the supply dries up? They have helped and guided us in remote areas well beyond the range of an engine whistle.

A sleeper bridge is crossed to join a lane leading to the road and the ruined Mill of Aber, a reminder of the days when Townhead of Aber was a thriving rural community. Another lane at the postbox winds towards the loch. Follow the signs for a walk through Shore Wood, part of the Mainland South Nature Reserve which is controlled by the Nature Conservancy Council. A permit is required for access to most of the remaining area and can be obtained from the Reserve Warden, 22 Muirpark Way, Drymen. After seeing the loch from a distance, it is a pleasure to stroll along the shore. The Endrick estuary is a well-known habitat of native and migratory birds so bird-watchers should be kept busy.

To return, walk back to Aber Mill then uphill towards the main road. Just before the junction, a lane runs parallel to the road, with views towards Loch Lomondside and overlooked by Duncryne. At the Community Centre we pass our way of the railway sleepers.

Both these rambles are short, for those with a few hours to spare.

Burns Country

With golden sands a pebble-throw away and a hinterland of lovely countryside, the town of Ayr is ideally situated for a variety of recreations. Add the romantic associations with Robert Burns and Auld Ayr has all the ingredients of a popular resort. On this ramble we sample the beach, two beautiful parks and a fraction of the area. We also visit the best-known places connected with the poet.

Make your way to the seafront and walk along the esplanade or, if the sand is firm, take to the beach. Join the lane by the River Doon, then enter Bellisle Park, where there is something for everyone, including a pet's corner and aviary for the kids.

Bellisle, Rozelle and the Monument Gardens are worth a visit any day of the year although May is a favourite time, when the cherry blossom is in bloom and the gardens are a glorious profusion of colour. Follow the track from the back of the Mansion House through the golf course to emerge on Monument Road opposite Rozelle, another former estate. It has wildlife ponds and a nature trail. Conservation is the keynote here. From Rozelle it's a short walk to the thatched cottage where the poet spent the first seven years of his life.

The Auld Kirk, a ruin before Burns's time, is further along the road and nearby are some relics immortalized in his epic poem 'Tam O'Shanter': '. . . the cairn, whare hunters fand the murdered bairn' was excavated prior to it being rebuilt in 1963, and proved to be a Bronze Age burial site. The hunters of long ago probably surmised that the small bones were a child's. Even in Burns's day the cairn's story was an old legend. The well 'where Mungo's mither hanged hersel' is on a bank of the Doon close to the railway bridge. Burns's Monument and the Brig o'Doon are down the lane from the present church. Pause on the centre or 'key-stane' of the bridge where Tam's steed Meg leapt to save them and in so doing lost her grey tail.

Where the lane meets the road you can either walk back into Alloway (there is a fine view of the old arch from the road bridge at the hotel) or walk uphill to enter a lane running almost parallel to the B7024. Climb Newark Hill for a view of Ayr Bay and the Firth of Clyde, then descend to the main coast road and the shore at Greenan Castle. If you have had your fill for the day, there are buses from Doonfoot and Alloway.

On the Pentlands

Lying so close to Edinburgh, the Pentland Hills are an obvious choice for rambles near the city. They are quickly reached by car or public transport and contain many interesting walks of moderate length and nature.

Hillend Park on the A702 Biggar road is one of several convenient starting points. Hillend ski slope, the longest artificial slope in Europe, is a prominent landmark on the hill above Hunter's Tryst. An alternative start can be made through the picturesque village of Swanston, or continue to the park, where the start can be made easier by the novelty of a chair lift.

From Caerketton Hill to Allermuir take in the extensive view of Edinburgh and the Firth of Forth, then turn to face the Moorfoot Hills and descend towards Glencorse Reservoir. The return journey can be made by the path between Harbour and Capelaw hills, then down by Bonaly Tower to Colinton or join the path at the Howden Burn for Swanston and Hillend Park. The road from the reservoir follows the Logan Burn to a path by the waterfalls and a quiet glen leading to Redford Bridge and Balerno.

These two popular walks should whet your appetite for other Pentland walks—the book of that name by D. G. Moir is an excellent guide.

Maps

The areas described are covered by OS 1:50,000 sheets 63, 64, 65, 66, 70 and 71, and Bartholomew's 1:100,000 sheets 40, 44 and 45.

4
THE OCHILS
Rennie McOwan

The ancient Celts described the Ochils as *Uchil*, the high ground. Their 24-mile (39-km) length spread—until local government reorganization—across five counties, blocking what to the stranger would seem to be the obvious way to the north.

The tide of Scottish history has swirled around their base and the glens and tracks to the east and west have been used by the mysterious peoples of the past, by the Romans, by Jacobite armies, by packmen, smugglers and drovers, by royalty and by common folk.

They are mainly rounded grassy hills, split by wooded glens of great beauty and by chattering burns turning the machinery of the mills which sprang up in the small Hillfoots towns, clinging to the base of the hills and clear of the softer, marshy ground to the south.

The Ochil Hills are, in effect, a green island plateau of tranquillity and quiet. This is their great attraction.

They have no foothills. To the north they slope gently down towards Strathearn. To the east they gradually fade into the rolling farmland and forestry plantations of Kinross and Fife. To the south they seem to hurl themselves down in steep grass slopes or crags to the Forth valley.

Millions of years ago a natural break in the earth's crust occurred near where Stirling now stands and ran east-west for 20 miles (32 km). This is known as the Ochils Fault. It had the effect of 'throwing down' all the land south of it to an original depth of about 10,000 feet (3,000 metres) in the now silted-up flood plain. The Fault also made the Ochils an earthquake area and tremors reaching 4 on the Richter scale have been recorded.

To the north of the Ochils Fault in the Old Red Sandstone times the area was alive with violent volcanic eruptions and fires. These initial upheavals helped create the Ochil Hills. The ravages of the Great Ice Age marked out the fall of the Firth of Forth leaving scars and the harder volcanic lines of the Ochils.

Once the sea lapped against forest-clad hills. You can still see areas which were once ancient beaches and where the bones of great whales, shells and the remains of minute sea creatures have been found.

Now there is the green and silver of the twisting links of the Forth, the modern farms, mines, towns and villages, spreading bricks and mortar, and all good for an argument about the quality of life today.

Many people have loved the Ochils: poets have written about their burns and glens, Queen Victoria said the hills reminded her of parts of Italy and Switzerland, travelling pedlars from Italy thought they were like the Apennines, and both Sir Walter Scott and Robert Burns referred to them in verse.

Copper, silver and calcite have been mined here, and parts of the southern scarp are a happy hunting ground for people seeking semi-precious stones. There are many traces of vanished dwellings and of ancient cultivation terraces.

They are sheep territory although the eastern glen passes were once part of the many tributaries of the river of cattle that flowed from the Highlands to be sold at Crieff, Falkirk or further south.

The Ochils' main area of character is to the west of Glen Eagles (no connection with eagles, incidentally: the name is derived from *eaglais*, a church) and particularly between Glen Devon and the Sheriffmuir road.

Four main outings can give the flavour.

Dumyat

At the western end stands the two-topped craggy hill of Dumyat (418 metres, pronounced Dum-eye-att) on whose southwest top the Picts built a fort. There are many arguments about the name but the most likely derivation seems to be the fort or dun of the Maeatae tribe. Roman historians speak of the country to the north of the Antonine Wall being in the hands of the Caledonii and the Maeatae, with the Maeatae living closest to the wall.

There is not much to see now—the remains of stone walls lying on layers of scree (some of the stones are vitrified) with a ditch across the neck of the 'entry' to the peak. Skilled use has been made of the terrain because there are cliffs on three sides.

There are forts of a similar type on the Lomond and Cleish hills, at Ben Ledi at Callander, at the entrance to Glen Devon and (formerly) at the quarry at Tillicoultry. There is a case for thinking they were part of an early-warning system as they are within bonfire signalling distance of one another.

On the main top of Dumyat are the remains of an indicator cairn erected by Scouts in 1935 as part of a chain of bonfires to commemorate the silver jubilee of George V and now rebuilt with a brazier-type top to commemorate the 1977 silver jubilee of the present queen. Alas, it is too often used as a litter bin.

There is also a concrete replica of the Argyll and Sutherland High-landers' cap badge and plaque beside the summit cairn, in memory of the 7th battalion, which was disbanded in 1967.

With a Warlock Glen and a Carlin Craig on or fringing Dumyat there are also, clearly, witch associations: the parish of Logie had a notoriety in this field as the records of Church and State show.

Dumyat is a favourite short climb for visitors, joggers and for New Year revellers. Sadly, some of the paths are showing the effect of overuse and there is far too much litter.

A common way in is to drive up the Sheriffmuir road until almost opposite Bridge of Allan reservoir, where there is room for parking. Go through a battered wooden gate and follow the track east to the top.

Alternatively, walk in from the Sheriffmuir road by the cart track leading past Lossburn reservoir and then strike uphill by a prominent dip between the two peaks.

The district council have also created a car park in Blairlogie, just past the post office. Cross a stile at the back of the park, go left, and then follow a track up beside the burn until it links with the one coming in from the Sheriffmuir road. Because of publicity, an indicator board and the car park this is becoming a popular route but it is not the best.

For this you should go to Menstrie. From the old bridge a path leads up through the fringe of Menstrie wood. Follow it uphill (with the waterworks on your left) until you come to a fence and stile. Most people then go uphill by a series of knolls.

A better way is to take the path beyond the stile until you reach the cart track. Follow that north until you see a small burn on your left coming down from Dumyat. Go up that way: the magnificent view to the west and northwest and particularly to the Grampians is hidden until you are almost on top.

Dumyat is a small hill. Many would argue that it has few rivals as a viewpoint.

Alva or Tillicoultry to Blackford

The cross-Ochils trek from Alva or Tillicoultry to Blackford is a pleasant excursion of about 7 miles (11 km) of green glens, with peat hags in the centre section, the quiet waters of the Upper Glendevon reservoir, and the attractive descent to Blackford (bus service back to Stirling).

In the sixteenth century coarse handwoven woollen cloth was produced in Tillicoultry and known as Tillicoultry serge. The right of way from Tillicoultry's Mill Glen to Blackford (now waymarked, unnecessarily in my view) is a relic of the time when the Blackford cobblers came to trade their wares with the Tillicoultry weavers.

When you go up Mill Glen to do the cross-Ochils walk remember to take the upper path, on the *east* side of the Gannell Burn. If you follow the lower path you will find yourself at the foot of The Law which is a common route up to Ben Cleuch, the Ochils' highest peak (720 metres).

Its name derives from the Gaelic word for a long sloping ridge. Personally, I have never thought it an attractive top. It has wide views, which in clear conditions can stretch from Ben Nevis to Ben Macdhui. In the past it was suggested that a railway be run to the top, an obscene suggestion that happily has never materialized. As it is, a large weather tower looks unsightly enough.

Ben Cleuch itself is often climbed from Alva via the Silver Glen or from Tillicoultry via The Law but a better expedition is to take the old mining road from Menstrie up behind Craigomas (Craig o' the Moss) and then walk round the south side of the Myretoun Hill to the remains of old calcite mines. (Calcite was used as a fertilizer and in the processing of iron-ore, particularly when the Napoleonic wars caused a shortage.) Continue up and over the west shoulder of Myretoun Hill (in snow or mist watch out for a ravine-like mining borehole now used as a sheep pen) until you reach a gate at the base of Cul Snaur. A steep pull-up follows beside a strong dry stone dyke. A little hollow on top of Cul Snaur is a good resting place.

Continue northeast until you reach the central Moss and then contour along the 'flat' to Ben Cleuch. Descend to Alva or Tillicoultry (bus back).

Round the Ochil Tops

An attractive expedition is the round of the nine 610 metre Ochil tops. There are arguments that there are really ten or eleven but the nine are those defined as such in the Scottish Mountaineering Club's guide. The others are really shoulders or offshoots.

If you don't want the hassle of arranging cars at either end you can use public transport.

Take a bus to Dollar. Go up the beautiful gorge-glen to Castle Campbell and through Glen Quey until opposite the reservoir, then up the steep grass slopes to the top of Innerdownie (611 metres) where there is a cairn and a wall. Two miles (3 km) of easy walking southeast (with plantations to the north as a marker) take one to Whitewisp (643 metres). It holds snow, and its southern slopes have been known to avalanche.

A mile (1½ km) west takes us to Tarmangie (645 metres, The Hillock of the Young Goats) and then comes a descent to the Burn of Sorrow and the fringe of Maddy Moss before following a fence to the top of King's Seat (648 metres). There are several theories about this name but it may derive from the Gaelic word *ceann* meaning head, or could possibly be linked to Castle Campbell as the seat or representative of authority.

A mile and a quarter (2 km) northwest brings us to Andrew Gannell Hill (670 metres), not named on the one-inch map. There is no such person as Andrew Gannell: the name is a corruption of the Gaelic for a sandy-bottomed burn. This knoll is a good resting place to linger and savour the scents and feel of the central section of the Ochils.

The route now curves southwest to The Law (638 metres) and then straight back to the top of Ben Cleuch: shelter can be had in the wall around the cairn.

Ben Ever (613 metres) to the southwest is an easy plod and then comes a 2½-mile (5-km) walk across hags and heather to the mound of Blairdenon (632 metres). It has a flat top but the highest bump is beside a fence junction. A strong pole used to stand here. Just down from the top is a cross and memorial to a student pilot whose training plane crashed in these hills. The source of the River Devon is also on the slopes of Blairdenon.

Descend to the Sheriffmuir road by Glen Tye and thence to Dunblane (if you are within hours you can halt at the Sheriffmuir Inn before plodding down the metalled road to Dunblane: train or bus back to Stirling). There is a bus service from Menstrie, if the walker prefers to descend to there.

This expedition generally means a walk of 18-20 miles (29-32 km) and a total ascent of over 1200 metres. The all-round views to Kinross and Loch Leven, to the Lomonds of Fife, to the northern hills, to the Forth plain and to the Grampians, are marvellous.

The further east you go the more indeterminate the Ochils become. But the little hill of Ben Shee (fairy associations), near the Glensherup reservoir, gives excellent views north and has a fey character.

Scott's View

A picnic or family day can be had to Scott's View, near the village of Glenfarg, north of Milnathort. In Sir Walter Scott's novel *The Fair Maid of Perth* this view towards Perth is described as 'one of the most beautiful which Britain, or perhaps the world, can afford'.

There has been controversy over the exact spot, but it has in fact been pinpointed.

Half a mile (¾ km) north of Glenfarg village a minor road known as the Wicks of Baiglie road strikes off to the west. Follow this for about a mile (1½ km) to the north and on the west side look for a sign pointing to the farm of Lochelbank. Don't take the track between the road end and Lochelbank which goes off right to Scarrhill Cottage, but carry on past the farm and pick up the path leading northwest (it is shown on the map but disappears).

Head for Dron Hill. Just south of the hill two buildings are marked on the map. This is Dron Hill Farm, now in ruins. The track appears again and passes between the buildings and some trees. About 300 yards (275 metres) further on, where the track turns left, there is a little ridge with some rusty fencing marking the spot. Look your fill.

The way from Lochelbank is part of the old Wallace Road, once the main road to Perth, and traditionally used by William Wallace, Mary Queen of Scots and other renowned figures. It was on this road that young Sir Walter, about 1786, stopped his horse and gazed on the view which he described in *The Fair Maid of Perth*.

It is a wise precaution to have a word with the farmer at Lochelbank: there are sometimes bulls around.

The Ochils are not large, but they have a special appeal.

An old rhyme goes:

> What hills are like the Ochil hills?
> There's nane sae green tho' grander.
> What rills are like the Ochil rills?
> Nane, nane on earth that wander.

Maps

The Ochils are covered by OS 1:50,000 sheets 57 (Stirling) and 58 (Perth and Kinross); and by Bartholomew's 1:100,000 sheets 45 (mid-Scotland) and 48 (Pitlochry and the Trossachs).

5

THE SOUTHERN HIGHLANDS
Rennie McOwan

I spent part of a day once in search of a vision. It was into a land of high mountains, of secret glens, remote, wild, fascinating and heart-gripping. Come and see for yourself, the messages said. Over the next shoulder, beyond that blue hill, through the green woods, past black lochans fringed with golden sand, there's treasure waiting for you. Fanciful? Embarrassingly romantic? Precious, over-flowery reminiscences coloured by the years? The imaginings of a young boy?

No, I don't think so. The feeling was very real and, along with other experiences around the same time, marked a stage where I later realized I had caught the mountain and outdoor bug, an affliction that cannot be cured and which intensifies as the years pass.

It came when a group of young Scouts were preparing cooking fires on the shingle shores of Loch Lomond as part of a long trek. It must have been spring because I remember that when we walked along the shore some oyster-catchers got very excited, angrily piping, their red beaks and black and white plumage startlingly clear, as they made belligerent fighter-plane runs at our ducking heads.

Later, we lay on the shingle and basked in the sun, and a mountain across the loch loomed large and blue-grey and dominating and drew the eye. We were very young, and had to ask what it was. It was the legendary Ben Lomond, annual mecca of thousands of youth hostellers and once-only hill-trampers, the second most-ascended mountain in Scotland, the Ben of the sad song that tells of the Highlander who was to be executed following the surrender of the ill-fated Jacobite garrison at Carlisle during the 1745 Rising, and of his spirit taking the 'low road' back to Scotland.

It is the mountain, too, of the winter snow, the steep north sides reaching down to the old Macgregor homesteads, and of the lonely country on the east side of the loch, now under threat from the hydro-electric board. You cannot go to the Southern Highlands and not visit it. The views are marvellous. Arran, Jura, Mull, Ben Nevis and all the nearby hills can be clearly seen.

I remember with great clarity an exciting feeling of wanting to get up and go there and see what the hill was like. There was an urge to explore the now-familiar Ben which then had all the attractions of distant lands, a feeling which I have never forgotten. It was such a nostalgic and pleasurable feeling that one day many years later I went back to try to find the spot but could not. Perhaps I walked over it, and it was the same, but I was not. The point of all this is that the Southern Highlands are—for all ages and for all natures—a magnificent area for personal fulfilment. Seek and you will find. It is territory for all men and all seasons.

It cannot be exhausted. 'Scotland small? Our multiform, our infinite Scotland *small?*' wrote Hugh MacDiarmid in a poem telling of all the beauty and interest of one small patch of hillside. The difficulty in describing the Southern Highlands is in compressing the goodies, but a useful start is to go to the royal and ancient Burgh of Stirling, Gateway to the Highlands, with castle perched on grim rock, commanding in past centuries the crossing of the River Forth and all traffic north and south.

Stirling has been described as 'the buckle that clasps Highland and Lowland together'. From its high ground you see a gradual end to extensive farmland, rolling moorland, and rash of town and villages on the plains, the lower and gentle hills round about.

In the distance to the west and northwest rise the bold ramparts of the Grampians.

Here is the true division between Highland and Lowland. Here Lowland gentleness and order ends and rugged harsh beauty takes over. Beyond this line of hills—the start of the Southern Highlands— an endless sea of mountains stretches into the central, northwest and northern Highlands until they tail off to the farmlands and fishing villages of the northeast and the moors and vast flatnesses of Caithness.

In the past, anxious eyes have looked to these hills because there the rule of law frequently did not run. From thence came the thieving clansmen to steal southern cattle. There, too, were their hidden fastnesses secure from reprisal. From this unpromising territory came tough, hardy, quarrelsome and hospitable hillmen who served in many armies, and a lovely culture of Gaelic songs and poetry much of which praises the hills, lochs, straths and glens in language of great sensitivity.

There are now modern and busy roads through the glens and passes

and the days of sword and targe are over, but as you head up Loch
Lomond-side for points north or westwards, for Inveraray and Argyll,
or through Stirling and Callander to Crianlarich or Killin, it is worth
remembering what this wall of mountains once meant.

Neil Munro in his magnificent historical novel *The New Road*—the
title refers to the military roads built by General Caulfeild and his
commander, General Wade, to try to keep the unruly clans in order—
speaks of the Grampians, like ramparts, standing between two ages,
one of paper, one of steel.

On either side were people foreign to each other. Since roads had
been in Scotland they had reached to Stirling, but at Stirling they had
stopped, and on the castle rock the sentinel at nightfall saw the mists

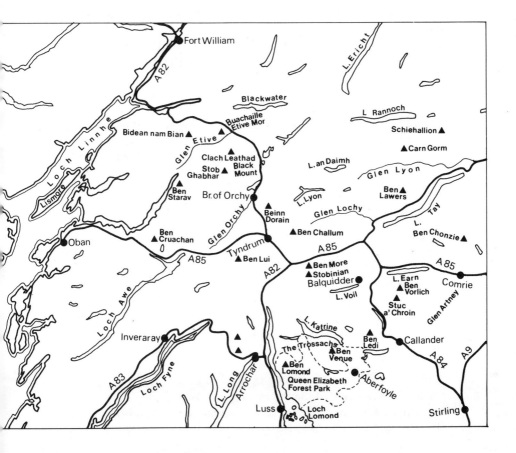

go down upon a distant land of bens and glens on which a cannon or a carriage wheel had never yet intruded. Only the bridle-paths to kirk and market, the drove-track on the shoulders of the hills.

But it is these once-remote hills we are concerned with, so to start with get hold of a motoring atlas and have an initial look at the boundaries.

At the top the boundaries move inland from the west coast port and resort of Oban, along the line of the railway, through the ancient Pass of Brander where fugitive King Robert the Bruce ambushed his would-be ambushers, the Macdougalls of Lorn, in the Scottish wars of independence. Today the main corrie of Ben Cruachan, one of Scotland's great mountains, holds a hydro-electric dam and its heart contains an underground pump storage cavern which is one of the largest in Europe.

On northeast through Glen Orchy, with its rippling river, deep pools and green hillsides, and out again to the hotel and railway station at Bridge of Orchy, dominated by the slopes of Beinn Dorain, the cone-shaped Mountain of the Otter, beloved of the Gaelic bard Duncan Ban MacIntyre, Fair Duncan of the Songs.

The line then bends round through lonely tracts of heather, grey rocks and peat hags, bounded by a steep wall of hills, until the fringes of Rannoch Moor are reached. Here is one of the last wildernesses of Scotland, once the site of great forests, the home of elk, bear and boar, the haven for broken men and fugitives, the scene of the flight of David Balfour and Alan Breck Stewart in Robert Louis Stevenson's *Kidnapped*. Its 56 square miles (145 sq km) of moor and lochan are now given over to grouse, deer, heather and bracken (it takes its name from the Gaelic word, *raineach,* bracken).

Loch Rannoch, of 'Road to the Isles' fame, is the next section of the northern boundary, and we come southwards again by the busy A9 which frequently runs over now-buried tracks well-trodden by drovers and packmen and by warring armies.

Down through Pitlochry with its summer visitors, salmon-viewing point and attractive 'theatre in the hills', we reach the cathedral city of Dunkeld with its woodland walks, neighbouring Craig-y-barns for rock climbers, and associations with Shakespeare's *Macbeth* (you can stroll in Birnam Wood).

Finally, our borderline curves in again to Loch Tay, fringed to the north by a fine array of mountains, topped by high Ben Lawers, the ninth highest mountain in Britain at 1214 metres and renowned for its alpine flowers.

It is an area of great contrasts, from bare windswept moors in the east near Comrie to the knolly, tree-covered, loch-besprinkled Trossachs, made famous by Sir Walter Scott in *The Lady of the Lake*. It has long wooded glens like Glen Lyon, slashed like a sword cut through the hills and arguably the most beautiful glen in Scotland, contrasting with the wider, stony, barren upper reaches of its neighbour Glen Lochay.

It has rocky tops like the summit of The Cobbler, at Arrochar, and moss and grass plateau tops like Meall Buidhe (The Yellow Mound) looking to the lonely country between Glen Lyon and Rannoch Moor. It contains more than 70 tops over 914 metres and 46 of Scotland's 276 Munros, including its most southerly, Ben Lomond.

It is very much loch and hill pass country, with Loch Lomond, Scotland's largest inland loch, forming a north-south boundary with the fringes of Argyll and the many lochs of differing character and sizes in the Trossachs.

A series of parallel glens and straths runs east-west, like outspread fingers: Loch Earn, then northwards to Loch Tay, and into the ancient area of Breadalbane, and Glen Lochay, Glen Lyon and Loch Rannoch. Right across Scotland from the west runs an interlinked series of passes from Oban through to Tyndrum, then Strath Fillan and Glen Dochart and on to Strath Tay and out to the lower eastern ground.

Each walker's assessment of hills and glens is to some degree a subjective one, and the choice given here can be no more than a taster.

Stuc a' Chroin and Ben Vorlich

If you want to be fairly certain of seeing deer take yourself off to two mountains that dominate Loch Earn and the ground between it and Callander: Stuc a' Chroin (972 metres, The Hill of the Cloven Foot) and its neighbour Ben Vorlich (984 metres)—meaning obscure—are fine viewpoints of the Crianlarich, Balquhidder and Breadalbane hills and the lower ground to the east.

They are prominent landmarks: the traveller approaching Stirling via Strathearn from Perth, sees Ben Vorlich as an attractive cone. Both are clearly seen from Stirling with the notch that gives Stuc a' Chroin its name distinctly etched. Travelling southwards down Glen Ogle both dominate the A85 road.

They are contrasting hills: Vorlich is shaped like a twisted propeller and is basically grassy. Stuc a' Chroin has steep cliffs falling to the fastnesses of the Gleann an Dubh Chorein at its southeast side, and they are linked by a broad bealach. Taken singly, they are easy days;

together, a not too strenuous twosome. One of their main attractions is that the glens and corries at their foot are well-known deer sanctuaries.

Ben Vorlich is also a favourite place for seeing the sunrise in mid-summer, situated as it is on the fringe of high hills and because it can be safely ascended in the half-dark.

But if you do decide to do that—and it can be an unforgettable experience of scents and sights—remember that there is not much shelter on Vorlich's bare top. Those getting there first can instal themselves in a tiny hollow just to the south of the cairn—it'll take three or four.

Nowadays it is fashionable to ascend these hills from Ardvorlich, on the south Loch Earn road, an attractive spot with unpleasant memories. The old keep at Ardvorlich is the seat of a branch of the Stewarts. In the sixteenth century one of them married a sister of the Drummond keeper of the royal hunting forest of Glen Artney (running from near Stuc a' Chroin to Comrie). It is said he cropped the ears of some MacGregors found poaching deer. They swore revenge, killed him, cut his head off and having stuffed its mouth with bread and cheese placed it on the table at Ardvorlich. The crazed wife, who was pregnant, rushed off into the hills and the baby was born there by a small loch called the Lochan of the Woman. The baby, a boy, grew up to become the infamous Mad Major Stewart of Ardvorlich, who slew MacGregors on sight, and also killed his friend and fellow officer, Lord Kilpont, in a frenzied rage when they were both serving in Montrose's army.

Take the path for about a mile (1½ km) up through pleasant Glen Vorlich as if going to the bealach on the east of Ben Vorlich (an ancient hill pass to Glen Artney and Callander). Turn on to the north ridge which is steep but broad in its upper parts and which links with the summit near the top. An old fence is followed due east to the twin tops and the cairn.

It's an easy matter to tramp down to the broad bealach and cross over to Stuc a' Chroin. The line of the old fence is a good marker in mist. The steep, stony sides of Stuc can look intimidating viewed straight on, but they are not so bad as they appear and can be easily scrambled, particularly if you bear right.

Provided the walker has transport at the other end, the knobbly ridge can be followed southward over the subsidiary peak of Ben Each, the Peak of the Horses, down to the white house of Ardchullarie, on Loch Lubnaig-side. This early eighteenth-century house was the home of the Abyssinian traveller, Bruce of Kinnaird, whose discovery of the source of the Nile was ridiculed by society.

Tinto Hill, Southern Uplands
Lee Pen, above Innerleithen, from the Moorfoots ridge

From Birkscairn Hill to Glensax,
Peeblesshire

The old drove road from Peebles
to the south, above Glensax

The entrance to Loch Doon, Galloway

The view up Glen Rosa to Cir Mhor, Arran
On the ridge over the Witch's Step to Caisteal Abhail, Arran

West Highland Way — Craigallian Loch and Dumgoyne

West Highland Way — the path along the Allander Water
West Highland Way — in the Blane Valley

Blairlogie village from the slopes of Dumyat

Looking north-west from the summit of Ben Cleuch, Ochil Hills

Ben Cruachan, on the ridge from Stob Garbh to Stob Daimh

Ben A'an, Trossachs
Ben Lomond from Loch Ard

Carlin Maggie — a landmark in the Lomond Hills

Largo Law from the north
Invermark Castle, Glen Esk

Buachaille Etive Mor
The Devil's Ridge, Mamores
The hills of the Blackmount from the Glencoe road

The hills around Glen Etive
The pap of Glencoe across Loch Leven

Braeriach from Loch Pityoulish, Cairngorms
Cairn Toul and the Angel's Peak, Cairngorms

Chalamain Gap, Cairngorms
The cliffs of Coire an Lochain
The edge of Coire an t-Sneachda, Cairngorms

Ben Resipol from Acharacle
South-west from Streap to Loch Shiel and Moidart

Loch Quoich skyline — (l. to r.) Sgurr Mor, Sgurr na Ciche, Ben Aden
In the Grey Corries — Sgurr Choinnich Mor from Stob Coire Easain

The Falls of Measach in the Corrieshalloch Gorge, Dearg hills
Slioch from Grudie Bridge
Braemore — the view down to Loch Broom

Stac Polly from Cul Mor
Liathach, looking towards Spidean a'Choire Leith from the east

Coire Lochan and Coire Ghrunndha from Rhu Point, Skye
The Kilt Rock, Skye
The Quiraing, Skye

Loch Coruisk, Skye
Sgurr nan Gillean (left) and Marsco (right), Skye

Black house at Ardhasig, Harris
The Lewis landscape — water and hills

Tolsta beach, Lewis
Standing stones at Callanish, Lewis

A pleasant way to visit both Ben Vorlich and Stuc a' Chroin is to walk up Glen Ample from Edinample, again on the south Loch Earn road. (Edinample is a former MacGregor castle taken over by the Campbells.) This glen, which runs through to Ardchullarie, is now a re-marked right of way with a new bridge: it is also marred by the landowners erecting signs giving stalking dates and wrongly interpreted by some walkers that there is no access at any time. If in doubt, check with local climbing clubs.

Follow the beautifully wooded glen for about 1½ miles (2½ km) until you reach the house at Glenample and turn uphill by a bulldozed road which in turn takes you on to the base of Ben Vorlich's west shoulder. Watch out for the ruins of old shielings across the glen not long after turning up the bulldozed road. Descend by Stuc a' Chroin's northwest ridge and back into Glen Ample again.

The best round, if one has not arranged transport at the other end, is to drive from Callander up the Bracklin Falls road (the falls are worth a quick deviation or an evening stroll). Drive up the metalled road, alongside the brawling Keltie Water, until you reach a junction near Braeleny Farm where you can park. (If the houses of Callander and the farms look familiar then you have seen the TV serial *Dr Finlay's Casebook*, much of which was filmed here. You pass Arden House on your left just before leaving the town and entering the wooded part of the Keltie Water road.)

Tramp up the rough track until you are near Callander reservoir and the right of way junction path to Glen Artney. Ahead lies the repaired (and locked) steading and bothy of Arivurichardich, which was inhabited in living memory and has been haven for many a hill walker. If wet, you can still shelter in the lean-to section which is open. Most people walk along Glen a' Chroin until a prominent burn is reached and then turn up to the bealach at the end of Stuc a' Chroin's long east ridge.

This is the old pass that goes via Gleann an Dubh Chorein round the east side of Ben Vorlich and over to Loch Earn. But—and weather will soon prove the key element—a better way is to tramp straight uphill from the bothy until the second fence is reached.

Follow the fence west until a tiny, frail wooden stile is found: on the other side a faint path strikes diagonally up the hillside through the bracken and ends amid the peat hags of the bealach. It is a time-saving and pleasant ascent, and is moreover becoming increasingly less used. Once on Stuc's ridge, there are good views to Ben Vorlich's steep southern side, and the wide, peat-hag-sprinkled Gleann an Dubh Chorein is clearly seen. Sit down for a bit and look for deer.

The broad ridge is easily followed on to Stuc's top, and the main view
is hidden until it bursts upon the eyes when the final knoll is scaled.
Follow the ridge round to Ben Vorlich, and descend from Vorlich into
Gleann an Dubh Chorein by the southeast shoulder. The path patchily
winds its way across the glen and after some re-ascending brings the
walker back on to the Stuc bealach.

Plenty of variety here, good views, sheltered nooks and a feeling of
remoteness and wildness on the fringes of the hills. Unless you are very
unlucky, you will see many deer, a sight that made this corner much
favoured in past centuries for sport by Scottish monarchs and for
poaching by the hardy clansmen.

Ben Lawers

If the Loch Earn area is good for deer hunters then Ben Lawers is a
paradise for botanists. To the north of Loch Tay lies a sprawling group
of bulky mountains, containing six Munros (seven if you include Meall
nan Tarmachan to the west), and dominated by Ben Lawers, the
highest mountain in Britain south of Ben Nevis.

To find Arctic flora in similar profusion in spring and summer
(particularly June and July) you would have to go as far north as Arctic
Norway and as far south as the Sierra Nevada.

These hills combine remote corners with easy access from roads and
are very much walkers' territory, with massive grassy shoulders,
avoidable bluffs, wide ridges and colossal views ranging from the
Atlantic to the North Sea. Until skiing facilities opened up at Glen Shee
and Glen Coe these hills were popular with skiers. There is still a ski hut
in Coire Odhar but numbers have now diminished.

The Lawers group of hills tends to be underrated because they are
not spectacular to look at from most road points, but Lawers in particular is of huge bulk. They are also hills that are good for a conservation argument, for parts of Ben Lawers and its southwest shoulder, Beinn Ghlas, are owned by the National Trust for Scotland and
operated as a nature reserve in conjunction with the Nature Conservancy Council. There is a mountain visitor centre, pay-parking,
guided walks and a Ranger-Naturalist Service. Arguments between
those who approve of such development and those who do not have
raged in recent years, and still go on.

There is much beauty here: the straight lines of 17-mile-long (27 km)
Loch Tay in Gaelic *Tatha*, the peaceful loch), the remoter slopes

reaching down to Glen Lyon, the remnants of old habitation, the long-distance views (on Ben Lawers you are almost exactly midway across Scotland).

Walking permutations are endless but three in particular give the flavour.

Those wanting a basically one-mountain day—or who have a split party—should drive up through Killin and about 4 miles (7 km) along the north side of Loch Tay (A827). A sign-posted road to the Trust's visitor centre goes off left into the hills. This is the old Lochan na Lairige hill pass to Glen Lyon (the lochan is now a dam) and the visitor centre and car park are on the right of the road. Those wanting to poke around can get leaflets in the centre, and there is a nature trail.

Those bound for Ben Lawers follow a clear path up beside the burn into Coire Odhar, then northeast up the steep slopes of Lawers' southwest and connected neighbour, Beinn Ghlas (1118 metres, The Grey Hill) until they arrive on this top. There is some erosion caused by heavy use of the waymarked path, and in foul weather it should be remembered that a nook in some rocks just below the top of Beinn Ghlas is the last shelter before the top of Lawers.

From Beinn Ghlas the walker descends about 120 metres to the foot of the drop between the two peaks (small lochan pools are a marker) and then up the southwest ridge of Lawers. There is a large cairn on top, the remnants of one vainly built to try to raise the mountain to 1220 metres (4000 feet), and in the Cat Corrie to the northeast is the beautiful Lochan nan Cat, another helpful marker.

For those who dislike crowds, tarmac and development, Lawers can also be easily ascended from Lawers village, 8 miles (13 km) from Killin. Just beyond the old school a path runs uphill beside the Lawers Burn. Another route takes one near to the Coire nan Cat, but you should turn left before reaching it and go up the east ridge of the mountain. Watch out for an old sheep fold not far from the top: it is a good shelter. Beinn Ghlas and Ben Lawers are an easy climb for a fit party and are pleasant hills for sitting and relaxing.

Lawers to Killin

A magnificent expedition is to traverse some or all of the six Munros (and then to cross the glen to Meall nan Tarmachan, finally descending to Killin). This is normally done from Lawers village, and is rightly featured in Ken Wilson and Richard Gilbert's book *The Big Walks*. It totals 20 miles (32 km) and for experienced mountaineers can take 11 hours plus. Those less fit will need longer but the journey can be broken off in many places and a descent made to the Loch Tay road. From Lawers village take the path up the east side of the Lawers Burn. After a mile, turn up the south ridge of Meall Greigh (999 metres, Hill of the Herd). It's an easy 2 miles (3 km) to Meall Garbh (1116 metres, The Rough Hill), but if there is mist, care is needed on two subsidiary tops, An Stuc and Creag an Fhithich. The ground rises steeply over 300 metres to the top of Lawers. Beinn Ghlas is only a mile (1½ km) away, and a broken ridge (some care needed) leads to Meall Corranaich (1076 metres, Hill of the Corrie of the Brackens). Some people ignore Meall a' Choire Leith (924 metres, Hill of the Grey Corrie), the Munro outlier to the north, and descend to Coire Odhar and the Lochan na Lairige road. But it's worth including, although it does mean retracing your steps back until you can easily descend to the Coire Odhar.

Personally, I feel to include Meall nan Tarmachan, (1043 metres, The Round-topped Hill of the Ptarmigan) is an artificial addition, but there it is across the glen, a knolly, attractive and twisting ridge from which you can descend to Killin (the odds are you *will* see ptarmigan in many parts of this range).

With so many connecting peaks the choices are endless and the rewards are great. To do 'the six' from one car, drive to Camusvrachan in Glen Lyon, cross the river to Milton Roro and ascend Meall a' Choire Leith via the Allt a' Chobhair. Descend off Meall Greigh to Invernain and back to Milton Roro.

Glen Lyon

Temporarily and regretfully turning our back on Glen Lochay, running west from Killin, let us head for wooded Glen Lyon. I say regretfully because Glen Lochay has some fine hills although its tops are duller than elsewhere. The magnificently named Ben Heasgarnich, The Peak of the Roaring Waterfall of the Horses, is a hill of character and so is Ben Chaluim, Malcolm's Mountain, seen as a strikingly pointed hill as you near the head of the glen.

But if Loch Earn-side is deer, and Lawers is alpine flora and mountain bulk, then Glen Lyon is ancient pedigree, loneliness and solitude. You could spend years simply exploring the glen and endless articles have been written about it. It is one of Scotland's best-loved glens. The hills at its northwest end form part of the high ground described by the revered Seton Gordon as part of the Wall of Rannoch, the mountains fringing the moor.

The Lochan na Lairige road descends into it at Bridge of Balgie or, alternatively, you can drive to Fortingall, at the mouth of the glen, renowned for its trim cottages, ancient yew tree and as the alleged birthplace of Pontius Pilate, whose father reputedly served with the Roman legions in this area when they tried in vain to subdue the tribes. Once a MacGregor glen, it was later dominated by the Campbells. It has a MacGregor's Leap, near the mouth of the glen, where in 1565 the landless MacGregor chief jumped the river pursued by Campbell dogs.

The glen winds for 25 miles (40 km), initially narrow, rocky and wooded and then opening out into attractive straths and finally fading out into the wild country at the head of Loch Lyon. It connects by a series of passes with the farm at Auch, near the foot of Beinn Dorain. It was once well populated and the remains of mills and houses can be clearly seen. At Innerwick stands Glenlyon parish church, built on an earlier site, where the bell of St Adamnan, St Columba's biographer, is preserved. Here, too, is sixteenth-century Meggernie Castle, originally built by Mad Colin Campbell in 1580, who hanged his enemies outside his front door and who made abduction and clan war a hobby. It was the sacking of the Campbell lands in this glen by the Keppoch Macdonalds and the MacIans of Glen Coe that finally ruined Robert Campbell and led to his part in the infamous Massacre of Glen Coe.

There are prehistoric structures like the remains of large towers near Cashlie, now thought to be a gathering and training ground for warriors, rather like present-day territorial camps. There are modern hydro-electric installations and communities. It is a glen for picnics, resting, strolling and exploration. The Carn Mairg range near the mouth of the glen on the north side makes for attractive walking and a round of all the tops can total over 14 miles (23 km) with the advantage of starting and finishing at Invervar.

Near the head of the glen are two peaks which demonstrate the Glen Lyon of old and of today. They would suit a family day if taken singly or an easy day for a fit party if taken together. Just over a mile (1¾ km) west of Meggernie Castle a road swings off right, passes a stalker's modern white house on the left and ends at a dam. Here once stood two lochs, Giorra and Daimh, and a hamlet appropriately called Lochs. The lochs are now joined up, the hamlet is submerged and this once remote and lovely corner has been opened up. However, situated as it is overlooking the wild country at the head of the glen and above Rannoch Moor, it is a fine place to go to savour past and present.

Stuchd an Lochain and Meall Buidhe

The joined loch is dominated by two peaks, Stuchd an Lochain (958 metres, The Peak of the Little Loch), and Meall Buidhe (931 metres, the Yellow Rounded Hill). Stuchd an Lochain lies to the left of the dam, as you face it, Meall Buidhe to the right, and they are often walked together. Mad Colin Campbell climbed Stuchd an Lochain around 1590 and saw wild goats. It can easily be climbed from Cashlie, in Glen Lyon, and even more easily from the dam. Watch out for cliffs around Lochan nan Cat (here is another lochan of the same name as that on Ben Lawers). The views are what make this hill; Glen Lyon's character and shape are clearly seen, the Lawers and Carn Mairg hills show up well, and so do the other sections of the Wall of Rannoch. The Bridge of Orchy hills hold the eye.

To include Meall Buidhe means descending again to the dam. A little ridge of mounds and bumps runs uphill to a section of peat hags. The mound of Meall Buidhe lies ahead to the left and the walker gains this and strolls round the wide and flat top to the final cairn. Here you are on the fringe of the wall, with the moor spread out and all the northern peaks clearly seen.

If you are looking for a safe, easy hill, Meall Buidhe has many attractions: pleasant drive, easily reached, fine views and safe. (In winter, of course, its exposed plateau can become boiler-plated with ice and blasted by gales.)

Bridge of Orchy Group

Glen Lyon ultimately connects with the great Bridge of Orchy group of mountains so let's head for them. There is no through road and, hopefully, there never will be. One must drive via Crianlarich and Tyndrum. The scene here is of increasing wildness. The mountains overlook a vast emptiness, the former territory of Drumalbain, the watershed barrier between Alba of the Picts to the east and the Dalriadic kingdom of the Scots to the west. Drumalbain is, literally, the Ridge of Alba. The main West Highland road, the A82, is lost amid this bleakness as it snakes north over the Blackmount to Glen Coe.

Four connecting and wild hills, running north and then northeast, part of the Wall of Rannoch, provide an interest-packed hill walk although it is as well to have a good day to do it as parts of the route are puzzling in mist and there are plentiful crags, deep corries and steep rock and grass. They have the advantage of being easily gained from the west by road and yet they overlook remoter country to the east and north.

They are hills of differing character. Some people prefer to take the eastern peak, Beinn Dorain (1076 metres), by itself because including its three neighbours means retracing your steps. It is one of Scotland's most photographed mountains, dominating the road and railway as you drive north from Tyndrum to Bridge of Orchy, and with the trains reduced to a puny size crawling along the foot of its steep sides. For its situation, its views are disappointing, being blocked by neighbours to some degree. You can peer down from the summit into Auch glen where the MacGregors came from Glen Lyon to bury their dead.

A prominent dip between Beinn Dorain and Beinn an Dothaidh (1003 metres, The Mountain of Scorching—possibly lightning), is clearly seen from Bridge of Orchy railway station. For Beinn Dorain the walker heads straight for it to about 450 metres, and then turns right on to the long shoulder.

Careful route-finding is needed when descending back into the dip in bad weather: it is easy to head for the lip of the cliffs. From Auch, the hill is wearyingly climbed in a steady uphill grind.

From the bealach north to the top of Beinn an Dothaidh is easily achieved: this hill is flat and moundy on top with a small cairn near the edge of the northern cliffs. Its views to Loch Tulla and the Blackmount peaks are outstanding.

Both Beinn Dorain and Beinn an Dothaidh are easy days, either taken singly or together, particularly if the day is fine.

An attractive threesome is to combine Beinn an Dothaidh with Beinn Achaladair (1037 metres, The Mower) and Beinn a' Chreachain (1081 metres, The Drinking Shell). Start from Achallader Farm, a historic spot.

It was once owned by the Fletchers who were ousted by the Campbells. The notorious Black Duncan of the Cowal, Campbell of Glenorchy, built one of his seven castles there to defend his lands. You can see it beside the present-day farmhouse. (You can leave a car there, but ask the farmer's permission.) The castle guarded the way over to Rannoch, and to the north and south, and is handy for Glen Orchy. In 1691, the Jacobite clan leaders and the Earl of Breadalbane held a peace meeting at Achallader which was uneasily concluded. Campbell of Glenlyon rested there en route to Glen Coe for the infamous massacre.

Cross the railway by a bridge above the farm and follow a track beside a stream. Make for the obvious shoulder of Beinn an Dothaidh which partially obscures the corrie. The going is easy to the top although rocks and cliffs are passed. When descending to the col (east, then southeast) between Dothaidh and Beinn Achaladair watch out for three knolls and a twist in the ridge, which can be puzzling in mist. The slopes to Achaladair are long but easy. This is a fine mountain, big and craggy, overlooking the way to Rannoch Moor and the famed Crannach Wood, one of the remnants of the ancient pine forest that once covered most of Scotland.

The descent down to the long connecting ridge (Meall Buidhe) to Beinn a' Chreachain is steep at first, with rock outcrops, and the route then goes along lovely turf with a final pull-up to the top. The ridge twists round to the east, with the lovely Lochan a' Chreachan cradled on the north side.

Beinn a' Chreachain must be one of the finest viewpoints in Scotland. The moor spreads out, all the Lochaber peaks are in view, and the Cairngorms can be seen, as well as Ben Alder and other neighbouring hills.

Descend by the northeast ridge to the Water of Tulla again, but don't wade the river to get to the Achallader track side. A plank bridge has been erected at the former bothy of Gorton, now an open hut maintained by the Mountain Bothies Association, and the track runs from there back to the farm. The bothy is a good refuge and once marked a special rail siding and halt built in the heyday of stalking. On the way back to the farm you can rejoice in the splendid view to be had of the shield-like Beinn Achaladair, its crags and corries.

This high-level walk across the three (or four) peaks is a genuine wilderness experience, and is highly recommended. In distance it is a fair day for a fit party but good route-finding is essential in bad weather. If break-off descents have to be made caution is needed with so many crags and bluffs. Remember, if doing the four, you have to get back to your starting point; two cars are best.

The Cobbler

Going to Arrochar, at the head of Loch Long, is like going down memory lane, said one mountaineer. Another described it as a nostalgia kick. Here is one of Scotland's best-known hills, the 881-metre Ben Arthur, better known as The Cobbler, its jagged three-peak outline well known to motorists and rail passengers.

Its accessibility by road and rail made it a favourite hill for generations. In the Depression days between the wars many a hardy Glasgow youth, fed up with unemployment or city life, took his mother's clothes-rope, put together what food and gear he could in an ex-army or home-made rucksack, and set out to get to Arrochar.

They were rightly known as hard men. Many hitched to and from Arrochar at the weekends, put up new rock-climbing routes of great severity on The Cobbler, played around on Beinn Narnain and explored other nearby peaks. They slept below walls, in culverts, in barns and in the open. They used old newspapers as extra blankets and became experts in finding suitable caves and in constructing stone and turf shelters in corries and glens near their favourite rock climbs.

The Depression years added a noteworthy chapter to Scottish mountaineering achievements. Many of these hard men are still alive and are rightly revered.

The mood of this period is brilliantly caught in Alastair Borthwick's classic book *Always a Little Further*, one of the funniest and best-ever mountaineering books. You can see the caves he spoke about in Glen Loin to this day, but they are now surrounded by trees and the entrances to some are partially blocked by boulders.

Sleeping in caves is not new, of course. The fugitive King Robert the Bruce is reputed to have slept in the Glen Loin caves, and they must have been used by local people when the Vikings brought their ships up Loch Long, hauled them on rollers across the isthmus at Tarbet to Loch Lomond and then sailed down the loch to plunder the settlements of Lennox.

This is wild country, on the fringes of Argyll with plenty of backdrops to the head of Loch Lomond and beyond. It is reiving country: much of it was Macfarlane land—expert thieves and warriors, so much so that it was said that they paid their daughters' tochers by the light of the Michaelmas moon (i.e. they stole to pay for their daughters' dowries). Another name for the moon was Macfarlane's lantern.

The hills in their lands by Loch Sloy now are an eyesore with hydro-electric structures, but nevertheless both Ben Vane and Ben Vorlich (same name as the Loch Earn Munro) are worth a visit.

But The Cobbler is the real hill of character in this area with its fine views across to Ben Lomond and down Loch Long and over to Cowal and Argyll. Loch Long, incidentally, does not mean long (although it is that) but is derived from a word meaning straight. The name Cobbler has long been a puzzle and there are many theories, but the likeliest seems to be that from some angles the three prongs look not unlike a cobbler's last.

About a quarter of a mile (½ km) south from the head of the loch the prominent score of an old rail track can be seen coming down the southeast slopes of Beinn Narnain. If you have trouble locating its start then follow the Allt a' Bhalachain (The Buttermilk Burn) uphill.

This score brings you on to a level path following the line of an aqueduct which is an excellent place to stop for a breather and to admire the length of Loch Long and the top of Ben Lomond now peering over the lower hills across the loch.

(If you want to ascend Beinn Narnain first then continue straight up from the terrace: a way can be picked between the bluffs which brings you out at the foot of the final small cliffs just beneath Narnain's flat top. But caution is needed when descending this way as the turn-offs can be hard to find in mist.)

This terrace leads the walker in a southwesterly direction and links up with the mucky path on the east bank of the Ailt a' Bhalachain. Follow that up into the corrie where the spectacular view of The Cobbler bursts upon the eyes as you top a rise.

The Narnain boulders lie ahead, and are worth a stop: they provide shelter, entertaining scrambling and are a good marker in mist.

The walker has a choice of routes but the two normally taken are either to follow the burn to the bealach between The Cobbler and Beinn Narnain and then to turn up the stony slopes to the North Peak, or to go into the Cobbler corrie and then to head for the dip between the North and Centre peaks.

A traverse of The Cobbler peaks provides some moderate scrambling, but is really only for those with a genuine head for awkward places.

There is no way round some climbing if you want to stand on the Centre Peak. Cobbler rock is often greasy and wind can be a problem, so care is needed. Go to the grassy hump at the back (west) of the true summit. It consists of a narrow wall of rock, vertical on three sides, steeply sloping to the south. Some fallen rocks abut on the northeast corner. The wall is split by a narrow crack: go through. There is a large ledge on the west side: follow that towards the southwest corner of the tower where there is a second opening. Go through that and up. It's not so complicated as it sounds, but it is not everyone's cup of tea.

The Cobbler is often combined in a round with Beinn Narnain and/or Beinn Ime (1011 metres, The Butter Mountain). It is lower than both, but it is the real hill of character and is rightly one of Scotland's best-known and renowned peaks.

Ben More, Stobinian and Cruach Ardrain

Every year it is a fair bet that some calendar will include the familiar view of Ben More, Stobinian and Cruach Ardrain towering above Strath Fillan. It is a popular subject with artists. Ben More, in particular, sweeps down in unbroken lines to the Crianlarich road and the hills hold snow on their tops well into the spring.

Here is a fine group of inter-connected mountains, well worth a visit. Their position beside the main road and railway at Crianlarich makes them easy for access. They command fine views. Hills of great character are nearby at the head of Balquhidder glen and at the head of Loch Lomond, and—perhaps above all—they are beautiful to look at. No visit to the Southern Highlands would be complete without going to them.

Ben More, 1174 metres, is simply translated—The Big Mountain.

Benmore Farm, two miles east of Crianlarich, is the normal starting point. The way up is rather like Beinn Dorain from Auch Farm, an unrelenting grind up steep slopes with no natural resting places until the top. It is normally a safe hill, but the scooped out near-corrie on its northwest side should be avoided in snow conditions as it avalanches from time to time. The views are vast, from the Merrick in Galloway to the Cairngorms. Rum and Jura can also be seen.

Ben More is frequently ascended. Its connecting neighbour Stobinian (1164 metres) is easily identified from afar because of its 'sawn-off' top. Its name is really Am Binnean (The Pinnacle) but it, too, is a large hill with steep sides. These hills can also be climbed from the Balquhidder side, which some people regard as the more attractive way up.

Cruach Ardrain (1045 metres, The High Heap), is the third mountain to figure in the drawings and photographs and its bold face, split by the well-known Y Gully, draws the eye. Forestry planting has marred the old route up the corrie. The hill is sometimes combined with a traverse of Ben More, Stobinian, the subsidiary peak of Stob Garbh and then Cruach Ardrain.

Ben More to Glen Falloch

Several permutations are available to the walker and an outstanding expedition for the fit—best kept for summer—is to traverse Ben More, Stobinian, Stob Garbh and Cruach Ardrain, then to cross over to the group of three fine Munros at the head of Loch Lomond, Beinn a Chroin (946 metres, Mountain of the Cloven Hoof), An Caisteal (995 metres, The Castle) and Beinn Chabhair (930 metres, Mountain of the Antler), descending to Inverarnan in Glen Falloch.

Between 12 and 15 hours are needed, and the distance is about 19 miles (31 km). This is a cracker, but it is long, has craggy sections, good route-finding is necessary and some retracing of footsteps is involved. A late spring day or early summer is the best time.

Ben Lui

While on the hunt for beauty no one could leave the Southern Highlands without going to Ben Lui (Laoigh, 1130 metres, Mountain of the Calf), six miles (10 km) east of Dalmally and clearly seen from the road between Crianlarich and Tyndrum.

Here is one of the most aesthetically attractive peaks in Scotland. It is sometimes climbed via its neighbours Beinn Dubhchraig and Ben Oss, but if it is described singly then that is because it merits it. In every sense of the word it is a big mountain. To walk up the track to Cononish Farm, from the Tyndrum road, in the spring and to see the mountain opening up with the twin horns of its shoulders cradling its renowned northeastern corrie, and the snow mantling its two distinctive little tops, is a magnificent sight.

In summer it is merely a walk up steep grass slopes: in spring or winter plenty of time should be allowed because its steep sides, bluffs and rocks can slow you down and many a person has been benighted or held up coming off Lui.

It is essential, too, to be able to see where you are descending. Many prefer to climb up from the Ben Oss bealach and to descend the same way to the Allt Coire Laoigh on the mountain's eastern side and to follow that burn until it joins up with the River Cononish, rather than to ascend or descend one of the shoulders of the corrie.

Ben Lui dominates its neighbours and can easily be identified from far afield. The summit is narrow with a small cairn, and the views are varied and extend from the Campsie Hills to Ben Nevis. Ben Cruachan stands up very well, and most of the neighbouring hills can be scrutinized in detail. Definitely a special hill, and worth a day to itself.

Tyndrum to Dalmally

Ben Lui used to be climbed a lot from the northwest, from the other Glen Lochy (Tyndrum to Dalmally) and combined with its western lumpish neighbour, Beinn a' Chleibh (916 metres, Mountain of the Chest), but forestry planting has made this an unattractive route.

A frequently followed high-level expedition of over 17 miles (28 km) (taking at least ten hours) is to walk from Tyndrum to Dalmally over Beinn Dubhchraig (976 metres, Mountain of the Black Rock), Ben Oss (1028 metres, Mountain of the Elk), Ben Lui and Beinn a' Chleibh—plenty of variety, outstanding views, and hardly any route problems.

But, above all, Ben Lui is the King.

Individual Gems

There are several individual gems to be gathered. The graceful cone of Schiehallion (1083 metres) above Loch Rannoch appears in photographs and prints almost as often as the Strath Fillan hills.

Its fairy associations and smooth contours make it an intriguing hill: Maskeleyne, an eighteenth-century astronomer-royal, carried out his pendulum experiment there to determine the earth's mass. It is so frequently ascended that erosion on the paths is unsightly. Climb it from the Aberfeldy-Tummel road, two miles (3 km) north of Coshieville Inn or from Braes of Foss.

Ben Ledi (879 metres) at Callander is a splendid viewpoint for the Trossachs lochs. But go there from the side via the Stank Glen, and enjoy its northeast corrie, boulders and pinnacles. An almost hidden path goes beside the burn, crosses the forestry tracks, and goes up into the corrie. It's a bit lost in trees early on, clear higher up.

The shapely Ben A'n (463 metres) near the Trossachs Hotel is a lovely spot to view the length of Loch Katrine and get the feel of the Trossachs. There is a car park near the hotel, and the path is signposted. Don't worry about the crags: the path goes round them to the right and back. The top is narrow.

Ben Venue (732 metres) is also a good Trossachs viewpoint but marred by signposted paths and similar junk.

For those seeking an evening jaunt or rest day, Beinn an t-Sithein (580 metres) at Strathyre gives a surprisingly good view down Loch Lubnaig and to the lonely country at the head of Glen Finglas and over to Balquhidder (signposted path from near the bridge to the top).

A noteworthy characteristic of Ben Chonzie (Ben-y-Hone, 929 metres, Hill of the Cry of Deer), near Comrie is the number of hares which haunt its flanks.

But don't forget Ben Lomond. From the Forestry Commission car park at Rowardennan a broad and often mucky path takes walkers close to the top. From Comer, at the back, it is a steep pull. In summer it is thronged. In winter, transformed. Its views are magnificent. For many, its name—Beacon Hill—and siting and history make it their favourite.

Maps

The Southern Highlands are covered by OS 1:50,000 sheets 50, 51, 52, 56, 57 and 58; and by Bartholomew's 1,100,000 sheets 44, 45, 48 and 49.

Bibliography

Bennet, Donald, *The Southern Highlands*, SMC District Guide, West Col Productions

Gordon, Seton, *Highways and Byways in the Central Highlands*, Macmillan

Holmes, W. K., *On Scottish Hills*, Oliver & Boyd

Kilberry, Marion, *Argyle, the Enduring Heartland*, Turnstone

Nairne, Campbell, *The Trossachs and the Rob Roy Country*, Oliver & Boyd

Parody

O there's bawbees in Lanark and siller in Skye
And profit in Hielans and Lowlands forbye,
But there's nae greater love that the heart could desire
Than to fleece the fine tourists in bonny Strathyre.

For it's up in the morn and awa' to the till
Where the lang summer days put a pound on the bill
And the peak of Ben Vorlich is no' muckle higher
Than the price you can charge for high tea in Strathyre.

O there's mirth in the shielin' and love in ma breast
For the globe-trotting Yank and the Sassenach pest,
And Carnegi himsel' wad be proud to aspire
To ma current account in the bank at Strathyre.

For there's some in the toons o' the Lowlands seek gain
And there's some risk their capital far frae their hame,
But I'll aye milk ma tourists like coos in the byre
And hing into ma gold mine in bonny Strathyre.

6
FIFE AND ANGUS
Dave Forsyth

Fife

'**A** beggar's mantle fringed with gold' was how King James VI described Fife, referring to a county with a barren and inhospitable interior, but with a prosperous coastline of busy ports and thriving fishing villages. In shape, Fife resembles a terrier's head sniffing out into the North Sea. Having water on three sides, and the barrier of the Ochil Hills on the fourth, its comparative isolation gives it an independence unknown to other parts of Scotland. It is a gentle landscape with hills which swell, rather than rear up, from the rich agricultural land.

They are not high, as hills go, yet they provide easy, safe walking on rolling moorland, and despite a sense of isolation one is never far from civilization. Most of the hills are volcanic in origin, for Fife has more extinct volcanoes than the rest of Scotland put together.

The Cleish Hills
In the west the Cleish Hills, 20 square miles (52 sq km) of high ground, have as their highest points Knock Hill at 364 metres, and Dumglow at 379 metres. Loch Glow is a popular spot for anglers and there are a number of smaller lochs in the vicinity, yet fishermen apart, this area is not visited by many people. Perhaps it is a perverse streak in the make-up of many walkers who consider that hills that are so easily accessible are not worth visiting.

Climb Saline Hill, 5 miles (8 km) northwest of Dunfermline. From its modest elevation the prospect is wide and varied. In clear weather the view ranges from the North Sea in the east to Ben Lomond and The Cobbler in the west; from the Lammermuirs and Tinto Hill in the south to the Cairngorms in the north. Nearer at hand, the whole Forth estuary from North Berwick to Stirling stretches on one side, while the ramparts of the Ochils march westwards to meet the Touch Hills, it seems, beyond Stirling.

From Saline Hill it is an easy dip and rise to Knock Hill, with its motor-racing track, and views over the main Cleish range and West Fife.

Dumglow lies just over 2 miles (3 km) away to the northeast, and access can be gained from the minor road which runs east of Loch Glow. A Land-Rover track goes down to the loch-side, and a path continues round its northern side, which leaves you with only a half-mile (¾-km) climb to reach the summit, once the main hill fort of the area. A descent can be made eastwards via Dummiefarline to rejoin the road about a mile (1½ km) north of the point of departure. It's a knobbly, hummocky landscape, thrown up by cataclysmic forces in the agony of creation, but the leisurely walk up Dumglow should take only a couple of hours.

From it the view is northeastwards towards Benarty, on the south side of Loch Leven, its steep western end normally rushed past on the motorway between Edinburgh and Perth. This is another hill worth a visit from anyone with an hour or two to spare.

A wide track climbs Benarty in easy loops from Paranwell at the western end, and finishes almost above the tree line. From there it is but a gentle climb over rising moorland to the summit.

The view southwards is grimy and industrial—the West Fife coalfields, and the former mining towns of Cowdenbeath, Lochgelly and Kelty; names which conjure up visions of gloom and dirt, gas lights, and tin baths in front of the fireplace. It's not like that nowadays, of course, but it is refreshing nevertheless to turn northwards where the vista opens out across the shining waters of Loch Leven to the farms and villages nestling under the Lomond Hills on the far side.

It's time well spent to pay a visit to the Vane Farm Wildlife Centre, by Loch Levenside, beneath Benarty. Here the whole gamut of the area's wildlife is laid out, with guides (both printed and human) available for the uninitiated.

Leave Benarty by the road going north to Kinross, and pause in the neighbourhood of Gairneybridge to look back at the Sleeping Giant, the local name for Benarty's striking skyline of crags resembling a somnolent warrior stretched out with his head pillowed.

The Lomonds

Over to the east lie the Lomonds, probably the best-known, and certainly the highest of Fife's hills; 20 square miles (52 sq km) of high moorland and forest containing six reservoirs and three definite summits. East Lomond and West Lomond, at 447 metres and 523 metres respectively, form a triangle with the slightly lower and flatter Bishop Hill to the southwest.

Again, these are volcanic remains, and the two main summits make a familiar outline when seen from the Cairngorms in the north, or the Pentlands to the south.

They are encircled by roads, and one even runs over the saddle between East and West Lomond on its way from Leslie to Falkland. In recent years Fife Regional Council has made a determined attempt to open up this area to the public with the provision of a car park, picnic site and toilets at the top of the road over the saddle, as well as erecting

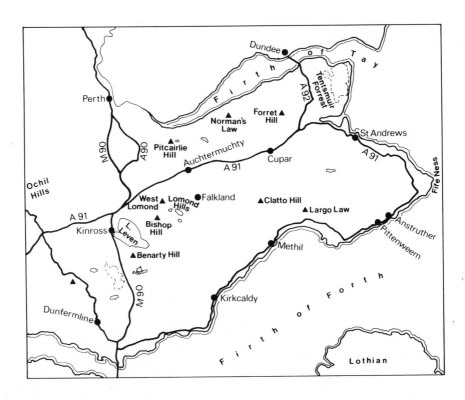

signposts at intervals: from the car park tracks lead outwards in various directions across the moors.

However, for the rambler dependent on public transport, the nearby village of Falkland is served by buses from Kirkcaldy and Perth, and there is a youth hostel and hotel there for those who wish to linger in this attractive corner of the county.

From Falkland the easiest way on to the Lomonds is to take the Leslie road as far as the car park, then strike off east or west as desired.

There is an indicator on the summit of Falkland Hill, as East Lomond is known locally, pointing out Ben Lawers, Beinn y Ghlo, Schiehallion and all the familiar northern peaks. The view westwards takes in the whole Lomond range, with the bulk of West Lomond dominating the scene 3 miles (5 km) away, and the reservoirs glinting in the hollows. It's an easy drop back down on to the Road of the Bloody Feet, a track which skirts the southern flanks of the hill, said to have been used by pilgrims in olden times on their way to St Andrews.

The grassy road leads westwards from a radio relay station and car park just below the summit, and past old lime kilns to the car park on the Leslie-Falkland road. A short distance north from there another track continues towards West Lomond, and it's a fine, easy stroll along the high, wide ridge which connects the two hills.

The track ambles on for a mile (1½ km) then peters out, and you are left to make your own way to the top. From the summit you look out to the Ochil Hills and beyond, taking in Loch Leven and the surrounding towns and villages. To the south, the flat moorland top of Bishop Hill rises heavily on the other side of Glenvale.

This is the direction of descent to take to see the Devil's Burdens, a jumble of rocks with a tale to tell, of which more later. Dropping into the tranquil Glenvale is as pleasant as it is unexpected. A little stream sparkles along under John Knox's Pulpit, a sandstone rock formation said to have been used as a speaking platform by the great man when addressing secret gatherings of his persecuted followers. There is no firm evidence to support this theory, but the name sticks.

Looking upwards from the other side of Glenvale, West Lomond rises with a majesty out of all proportion to its modest height. Keeping round the base of the hill, one finds on its northern side another curiosity—the Bannet Stane, or Bonnet Stone. Wind and weather have sculpted differing hardnesses of rock, until now there is a three-ton slab perched flatly upon a slender pillar. It has been suggested that this was an ancient sacrificial table, but again there is no proof. Underneath it is the Maiden's Bower, a little room carved out of the rock. A number of legends exist about it, all concerning a wealthy local maiden and her lower-class lover. How many legends have been born out of just such a situation?

Moving eastwards you are soon on tempting forest roads in the shadow of Arraty Craigs. At one point the Arraty Burn cascades over the edge of the hills, and tumbles down conifer-clad slopes in the style of the Canadian Rockies. Falkland is within easy reach, and completes a walk of about 10 miles (16 km).

Much easier, however, is the ascent of the Bishop Hill from Leslie. A tarred road leaves the Leslie-Milnathort road (A911) about a mile west of the town and rises northwards to a crossroads just south of Holl Reservoir. The left branch is a delight under any conditions, and climbs westwards so gradually that it is hardly noticeable, until you turn to see the spread of the Lomonds beneath you. Crossing farmland, forest and moorland, the road reaches the tussocky summit of Bishop Hill after about four miles (6 km).

Here you will find the derelict limestone quarries which for years have been rich sources of fossils. Even though they have been plundered for generations there always seems to be plenty left, and interesting finds are almost guaranteed.

The outlook is high, wide and handsome, and invariably breezy, for here the prevailing winds sweep in from the west, across Loch Leven and up the steep front of the Bishop. Nearby, at Portmoak, is the Scottish Gliding Union's headquarters, and in good weather groups of gliders using the upcurrents perform their silently graceful aerial ballets overhead, or swish past in fast runs, often below summit level.

Just over the crest of the hill on the west-facing slopes, stands the Lomonds' most famous landmark, Carlin Maggie, a 40-foot (12-metre) column of basalt, which until recently had a number of boulders balanced precariously on its top. Some of these are gone now, but it is still an impressive sight with those that remain.

Legend has it that Maggie was head of a coven of witches in these parts, and her ability and authority grew to such an extent that she entered into a power struggle with the Devil himself. Auld Nick was so incensed at this audacity that he gathered up a load of large boulders and dropped them on the coven. As mentioned earlier, these Devil's Burdens can still be seen on the slopes of West Lomond. For Maggie he reserved a special punishment. As she fled across the hillside he struck her with a bolt of lightning, turning her to stone for all time. Maggie still stands there, aloof and tall, gazing silently out over the hillside and farmlands to the distant Ochils.

There are, of course, other hills in Fife; Largo Law in the east, the Binn at Burntisland, the Ferry Hills at North Queensferry, and Norman's Law and the hills of North Fife, where the Ochils tail off into nothingness. None of these exceed 300 metres, but they provide interesting outings for casual walkers.

From the North Fife hills the views across the River Tay are quite splendid, considering how little effort is required to reach the tops.

On the far shore the Carse of Gowrie rises to the Sidlaw Hills, and these are backed, in turn, by the higher mountains of Angus rolling northwards to meet their Cairngorm cousins.

Angus

Angus is an area *par excellence* for the walker, for it is a microcosm of the whole country. From its renowned beaches at Carnoustie and the rocky, cliff-bound coastline around Arbroath, it sweeps inland and upwards over rich farmland and rolling hills to culminate in the great wall of mountains which separates it from Aberdeenshire.

It has everything—bustling holiday towns, quiet villages, lonely hamlets, hills, glens, rivers, waterfalls, ancient castles and Bronze-Age forts; and a dialect all of its own. Although it is separated from Fife by only a mile (1½ km) of water, its people speak almost a different tongue.

From sea level the terrain rises to the Sidlaw Hills behind Dundee, a low range which runs parallel to the north bank of the River Tay. It then drops to the fertile Vale of Strathmore before once more rising even higher to the Braes of Angus and the Cairngorms, remote and beautiful, yet at the same time savage in their grandeur.

This high upland area is made the more interesting and dramatic by the glens which slice deep into the heart of the mountains. They run generally north/south; from west to east the major ones are Glenisla, Glen Prosen, Glen Clova and Glen Esk. These give access to the most remote areas, and are supplemented by other, lesser-known valleys.

With this barrier of mountains across the north of Angus, the roads up the glens are necessarily dead ends. However, they are dead ends only for the motorist; for the walker the end of the road is just the beginning of his world.

The ancient name for these Cairngorms was the Mounth, and the name is perpetuated in the Mounth roads, old highways which continue from the head of each glen over the high tops to Deeside. Now little more than tracks, they have been used as a means of communication for centuries. Black Highland cattle were driven south over these routes to the markets in Forfar; the same cattle were often stolen, too, by marauding bands of caterans, and brought over the hills rather than by the more open road through the Cairnwell Pass to the west. Tinkers and farmers, shepherds, bootleggers and royal messengers on their way to Balmoral have all used these hill roads, and Queen Victoria herself crossed them on horseback on several occasions on her famous 'expeditions'.

Glenisla

The most westerly of the main Angus glens is Glenisla, the mountains of its western side actually forming the boundary between Angus and

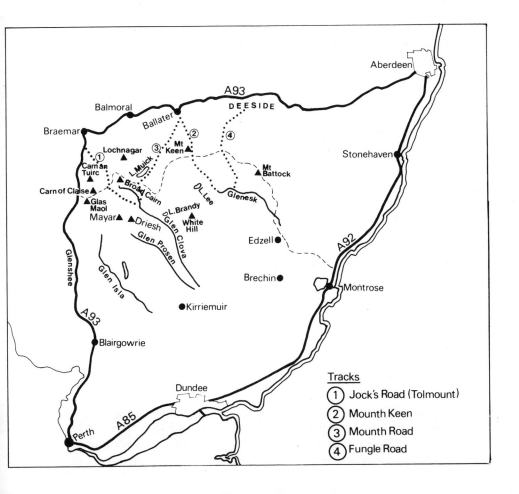

Tracks
1. Jock's Road (Tolmount)
2. Mounth Keen
3. Mounth Road
4. Fungle Road

Perthshire. For some reason it is not outstandingly popular with hill walkers, yet it has much to offer. This is the land of the Ogilvies, and the glen starts near the family seat of Airlie Castle, on the River Isla, 6 miles (10 km) west of Kirriemuir.

Approaching from the south via Alyth the road crosses the river upstream from Reekie Linn, one of the best known features of the glen. Here the Isla passes from the Highlands into the Lowlands as it roars over the Highland Boundary Fault and thunders 80 feet (24 metres) into the gorge.

There are two roads up the glen from Reekie Linn. The minor road is a hill road, and climbs to 400 metres before dropping to Bridge of Brewlands and rejoining the main road which follows the east bank of the Isla.

Just over halfway up the main road is Knockshannoch, or the Round House, a pleasantly-situated youth hostel which is said to owe its round shape to the owner's fear of being trapped in a corner by the devil.

North from Brewlands the hills start to crowd in, Mount Blair being the most prominent to the west. At 745 metres, its popularity stems from its accessibility, the good walking on its slopes, and the uninterrupted view from the top.

A secondary road continues up the glen from Brewlands for a further five miles (8 km) before degenerating into a track. At this point you are only a mile (1½ km) away from Perthshire over the hills.

The best-known of all the hill walks in the area is the Monega Path over the Mounth, which starts 2½ miles (4 km) further up the glen. It is a 6-mile (10-km) high-level walk, the highest public track in the country, in fact. Branching left from the main track, it crosses the Glas Burn and climbs steadily to the summit of Monega Hill to continue as a Land-Rover track along the top of the cliffs, where the mountains tumble steeply down into Caenlochan Glen. The route then bends northwest and climbs to its highest point at just over 1000 metres on the eastern shoulder of Glas Maol before starting its descent to cross the Angus/Aberdeenshire boundary, and down the spur of Sron a Gaoithe to join the Glen Clunie road 7 miles (11 km) south of Braemar.

From just below the county boundary the path is virtually non-existent, but by then journey's end is almost in sight, and you should have little difficulty in finding your way.

Glas Maol, at 1068 metres, is the highest summit in Angus, and a fine, if rather short ridge walk runs southwestwards from it to Creag Leacach. The view extends over the Devil's Elbow, up the Cairnwell Pass to the ski slopes on the Cairnwell and Carn Aosda, and beyond to the main massif of the Cairngorms. Southwards are the familiar twin summits of the Lomonds of Fife.

It is interesting to note that from Creag Leacach the Angus boundary runs along the hilltops rather than the valleys, and crosses the summits of no fewer than seven Munros. Little wonder then that this bastion of mountains has provided Angus with a solid barrier in the north, and channelled movement via the Mounth paths.

An alternative outing to the Monega Path is an exploration of the upper reaches of Glenisla. Here it splits into two short glens, each only a mile (1½ km) in length, Caenlochan Glen and Glen Canness. Both are steep-sided and craggy around their rims—'A very precipitous place' according to Queen Victoria.

Deep-cut and remote, their steep sides of consolidated scree topped by walls of split and fissured rock are in stark contrast to the gentle valley below and the featureless plateau above. However, it is possible to walk to the head of Caenlochan Glen and up through the rocks—without actual rock climbing—to join the Monega Path as it descends to the north.

These twin glens are justly famous among botanists for, with Glen Doll and Ben Lawers, they are the main locations of the rarer alpine plants in Britain.

Glen Doll

Just over the hills to the east of Glen Canness is Glen Doll, part of a similar geographical set-up at the head of Glen Clova. The main glen again divides into a Y formation, this time around the base of Craig Mellon.

For an extended stay in the area there are hotels at Clova and Rottal, plus a good youth hostel just north of Braedownie at the junction of the two glens.

The youth hostel is situated near the start of a hill path that is probably the most famous of them all. This is the Tolmounth, another high crossing from the Angus glens to Deeside which takes its name from Tolmount, a 958-metre summit near its highest point. However, it is better, if wrongly, known as Jock's Road. Strictly speaking this name applies only to a part of the route between Glen Doll and the summit, but common usage has lent the name to the whole 12-mile (19-km) track from Glen Doll to Auchallater, 2 miles (3 km) south of Braemar.

How did the name arise? Some say it came from the kestrels, or baddenjowks which used to hunt in large numbers in the area. Others say that it was named after Jock Winter, a countryman of these parts; it is interesting that there is a 'Winter Corrie' in the side of Driesh, a nearby mountain.

Names aside, it's a fine track which climbs steeply up the glen by the White Water. Once past the tree line the view back is quite magnificent, out across a blanket of conifers to the jutting cliffs of Craig Rennet. The route has been spoiled somewhat in recent years by this wholesale afforestation, but the walk is still well worth the effort.

The path steepens, climbing to the right to avoid the ravine at the head of the glen, and once away from the encircling rock faces you reach a bothy by the trackside.

In 1959 four Glasgow hill walkers died in a blizzard while crossing the Tolmounth from Braemar to Glendoll Lodge. One had almost reached this bothy, which was a ruin at the time, but might have provided enough shelter for him to survive. After the tragedy volunteers rebuilt the hut and it now stands as a place of sanctuary for future hill walkers.

Walkers venturing on these hills, as on all other hills in this area, should always be prepared for the worst. In summer a good map and compass are desirable; in winter they are essential. In a matter of minutes the weather can change from a bright, crisp day to a freezing Arctic hell.

The hillside is more open above the bothy, and the path is followed upwards over Crow Craigies, its highest point at 918 metres, before starting to descend, gradually at first, then more steeply into Glen Callater and along the northeast side of Loch Callater.

If time and energy are plentiful make a detour by Tolmount itself and around the rim of Corrie Kander. It's a stomach-churning experience to gaze down into this lonely, steep-sided corrie, with its inky lochan far below. On its far side is a ruin, near which a track can be picked up to take you down to Lochcallater Lodge, and from there it is a pleasant 3-mile (5-km) tramp to the main road at Auchallater.

Glen Clova's other Mounth path starts from the eastern arm of the Y at the top of the glen. From Braedownie a road runs northwards towards Moulzie, and after about a mile (1½ km) the Capel Mounth track strikes upwards through the trees on the right. On reaching the open hillside it zigzags steeply to attain the shoulder of Ferrowie. After a dip it develops into a broader track, and for the next couple of miles (3 km) undulates easily across the plateau before dropping to the Spittal of Glenmuick.

A slightly longer, but more spectacular way across the mountains is to continue up the road past Moulzie and round under the crags of

Juanjorge to Bachnagairn. At this point it seems that there is no way out of this dead end, yet the path somehow twists its way upwards to join a Land-Rover track near a hut on the col between the Sandy Hillock and Broad Cairn. Turning east the county boundary is crossed into Aberdeenshire, and there is a choice of routes, each equally stimulating.

The broad track continues along the top of the hillside overlooking Loch Muick, affording a dazzling vista to Lochnagar and the desolate mountain-hung valley of the Dubh Loch. A narrower track leads off northwestwards and swoops dizzily down to the shores of Loch Muick, then continues along the loch-side to the Spittal.

Although the head of Glen Clova is a walkers' Mecca the remainder of the glen should not be neglected. From the roadside between Rottal and the hamlet of Clova tracks lead up into the hills for those who prefer to do their own route-planning. Two of the finest walks encircle Lochs Wharral and Brandy, and once on the plateau the possibilities are endless.

Driesh and Mayar, the popular twin Munros, are usually tackled by the breathtaking track up the Shank of Drumfollow, and though this is probably the best route for scenery, a different approach can be made from the head of Glen Prosen, which runs parallel to Glen Clova, some 3 miles (5 km) to the southwest. From Glenprosen Lodge a path climbs up on to the Shank of Driesh, and an easy walk over rough moorland leads to the summit, with its memorial cairn. It's almost a tradition that you don't climb Driesh without taking in Mayar also, and it's a grand stroll from one to the other along a high path made by generations of pounding boots.

Glen Esk

Glen Esk, arguably the most beautiful of the Angus glens, must certainly be the most varied. From the fertile lowlands around Brechin it bores into the mountains, twisting and curving. At its head it forks, like its neighbouring glens, and the walkers' routes continue to the very roof of the Cairngorms.

A glance at the map will show many footpaths and forestry tracks leaving the road up the glen. Some of these provide easy, well-defined circular walks, while others fade away on the bare hillside and leave the more ambitious walker to his own devices.

One of the most popular tops in the lower reaches of the glen is the Hill of Wirren, along with its two outliers, East and West Wirren. These give a fine walk on broad ridges, with extensive views southwards.

A good 12-mile (19-km) tramp starts at the corner of the B966 road where it crosses the River North Esk, about a mile (1½ km) north of Edzell. From Gannochy, roads and tracks lead on to the main east ridge via the Hill of Corathro. From the Hill of Wirren a broad ridge drops northeastwards towards Craigangower, then by descending eastwards to a bulldozed track you can circle down to the River North Esk, and so back to Gannochy.

As you move up the glen the hills crowd in over the road, and the river, though generally not spectacular, passes through some fine rocky defiles. The glen gradually takes a westward direction before passing through birchwoods to reach the hamlet of Tarfside with its folk museum and tearoom, where the Water of Tarf spills down from its mountain fastnesses to join the North Esk on its way to the sea.

Tarfside is also noted as the start (or finish) of three more Mounth paths over the hills. Challenging walks these, though not beyond the capabilities of a normally active walker.

The Firmounth, Birse Mounth and Fungle Road all start as one route, following the Water of Tarf northwards. On the slopes of Tampie Hill they divide, the Firmounth continuing northwards over the summit of Tampie then down the slopes of St Colm's Hill to meet the forestry roads of Deeside to the west of Aboyne.

The other two drop steeply down the eastern side of Tampie to Ballochan in the Forest of Birse, then continue by tracks to Birse Castle and the hill of Carnfeg. Here they separate, the Birse Mounth heading down by Newmill to the main road a couple of miles (3 km) east of Aboyne, while the Fungle Road follows the Allt Dinnie down through the Fungle, the wooded glen which gives its name to the whole route. This route brings the walker right into the south side of Aboyne itself.

From Tarfside it is but 3 miles (5 km) to the head of Glen Esk where the public road ends. Although this is probably the most remote of the principal Angus glens, its popularity is borne out by the existence of a car park at this point. It is here that drivers take a back seat, as it were, and walkers come into their own.

If the glen seemed picturesque and rugged before, these descriptions pale beside the scenery ahead. In only a few miles the landscape changes from the soft hills of the lower glen to the high reaches of the Cairngorms.

It is a land which will throw out the ultimate challenge to the hardened hillman, especially in winter, yet it provides good terrain for the novice if it is treated with understanding and respect.

Glen Esk divides, both branches running into steep-sided valleys, craggy and boulder-strewn—a wonderful wilderness of high places, magnificent isolation and desolation, the home of the red deer and golden eagle.

To the north the way is by the Mounth Keen, the last of the Mounth paths of Angus, crossing over the shoulder of Mount Keen, Scotland's most easterly Munro.

From the car park the path follows the Water of Mark in a north-westerly direction for 2 miles (3 km) to the Queen's Well, a crown-shaped stone monument erected by Lord Dalhousie at the spot where Queen Victoria stopped to drink while on one of her expeditions over Mounth Keen from Balmoral to Fettercairn. It's a sad monument, for only a few weeks after she passed this way her beloved Prince Albert was dead, and the monarch, so often seen as a stern disciplinarian, was left alone in the world with her grief.

The path divides at the well, the Mounth Keen being the right-hand branch. It climbs steeply up the gorge of the Ladder Burn, and zigzags sharply to gain the southern shoulder of Mount Keen.

Once on the open hillside the way is clear across the western flanks of the mountain, though an alternative path crosses the summit. The paths meet up again and fall to the valley of the Tanar near the Shiel of Glentanar, then cross the remaining hills by Craig Vallich to the Bridge of Muick and Ballater. The total walking distance is 13 miles (21 km).

Westwards from the car park a road goes up Glen Lee by the northern shore of Loch Lee. Ahead is the rugged peak of Craig Maskeldie soaring a thousand feet (300 metres) above the valley floor, and jutting out arrogantly as if to bar further progress up the glen. However, the track curves around its lower slopes and edges between it and Monawee, then continues, twisting and snaking up the narrow glen.

A favourite and not too difficult walk is to proceed to a point on the track under the birch-clad slopes of Craig Maskeldie, about a mile (1½ km) beyond the western end of Loch Lee. Here a path leads into a valley on the left for ¾ mile (1 km) to the Falls of Unich where the river foams and crashes over a rocky staircase before leaping the final 30 feet (9 metres) as if glad to be free of the restricting gorge at last, and able to pursue a quieter course to meet Loch Lee.

Many people return by the same route, but to see this wild country at its best follow the Unich through the ravine between Craig Maskeldie and Hunt Hill. This path was originally constructed for stalkers' ponies, and gives a rewarding, if stiff, climb to the Falls of Damff, which are even more spectacular than their downstream relative.

Once past the falls the way eases and eventually leads to the featureless plateau which stretches southwestwards to Glen Clova. However, ¾ mile (1 km) past the falls you can double back up over the summit of Cairn Lick. From there a broad track descends a shoulder, the Shank of Inchgrundle, which gives awe-inspiring views down into the corrie beneath the crags of Craig Maskeldie on the left, and a wide vista along the length of Loch Lee ahead. To the north Mount Keen rises in the background, with the Mounth path to Deeside clearly visible.

It's an easy saunter down to the head of Loch Lee where the main track back to the car park can be rejoined, thus completing a round of 10 miles (16 km).

A little-known road runs southwards from the car park, and though it has deteriorated in places it is still possible to follow the route. This Priest's Road is so called because of its use by the local minister when travelling between his two charges at Invermark and Glen Lethnot. It was also used extensively by bootleggers moving whisky, illicitly distilled in the glens, to the lucrative markets in the Lowlands, and so its alternative name is the Whisky Road.

From Invermark car park it rises eastwards to Westbank, then round the western flanks of the Hill of Rowan to meet the main road. Crossing the North Esk at Dalbrack it then climbs Garlet Hill, over the saddle between it and Cowie Hill, and descends to the Berryhill Burn. From there it rises once more, round the eastern end of East Knock, and runs by the steep-sided gully of the Clash of Wirren on the last 2 miles (3 km) to the glen road at Stonyford.

The original road kept to the east of the main road, but this has all but disappeared. However it is still possible to pick it up on the hillside about halfway between Stonyford and Bridgend at the bottom of the glen. It runs along the flank of Craig Finnoch, parallel to the West Water, and indeed this last section, being better defined than most of the route, seems to bear out the story that this was to have been a 'super highway' over the Mounth. Alas, the new road was driven up only 2 miles (3 km) from Bridgend before the dreams of the builders faded, and with them the prospects of a modern road.

Using the Mounth Keen and the Priest's Road bootleggers were able to bring their illicit whisky by pack trains over the mountains from Deeside for sale in Brechin and the south, much to the discomfiture of the local excisemen.

The Sidlaws

Finally, it would be seen as a criminal injustice to have an account of the Angus Hills and fail to mention the Sidlaws. 'The Seedlies', beloved of Dundonians for generations, are not as popular as they once were, but being almost on Dundee's doorstep they provide easy walking with wide panoramas for anyone who cannot get further afield.

Stand on the Sidlaws and look northwards to the mountains and glens of Angus. Promise yourself that you will visit them some day, and you will be rewarded with some of the greatest hill walking experiences of your life.

Maps

Fife and Angus are covered by OS 1:50,000 sheets 44, 53, 54, 58 and 59; and by Bartholomew's 1:100,000 sheets 45, 49 and 52.

Change and Immutability

When I went up to Clova glen
And I was in my teens
And got there on a bicycle
And lived on bread and beans
And covered twenty miles or so
And got up Driesh and Mayar
The May month oystercatcher flights
Were madly piping there.

When I went up to Clova glen
And I was fifty-five
And lived on wine and caviare
And had a car to drive
And managed half a dozen miles
And halfway up the hill
The May month oystercatcher flights
Were madly piping still.

7
THE CENTRAL HIGHLANDS
Hamish M. Brown

T he Central Highlands are, by their very nature, reasonably accessible to the large urban areas of Scotland and some parts, like Glen Coe or Ben Nevis, can suffer from overuse. Nevertheless it is still easy to walk for days without meeting other people. The region has vast areas of wilderness, for sheep have long displaced man as the local population.

The area boundaries are, in the west, the Firth of Lorn, Loch Linnhe and Loch Lochy; across by upper Speyside in the north; in the east, down the line of the A9 (Drumochter-Pitlochry) road; then along the south, Loch Rannoch, the edge of Rannoch Moor, Glen Orchy to Oban. Apart from Loch Linnhe the area is landlocked, very much the centre of the Highlands.

Few areas of Britain offer such diverse interests to the mountain lover: the rock climber has the Buachaille and Ben Nevis to which the winter climber adds Creag Meaghaidh; there are great ridges like Cruachan, the Blackmount, Mamores and Grey Corries, while Ben Alder is one of the largest areas of high ground in Britain; the hosteller has several useful bases; there is a useful chain of bothies; there are wilds enough for the backpacker to crisscross the area on longer treks; Meall a' Bhuiridh offers a ski centre and the hills between Loch Ericht and Loch Ossian are splendid for ski touring. I can only mention a few places here (and some favourites not at all) for exploring a region is part of its enjoyment. With a railway leading to Oban, another over Rannoch Moor, and another forming the eastern boundary there is unique opportunity to explore cross-country without the tie of a car. The Munro-bagger will find about 80 of his magic mountains within these bounds, including four of the eight 4000-footers (or should we say 1219-metres, these days?)

A surprising amount *can* be done from a car as the country really remote from roads is generally less mountainous, but this does not mean liberties can be taken. Wide margins should be allowed in planning routes. In some areas heavy rainfall (not unknown) can provide serious river-crossing problems. Winters can be severe. Summers can be airless and hot. The Etive midge is not to be underestimated. For all our enjoyment of the hills we must not forget the regular hazards which are always lying ready to ambush us.

The main walking areas in the Central Highlands are really those with good groupings of Munros. I should think the majority of Highland walking is Munro-orientated. This certainly helps to ensure one comes to know an area generally rather than always repeating favourite hills. It spreads the numbers, gives enjoyable planning and the satisfaction of objectives accomplished. It is a natural spur, but should not be the *only* activity and if I have described plenty of circular walks which are basically Munro-hunting I equally emphasize the special delights of longer, linear routes, with which the area is peculiarly endowed.

They can be combined, of course. A friend and I on the first-ever *Ultimate Challenge* coast-to-coast trek reeled off several Munros from Ben Nevis eastwards, then enjoyed two days of extraordinary rough, empty, low-level trekking by Rannoch Moor, Loch Ericht and Loch Errochty through to the A9. We did not see a car between Fort William and Calvine and, off the Munros, we did not see a single human being. The *Ultimate Challenge* is, as its name implies, a longer and demanding trip, but on a smaller scale the Central Highlands provide good training in the art of trail packing. It has some superb expeditions in its own right.

Accommodation

It would pay the walker to be a member of the Scottish Youth Hostels Association simply to be able to stay at Loch Ossian hostel at some time. It is one of the few hostels which, perforce, you reach on foot. It is a good centre for Munro-bagging and an important stage on long multi-day through walks if you are trying not to carry a tent. Glen Coe and Glen Nevis are well placed for important hill areas but do tend, in the summer, to be swamped by the international hitching brigade. Speyside hostels, Pitlochry, Oban and Loch Lochy are all on the edge of the Central Highlands. At Fersit (north end of Loch Treig) is a private hostel (Fasgadh, proprietor Nancy Smith) which again is a good base or staging post.

There are many club huts in the area, most of which are available to members of other clubs and can be booked through club secretaries who have up-to-date information: CIC Hut on Ben Nevis (very historic and surprisingly little used in summer); Steall (head of Glen Nevis, Lochaber MC); Lagangarbh (under the Buachaille, SMC); Inbhirfhaolain (Glen Etive, Grampian Club); Blackrock (under Meall a' Bhuiridh, LSCC); Clashgour (west of Loch Tulla, small, Glasgow University MC).

There is an open shelter under Creag Meaghaidh (GR 435879, not in stalking season) and quite an extensive range of bothies. These are not publicized as overuse can spoil the atmosphere of such open shelters but those keen enough to tramp will find them and/or can join the Mountain Bothies Association.

The Bridge of Orchy Hotel does special weekend rates for walkers (even early breakfasts!) and is recommended. Inveroran (west of Loch Tulla), Kingshouse and Rannoch Station (on Rannoch Moor), and Laggan (east end of Loch Laggan) are hotels in isolated situations which backpackers may find useful. Hotels and/or bed and breakfasts are really only found round the periphery of our area, there being no roads in its heart, but some of these close in the off season and can be busy in summer. There are 'gaps' on the A9 and east from Roy Bridge.

Transport

The Highlands and Islands Development Board produces an annual timetable of all routes by train, bus, sea and air: *Getting Around the Highlands and Islands,* and the Post Office has a *Scottish Postbus Timetable* of its services into remote areas. For anyone without private transport these are invaluable. In this area the railway lines provide valuable stopping off points and there are bus services across Rannoch Moor and from Fort William to Speyside. A postbus links Rannoch Station eastwards.

There is no Sunday service on the Glasgow-Fort William line but there is on the Perth-Inverness line so weekend links using these should go west-east. Cycles can be carried free on British Rail and are a superb cheap means of transport which can be of great help to walkers. I keep a folding Raleigh *Stowaway* in my car; you can add many miles to the daily range this way. Services will in many cases not operate on Sundays.

Long Expeditions

Backpacking is one of the few transatlantic words which is concise and accurate. It is also a warning: it's your back you pack! This is not a handbook on methods but with the distances sometimes involved in Scotland, it is important not to carry too much and become exhausted. You still may have to carry all you need. To the coast-to-coast note earlier I could have added that we did not pass a single café, shop or pub in 50 miles (80 km) as the crow flies—which is the very reason we value Scotland as it is and must resist unwarranted development. The following are just two samples of long treks.

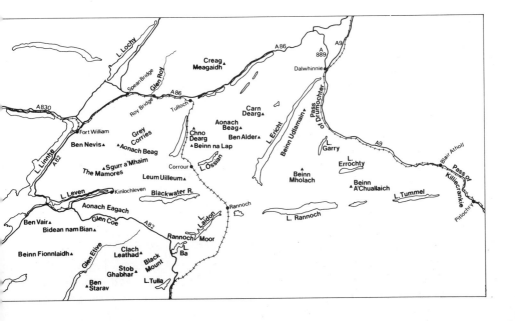

Loch Awe to Dalwhinnie

Four days; about 60 miles (100 km). Maps: Bart 48, 51; OS 50, 42. Start: Dalmally, conveniently on the Oban rail line. A variety of accommodation is readily available, in Dalmally or on the shores of Loch Awe if the back road by Stronmilichan is done the evening before.

Day One: The route goes up Glen Strae (an old Clan MacGregor homeland) by a Land-Rover track which has been extended a couple of miles (3 km) beyond what is shown on the maps. It ends where the waterfall is marked. A feeling of real remoteness begins once you leave the scar of track behind, and the going is rough and then steep as you make for the col, east of Beinn a' Chuirn, which leads to Gleann Fuar. The col is about 400 metres and is a place of character. You descend to a pretty remnant of the old Caledonian Forest, beyond which the valley bottom is peat-ridden and wet. Escape to the path shown to pass Druimliart (ruin, GR 260411), birthplace of Duncan Ban Macintyre. Inveroran and Bridge of Orchy have hotels.

Day Two: Round Loch Tulla and take the Land-Rover track eastwards by Achallader (ruin of an old Campbell keep), passing another forest remnant at Cranach, then Gorton, then pulling up on to the edge of the moor which is crossed to Rannoch Station (hotel). There are new plantings which complicate navigation but the railway line is a sure guide.

Day Three: Go east to pick up the track that runs north from Loch Eigheach to Loch Ossian. After crossing the Allt Gormag turn right on the line of track (shown on Bartholomew) to pass Loch Smeur, pass above the plantings and gain Loch Erichtside at the bridge in the southwest corner. A mile and a half (3 km) short of Alder Bay the track stops suddenly. Alder Bay is a good overnight stop (haunted bothy or camp).

Day Four: Several variants, all long: 1: Right up the loch-side (track underwater in parts to start) which is extraordinarily monotonous. 2: Up to the pass between Ben Alder and Beinn Bheoil (both Munros) to pick up the Bealach Beithe track which is followed to the east of Loch Pattack to reach Ben Alder Lodge and the weary road to Dalwhinnie. 3: Go northwest and round to use the Bealach Cumhann and Bealach Dubh paths. Cross after Culra to avoid the hard road. There are hotels, shop and railway at Dalwhinnie.

The mileages work out about 15-17-11-18 (24-27-18-29 km). The trip could be done over weekends: train to Bridge of Orchy and walk to Loch Awe; train to Rannoch and walk to Bridge of Orchy; Rannoch to Dalwhinnie over a Saturday-Sunday.

Fort William to Dalwhinnie

Three days; at least 50 miles (80 km). Maps: Bart 50, 51; OS 41, 42. Start: Fort William, on the West Highland Line. Major town. Youth Hostel in Glen Nevis.

Day One: Walk up Glen Nevis, a tarred road, which can be avoided by using the north bank of the river from the youth hostel to Polldubh. A water-worn gorge after the car park leads to the Steall meadow and the long miles up the watershed of Tom an Eite. Camp or bothy somewhere between there and Loch Treig, fine wilderness country.

Day Two: Take the path to and round the head of Loch Treig and on up to Corrour Station (keep west of the line). Road east to, and along, Loch Ossian (tempting youth hostel!) to either cross the Bealach Dubh towards Culra, or to turn through by the Bealach Cumhann to Ben Alder cottage.

Day Three: Continue to Dalwhinnie (see previous route description) or, if transport can be arranged, keep down the River Pattack to Kinloch Laggan, a more enjoyable route. Distances will depend on where you stop but day two could be over 20 miles (32 km). There is track, however, for most of the journey. Both these routes follow lines used in droving days.

Easy Day Walks

These are expeditions which can be done in half a day but some can be extended if desired. They are short but deserve the respect due to rough country.

Meall a' Bhuiridh (Hill of the Roaring)

Maps: Bart 48; OS 41 (GR 251503). This ski mountain overlooking Rannoch Moor has a car park and other facilities at its base and is well signposted on the A82. At weekends the chair lifts may be in operation, which gives useful uplift. The mountain gives superb views over the Moor and to Ben Nevis. It is 1108 metres (740 metres of ascent) but presents no problems. In summer there is a tempting narrow rocky ridge west to Creise for the more expert. The safest way off it is back over Meall a' Bhuiridh. Both are Munros.

Buachaille Etive Mor

Maps: Bart 48; OS 41 (GR 223542). This rocky mountain facing Rannoch Moor has easy approaches up Coire na Tulaich from Lagangarbh, on the A82, or Coire Cloiche Finne facing Glen Etive, but should only be attempted if clear of snow. From the saddle between the corries there is a well-marked path to the summit, Stob Dearg, 1022 metres. The whole eastern slopes are cliff-bound, the preserve of the rock climber. The ascent is best reserved for a clear day. About 800 metres of ascent. A grand viewpoint. Its neighbour, Buachaille Etive Beag (GR 179526), has its summit, Stob Dubh (958 metres), at the southwest end and can be climbed by the ridge dropping towards Glen Etive. The Lairig Eilde/Lairig Gartain circuit of the 'wee Buachaille' is a good low-level walk. Allow five hours.

Beinn na Lap

Maps: Bart 51; OS 41 (GR 376696). A very easy hill (937 metres) which can be done in a couple of hours from Loch Ossian youth hostel. This solitary Munro can be bagged between trains from Corrour Station. It is in the centre of some fine country. Leum Uilleim (William's Leap, 906 metres) on the other side of the railway (GR 332642) is a worthier summit, if below Munro altitude. Both offer about 500 metres of uphill going.

Some low-level walks

Glen Coe: The old road through the glen with a visit to the Lost Valley is popular. *Glen Nevis:* The gorge beyond the car park leads through magnificent scenery. *Kinlochleven:* Several paths run into the hinterland and, in various combinations, make good walks. *Glen Roy:* With its Parallel Roads it is quiet enough to give enjoyable walking and the forested northern foothills of the Nevis-Grey Corrie reaches are pleasant.

There are many glen tracks in Appin but most are dead ends. Glen Creran is linked by a marked path over a hill pass (400 metres) with Ballachulish on Loch Leven. Recommended. (OS Maps 41, 50.)

The West Highland Way

This runs right through the area and has always given a good walk without any need for officialdom's blessing. Consult the HMSO guide (R. Aitken) for details *and walk it* before it becomes soiled like the

Pennine Way. Its stages make excellent, fairly easy, day walks: Bridge of Orchy to Kingshouse; Kingshouse to Kinlochleven; Kinlochleven to Fort William, if you can arrange transport.

Easy Munro Days

Those not in the above are few, as several peaks are usually combined in any day's walking. Non-scramblers may peck at Sgor nam Fiannaidh (Peak of the Fingalians) and Meall Dearg separately rather than traverse the whole Aonach Eagach; the eastern A9/Drumochter summits of Meall Chuaich, Carn na Caim and A'Bhuidheanach Bheag are useful solitary ones while motoring by, as are the pairs of Gealcharn/ A'Mharconnaich (from Balsporran) and Udlamain/Sgairneach Mhor (from Coire Dhomhain) on the west of the A9 road. Beinn a' Chaoruinn (Hill of the Rowan) above Glen Spean is another single summit. Not Munros but also giving easy ascents and fine panoramas are the Pap of Glencoe (can be combined with Fiannaidh), Mam na Gualainn (north of Loch Leven, path from Lairigmor), Beinn a' Bhuiridh of Cruachan (from the dam), and Beinn a' Chrulaiste opposite the Buachaille.

Moderate Day Walks

These are rounds which will require a day rather than half a day but are straightforward in character.

Loch Treig Hills

The hills on both sides of the loch offer enjoyable walks. Turn off the A86 on the road signposted to Fersit. Park at the end of the tarmac.

Eastern Pair: Stob Coire Sgriodain (976 metres, Hill of the Scree Corrie) and Chno Dearg (1047 metres). Follow up one of the streams from Fersit—a unique splitting and splitting of the river flowing from Lochan Coire an Lochain—and then angle up on to the knobbly north ridge of the Munro. There are plenty of ups and downs on the round but Chno Dearg is grassy and easy in contrast. About 1000 metres of ascent.

Western Pair: Stob Coire Easain (1116 metres) and Stob a' Choire Mheadhoin (1106 metres). Start at Inverlair and follow right up Coire Laire, nearly to Coire na Cabaig, then simply up the ridge to Easain, returning over Mheadhoin and all the steps down to the Dubh Lochan. With 1200 metres of ascent and 14 miles (23 km), a full day.

Creag Meagaidh

Maps: Bart 51; OS 34 (GR 418876). This is a popular winter climbing ground but in spring or summer it can give the walker a good day in fine surroundings. Start at Aberarder by Loch Laggan and follow the footpath to Lochain a' Choire Ardair, then aim for The Window, the pass (used by Prince Charles after Culloden) at GR 426886 before turning south on to the summit plateau. There is over a mile (1½ km) of this to cross so good visibility is advisable. Some famous climbers have managed to become lost on its featureless acres! It is easiest to return by the same route. Munro-baggers can add Stob Poite Coire Ardair, GR 429889 (not named on map) and Carn Liath, GR 472903, to descend south back to the Aberarder path. At 1130 metres Creag Meagaidh is big, a 14-mile (23 km), 1000 metres of ascent trip.

Ben Nevis

Maps: Bart 50; OS 41 and several special maps (available from the Nevisport shop in Fort William). At 1344 metres Ben Nevis is Britain's highest point and deserves better than the standard plod up the tourist path (built originally for summit observatory ponies). Any straying from that clear way should only be made late in the season when the hill is free of snow—and with clear visibility. Start at Achintee House (parking) or the youth hostel and follow the tourist path up round to pass above Lochan Meall an t-Suidhe, then curve into the Allt a' Mhuilinn glen under the biggest cliffs in Britain. Go on past the CIC hut to Coire Leis and up the bouldery headwall to the lowest point towards the right as you approach. There are abseil posts visible. From the arête thus gained a toilsome climb up steep boulders leads to the summit. Descend by the tourist path. The Ben can also be climbed from the car park at the head of Glen Nevis by ascending beside the Allt Coire Eoghainn, then bearing right to gain the route up from the Carn Mor Dearg Arête. Descend by the tourist path. Ben Nevis is vastly overrated (and over-populated all summer). It is not even a very good viewpoint. Its lure is its supreme altitude.

Moderately full Munro Days

Moderately full days are probably needed for the following. Beinn Sgulaird (Mountain of Yelping) from head of Glen Ure or from Loch Creran; Beinn Fhionlaidh (Finlay's Mountain) from Allt Bharann or the head of Glen Ure; Sgor na h-Ulaidh (Peak of the Treasure) from the A82; Bidean nam Bian from the Lost Valley or Achtriochtan (not in winter); Carn Dearg and Sgor Ghaibhre from Loch Ossian; the east-end Munros of the Mamores; Stob Ban of the Grey Corries and 'combinations' from the A9 at Drumochter.

Strenuous Days on the Hills

These will demand long summer days and should only be attempted by the fit and experienced. In winter they are virtually alpine undertakings and not walks at all.

The Cruachan Ridges

Maps: Bart 47; OS 50. Start from the Pass of Brander (GR 050284) and follow up the stream to ascend the unnamed Taynuilt Peak (1101 metres). Three miles (5 km) of fine granite ridge take you eastwards (Pts 1126 metres and 997 metres are Munros) before turning off, steeply down, north to the pass at the head of Glen Noe (c. 550 metres). An equally hard pull up leads to Munros Beinn a' Chochuill (Peak of the Hood, 980 metres) and, 2 miles (3 km) east, Beinn Eunaich (Fowling Hill, 988 metres). Descend by dropping south from the col west of Eunaich or, if still full of energy, continue the traverse east over Meall Copagach to the col beyond, and from there follow the path down to Glen Strae. A very much shorter day can be had by simply doing the Cruachan Horseshoe: the ring of peaks holding the reservoir. Start and finish from the power station by Loch Awe. The main traverse will give about 13 miles (21 km) but 2250 metres of ascent. This is an excellent day with typical western atmosphere.

The Glen Etive Peaks

Maps: Bart 47; OS 50. The quickest start is to paddle the River Etive below Glenetive House, otherwise there is a bridge, 2 miles (3 km) up, to Coileitir. Whatever the start the ascent of Ben Starav (Stout Hill!) is brutal: 1078 metres in slightly more than 2 miles (3 km). Following the burn up to the northeast corrie can provide some interest; the ridges feel interminable! A good crest then wends east to a col where you skirt off to a lower col to make the ascent of outlying Beinn nan Aighenan (957 metres); Glas Bheinn Mhor (The Big Grey Lump, 993 metres) is then traversed, with a twisting drop to the col beyond (escape possible down the Allt Mheuran). A dull pull leads up to Stob Coir' an Albannaich (Peak of the Scotsman's Corrie, 1044 metres). Go well east from it before descending the col to Meall Tarsuinn (Transverse Peak). Traverse, rather than flank, this nuisance and from the odd col beyond, wet going leads to Munro number five, Meall nan Eun (Hill of the Birds, 926 metres). Descend by the Allt Ceitlein to Glen Etive. This is 17 miles (27 km) and 2350 metres of ascent. The day can also be done from Victoria Bridge by Loch Tulla, following an estate track west by Loch Dochard to GR 185403. A long ridge gains Aighenan. Descending off Eun to the Allt Dochard requires some care. Slightly less uphill, this route is at least 10 extra miles (16 km)—and worth the effort.

The Beinn a' Bheithir (Ben Vair) Horseshoe

Maps: Bart 47; OS 41. Start from Ballachulish village and ascend by the steep slopes to gain the Beinn Bhan ridge. (The view up Loch Leven is a good excuse for rests!) Once height is gained, fine crests lead over a top at 901 metres to Sgorr Dhearg (1024 metres), then down to a col at 757 metres before ascending Sgorr Dhonuill (Donald's Peak, 1001 metres) by a bouldery edge with cliffs to the north. The 3-mile (5-km) western arm will give one-mile-an-hour (1½ kph) going as it is rocky and knobbly (hence the many lochans) but the views are superlative.

Early in the day spot a fire break for the descent or risk fighting the forest. There are more tracks in the forest than the OS cares to show and timber is being felled. For this reason the alternative ascent by the north ridge of Sgorr Dhearg is not advised. Descent can be made to the sea near Kentallen Bay. The two Munros can be done quickest by a path up to the 757 metres col from GR 047569 on the forestry road. All southern flanks are steep and foul. If only about 9 miles (14 km) there is 1650 metres of ascent and the going is rough.

The Four Fours

Maps: Bart 50; OS 41. Aonach Mor, still *lower* than Aonach Beag, was promoted to over 4000 feet in the surveys that were incorporated into the metric maps we now use—so this fact was little noticed. Probably the easiest start if a car is used is from the Glen Nevis road-end car park and the waterslide but any of the routes mentioned earlier can do for climbing Ben Nevis. The descent to the Carn Mor Dearg Arête needs careful navigation. There have been many fatalities from sliding off over the cliffs on snow or ice. Marker posts guide. Once on the arête there is no problem in finding Carn Mor Dearg (1223 metres). This is an exposed crest of character. The east ridge down is interesting, dropping 400 metres in under a mile (1½ km). The col is c. 820 metres and a steep flank has to be slogged up to regain all the height lost. Aonach Mor is 1219 metres, an odd plateau above flanking cliffs. Follow the eastern crags south to gain Aonach Beag and descend the southwest ridge to the hanging valley and its stream leading down to Steall ruin. If linking on the Grey Corries, the descent is made from the col to Sgurr a' Bhuic. This day should not be attempted in winter by the inexperienced. It is 2100 metres of ascent and at least 10 miles (16 km).

The Mamores

Maps: Bart 51; OS 41. The full traverse of the eleven Munros of the Mamores is one of the great long days. Descriptions of it are found in *Hamish's Mountain Walk* and *The Big Walks* so, for here, it has been split into several day-walks, each long enough to satisfy the majority who will be collecting its summits in this fashion. The Mullach, Stob Ban, Iubhair and Sgurr a' Mhaim are often combined from the Glen Nevis side. The first three can equally well be done from the south by the Lairigmor Road. Sgurr a' Mhaim, Iubhair, Am Bodach (The Old Man), Chairn and An Garbhanach form another circuit from the head of Glen Nevis, as do An Garbhanach, Chairn, Na Gruagaichean (The Maiden) and Binnean Mor. Am Bodach, Chairn, Gruagaichean and Binnean Mor can be done from Kinlochleven which is also the usual approach for the eastern Munros of Eilde Mor, Binnean Beag and (perhaps) Binnean Mor. The paths shown on the OS map should be used for approach and descent lines as the hills form a rugged group with strenuous going everywhere. They merit many visits.

Long or Very Long Munro Expeditions

Apart from those above, there are the following. The Aonach Eogach ridge, which forms the north wall of Glen Coe, can be traversed in four or five hours but as it involves exposed scrambling the ordinary walker will find it challenging enough to possibly need a rope. The Grey Corries can be traversed from the head of Glen Nevis, from Choinnich Mor to Stob Ban, returning by the southern flanking glen. Approaches from the north have the problem of Stob Ban's outlying position in the south! A splendid really big day can combine these with the Ben-

Aonach traverse (see above). The round of Ben Alder/Beinn Bheoil, the traverse of the Beinn Eibhinn-Carn Dearg ridge and the round of Beinn a' Chlachair, Geal Charn and Creag Pitridh are all good days which, in the case of the first two, usually require a tent/bothy base as they are far from roads. The last is usually done from Luiblea on the A86; good paths help with all of them.

Maps

The Central Highlands area is covered by OS 1:50,000 sheets 34, 41, 42, 50 and 51; and by Bartholomew's 1:100,000 sheets 47, 48, 50 and 51.

Bibliography

Gordon, Seton, *Highways and Byways in the Central Highlands*, Macmillan

Steven, C. R., *The Central Highlands*, SMC district guide, West Col Productions

The area also features in the books by Borthwick, Brown, Gilbert/ Wilson, Haldane, Moir, Murray, Poucher, Prebble and Weir in the general list on page 31.

Loch Ossian

It was a heat to melt the mountains in,
The basking adder sunned his varnished span
And cooked the burning rock beneath his skin.
The aromatic resin swelled and ran;
Whilst, in the arid timber, tall and still,
Each needle nodded in the larch's shade:
And, bare above its plaid, the shapely hill
Seemed as the sunburnt shoulders of a maid,
Shyly disrobing by the shore alone.
Loch Ossian looked its very loveliest,
With lazing water warm against the stone,
The heron silent in his island nest,
And such a golden langour through the haze
That Summer seemed in love with idle days.

8
THE CAIRNGORMS
Cameron McNeish

For the purposes of this book, the Cairngorms are defined as that area bounded in the west by Glen Feshie, in the south by Glen Geldie and the River Dee, in the east by the Braemar to Tomintoul road, and in the north by the River Spey.

The Cairngorms have become, in recent years, one of Britain's foremost outdoor recreation areas. The great forests of Rothiemurchus, Glenmore, Abernethy and Ballochbuie on Deeside form an attractive foreground to the hills themselves, and offer attractive rambling in natural pine, birch and juniper-covered slopes. The lochs of Insh and Morlich seem to grow a dotted surface of sailing boats, canoes and windsurfers during the summer months, and the great granite cliffs and crags boast some of the finest rock and snow and ice routes in the country. Small wonder that Speyside now claims to be a tourist boom area. In winter the hordes of skiers have turned Aviemore, once a minor railway village, into Britain's only all-year-round holiday resort, so much so that expansion, in the village and on the slopes, is demanded by the various ski authorities and developers. There is unprecedented conflict between the skiers and the conservationists, and at the time of writing the argument has been put into the hands of the Secretary of State for Scotland.

The rounded masses of the hills are scoured by wind, an Arctic environment that demands respect. The vast glacier-scooped corries are unsurpassed in Britain for sheer grandeur, and the great fissures, valleys and trenches hold some of the most spectacular lochs in Scotland.

In winter these hills are demanding, and the visitor must be totally competent in the use of ice axe and crampons and well versed in the techniques of advanced navigation. There can be white-outs for days on end on the high tops, and a Cairngorm blizzard can be a killer which has caught, and continues to catch, many people unprepared.

However, please do not fear these hills; respect them. I think they are the finest in Britain. I hope you will enjoy them as much as I do.

The Passes

Seen from the air, the Cairngorms are sliced into three separate massifs; to the east the great bulks of Ben Avon and Beinn a'Bhuird lie alone, separated from the main Cairngorm massif by the great trench of the Lairig an Laoigh (The Pass of the Calves). The centre of the range is split by an even more imposing pass, the Lairig Ghru (The Gloomy or Forbidding Pass), a long narrow steep-sided defile running almost due north-south. West and south of the Sgorans and the Moine Mhor, the great wide glens of Feshie and Geldie separate the main Cairngorms area from the Drumochter Hills in the west and Tarff Hills in the south.

Each of these three passes offers the walker fine through routes from Speyside to Deeside, and of course vice versa.

The Lairig an Laoigh

The name of this pass, Pass of the Calves, originates from cattle-droving days, when the cattlemen of the north travelled south to the great trysts of Crieff and Falkirk. The Lairig Ghru was the main route through the barrier of the Cairngorms, but it was thought too rough for the younger beasts. The alternative, the Lairig an Laoigh, from Abernethy to Braemar, was less demanding.

Start from Glenmore, and follow the forestry track past Glenmore Lodge, the National Mountaineering Centre. This is a particularly attractive trail through an abundance of pine and juniper, with little Lochan Uaine, the green lochan, nestling in its hollow, making a fine point for a brief stop. Try the echo across the loch and hear it bounce back to you from the scree-covered slopes of Creag nan Gall. It is said that the almost translucent waters of Lochain Uaine were once used by the Glenmore fairies for washing their clothes; hence the green hue of the water.

Further along the trail, with the gable end of Ryvoan bothy on the horizon, the track splits in two. The branch in front of you passes by the bothy and leads down through Abernethy Forest to Nethy Bridge. The right-hand track is the one to follow, running over heather-covered moorland, past Loch a Garbh-Choire to Bynack Stable, or as it is locally known, the Nethy Hut.

From the hut, the cleft of Strathnethy lies immediately to the south, splitting the flanks of Bynack More and A'Choinneach on the left, and Cairngorm on the right. Cross the river by the wooden bridge and instead of continuing up Strathnethy, take the track which climbs steadily up the long north ridge of Bynack More. This track rises to a height of 770 metres, on a bleak and featureless plateau. Care and good navigation are needed in misty weather on this stretch, and records show that quite a few parties have lost themselves here.

Continue south past the eastern flanks of Bynack More and drop down to the rude shelter at Fords of Avon. This is a small howff, and often full, so don't count on it for accommodation. Cross the river Avon just below the hut, at a point marked on the OS map as Ath na Fiann, indicating an association with the legendary Celtic warrior hero Fingal. Be careful when you cross the river, as it is difficult when in spate.

For some miles south of the ford the route is fairly flat and obvious; past the Dubh Lochan and over the summit of the pass between Beinn Chaoruinn and Beinn Mheadhoin (Vane). Drop down into Glen Derry,

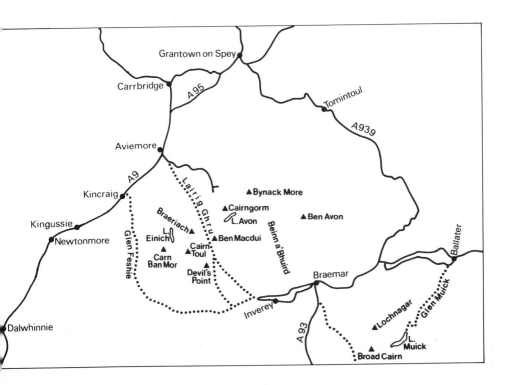

past the track which climbs up into Coire Etchachan, and continue over the alluvial flats and into the pines just north of Derry Lodge.

At Derry Lodge, take the Land-Rover track down Glen Lui to Linn o' Dee and Inverey. Braemar is another 4 miles (6 km) along the road.

Braemar to Derry Lodge—10½ miles (17 km); Derry Lodge to Fords of Avon—7 miles (11 km); Fords of Avon to Bynack Stable—6 miles (10 km); Bynack Stable to Glenmore—4 miles (6 km); Glenmore to Aviemore—7 miles (11 km). Total distance 34½ miles (55 km).

The Lairig Ghru

This is one of the most popular walking routes in Scotland and is a classic expedition in its own right. It is often walked as a climax to the long walk from Blair Atholl to Aviemore via Glen Tilt, and many backpackers link it with the Lairig an Laoigh route as a circular expedition.

Don't be misled by the fact that the Lairig Ghru is a pass; it is a strenuous mountain walk which rises to a height of 847 metres. It takes you through the very heart of the Cairngorms amid scenery of spectacular dimensions; in my opinion, the view up into the great Garbh Choire of Braeriach from the Lairig Ghru is one of the most impressive in Scotland, rivalling Coruisk in Skye and Loch Toll an Lochain of An Teallach.

Start at Coylumbridge, at GR 915106. Follow the signposted track up through the pines in Rothiemurchus to the Cairngorm Club footbridge which spans the waters of the Allt Druidh not far below the junction with the Am Beannaidh, which flows from Gleann Einich.

From the footbridge, follow the track through grassy meadows, with the great dark cleft of the Lairig Ghru splitting the mountains in front of you. You then come into the forest again, and a choice of four paths. The path to the Lairig turns sharp right and begins to climb rather steeply through the trees and heather high above the Allt Druidh. Look back over the superb views of Rothiemurchus to the Monadhliaths. Aviemore looks tiny in the distance, and the scene is totally dominated by pine trees, a vast mattress of them. On a day of light snowfall, the snow-speckled pine tops take on the look of brushed velvet, so dense is their natural formation.

As the pines grow more gnarled and stunted and begin to thin out, you will approach the bumpy moraines at the entrance to the path. Another path arrives from the left, from the Rothiemurchus Hut, used by the armed forces for outdoor activities. Sinclair Bothy, built in 1957, offers some shelter before the rough going in the actual pass. From here

the path climbs steadily through and over a maze of boulders and red
screes. On the left, the steep cliffs of Creag an Leth Choin loom high
above you, and on the right the scree slopes of Sron na Lairige are
almost as sheer. This is the Lairig Ghru proper, a narrow and steep-
sided defile, and strong winds are often funnelled through the narrows
even when the rest of the glen is calm. To many this may well be the
'gloomy, forbidding pass', but I am always thrilled in anticipation of the
prospect opening up in front of me.

As you descend from the summit of the path, the Allt na Criche, or
March Burn, plunges down from the Ben Macdhui plateau on your
left, to disappear underground below the boulders. It emerges again
south of the summit in three beautiful pools, the largest of which is
called the Lochan Dhubh na Lairige, the Black Lochan of the Pass.
Sadly, like other names in the Cairngorms, the old Gaelic names have
been anglicized thanks to the popularity of the area, and the three pools
are nowadays known as simply the Pools of Dee; a name sadly lacking
the poetic romance of the Gaelic.

Past the pools, the going becomes easier, and the view into Garbh
Choire gradually opens up on your right. You may see the large snow
wreath high in the left-hand corner of the corrie which has only melted
twice this century; the great corries will impress you, and in one, the
Garbh Choire Dhaidh, the infant Dee crashes down the crags from the
Braeriach Plateau at the start of its long journey to the sea at Aberdeen.

Braeriach, Sgor nan Lochain Uaine (Angels' Peak) and Cairn Toul
are the high points of these vast corries, Angels' Peak and Cairn Toul
being the shapeliest peaks in the area. Confusingly, Cairn Toul means
Hill of the Barn, an unusual name for such a shapely hill; but, when
viewed from the west on the Great Moss, the square-cut look of Cairn
Toul fully justifies its old Gaelic title.

Continuing south along the rough track you will cross the Allt Clach
nan Taillear, Burn of the Stone of the Tailors. Legend claims that three
tailors from Speyside wagered that on Hogmanay they would dance a
reel at the Three Dells—the Dell of Abernethy, the Dell of Rothiemurchus, and Dalmore in Braemar. After completing the first two parts of
the wager, they set off through the Lairig Ghru to fulfil the third part,
only to be overcome by a violent snowstorm. They sheltered, and
eventually died, beside the boulder which today bears their name.

A mile or so (1½ km) further on, Corrour Bothy can be seen below
the Devil's Point and Cairn Toul. The path then climbs uphill again,
and skirts around the flanks of Carn a Mhaim and into Glen Luibeg,
where the track meanders through superb pine and river scenery to

Luibeg and Derry Lodge. From Derry Lodge the route to Braemar is the same as for the Lairig an Laoigh.

Aviemore to Coylumbridge—2 miles (3 km); Coylumbridge to Cairngorm Club footbridge—2 miles (3 km); CCF to summit—5½ miles (9 km); Summit to Derry Lodge— 8½ miles (14 km); Derry Lodge to Braemar—10½ miles (17 km). Total distance 28½ miles (46 km).

Glen Feshie

From Achlean in Glen Feshie (GR 853976) a very fine route can be walked by way of the glen and by Glen Geldie to Inverey and Braemar. It is another long walk of some 21 miles (34 km) from Achlean to Inverey, or 25 miles (40 km) to Braemar, and can be made into a circuit by returning to Speyside via one of the two Lairigs.

This is the easiest of the three passes, but the going can still be difficult in bad weather. Glen Geldie in particular is open and remote, with little shelter, and you are not as likely to come across other groups of walkers as you are in the other passes.

Take the footpath south of Achlean beside the River Feshie and continue south to the bothy at Ruigh Aiteachain. This path wanders through a forestry plantation, but is quite easy to follow. Ruigh Aiteachain is probably the finest bothy in the Cairngorms, set amid natural pine woods close to the River Feshie. It was a favourite haunt of the artist Landseer, and it was here that he painted his evocative *Stag at Bay*. From the cottage, a bulldozed track follows the river and begins to climb through screes and pines on to the wild moorland of upper Glen Feshie. As the track, and the river, turn eastwards, known locally as the Turn o'Feshie, the scenery becomes bare and remote, with the hills of the Ring of Tarff seemingly far away in the south. The River Eidart is soon reached, rushing and foaming in its miniature canyon. A footbridge crosses the river higher up, and it is just as well it is there, as the Eidart is often completely unfordable.

The bealach between Feshie and Glen Geldie is quite low, a mere 560 metres, but nowhere else in the Cairngorms will you experience the feeling of spaciousness that you do here. It is an omnipotent sensation, a flat landscape unrelieved by steep crags or ridges, a real, in these days of clichés, wilderness experience.

The track continues eastwards through this open landscape, with the long slopes of Beinn Bhrotain and Monadh Mor on your left, and away in the far distance the boundaries of An Sgarsoch and Carn an Fhidleir on your right, in the south. Follow this track, turning northeastwards now past a forestry plantation to the White Bridge, straddling the River Dee. Turn right once you cross the bridge, and follow the Land-Rover track beside the Dee to the Linn o'Dee and then by the road to Inverey and Braemar.

The High Tops

The Cairngorm Mountains are a mass of granite thrust up through the schists and gneiss that form the lower surrounding hills, planed down by the ice cap, and split, shattered and scooped by glaciers, frosts, and the power of running water and wind. One important point must be made to the visitor: these hills are unlike any other mountain range in Britain. From the viewpoints of Speyside or Deeside the hills appear as large rounded masses, perhaps a little uninspiring at first sight. But the Cairngorms are reticent hills, carefully guarding their innermost secrets for those who have the inspiration and energy to penetrate their inner sanctums. You do not gaze upwards to spectacular peaks in the Cairngorms; you must first pay the price of expending some energy to reach the tops and gaze *downward* to spectacular fissures and chasms, corries of unequalled grandeur and high lonely lochans.

'The sculptured sides of Braeriach, seen from Sgoran Dubh, are in reality far richer in beautiful intricate mountain sculpture than the whole face of the Matterhorn, as seen from the Riffel Alp.' That was the opinion of Professor Norman Collie, and although many may feel that he was slightly overstating his case, the parallels most certainly exist.

Ben Avon and Beinn a'Bhuird

These are the easternmost Munros of the Cairngorms, best approached from Deeside, although you can reach Ben Avon from Glenmore in a long expedition by following the Lairig an Laoigh track to Fords of Avon and climbing the long slopes from there.

Ben Avon is not so much a single mountain, its complexities almost afford it the honour of being a small hill range instead. It is a vast agglomeration of rounded tops and vast corries, some 7 miles long by 6 miles wide (11 × 10 km). Beinn a'Bhuird, or Table Mountain, is a long stretched-out hill with a huge flat summit plateau. On one side of the hill, vast heathery slopes fall gently into the Moine Bhealaidh above Glen Derry and into remote Glen Avon. The other side offers a complete contrast to this gentle aspect. All along the east side of the hill, steep craggy corries show the true face of the mountain, corries which look their finest when filled with snow and rimmed by some of the most spectacular cornices you will ever see.

Start by the Linn o' Dee past Inverey, and take the track northwards up Glen Lui towards Derry Lodge. After crossing the Black Bridge over the river, you will come upon a copse of tall mature pines on the right-hand side of the path. Immediately after the copse, strike right up the hillside and follow a narrow track which leads you through a narrow defile, past some small lochans, and into Glen Quoich.

With Beinn a' Bhuird and Ben Avon rising steadily in front of you, follow the forestry road in Glen Quoich for half a mile (¾ km) and cross the Dubh Gleann river by the ford. Follow the road for another mile or so (1½ km) before heading northeast up the heathery slopes to the south shoulder of Beinn a' Bhuird. This is marked as Bruach Mhor on the map. Easy walking will bring you to the cairn which marks the south summit at 1177 metres, and you can wander happily across this great wilderness, past the three magnificent eastern corries, to the main summit 2 miles (3 km) further on. You are now standing at 1196 metres above sea level.

Follow the rim of the great Garbh Coire in front of you, being careful to avoid the deep cornices which form here in the winter and spring. Pass the summit of Cnap a'Chleirich, and then descend to the obvious bealach, known locally as the Sneck. Climb the loose slopes above the Sneck on to Ben Avon, and head 1 mile (1½ km) northeast to the very conspicuous granite tor which carries the summit cairn. These tors are a feature of Ben Avon, and of Beinn Mheadhoin above Loch Avon. The Ben Avon tors can be seen for miles in every direction and are a useful aid to recognizing the mountain.

Return to the Sneck and descend into the peaty glen for 5 miles (8 km) until you come across the Glen Quoich path among the trees. Cross the ford again and by keeping on the Glen Quoich road you will eventually reach the public road near Mar Lodge. After quenching your thirst in the hotel, it is only a few miles by road back to the car park at Linn o'Dee. Alternatively, you can cross over into Glen Lui again and finish on the Derry Lodge road.

Distance: 25 miles (40 km). Maps 36, 43.

Ben Macdhui from Deeside

Ben Macdhui, the highest of all the Cairngorms at 1309 metres and the second highest mountain in Britain, is equidistant from Aviemore and Braemar, and involves a fairly long day out. The trip can be vastly reduced in length (and in quality) by gaining quick elevation to the summit of Cairngorm by the chair lift in Coire Cas, and then wandering across the plateau, but we will look at this approach later when we also take in Coire Etchachan, Loch Avon and the Shelter Stone.

Ben Macdhui's best approach is undoubtedly from Deeside. Leave Linn o'Dee car park and take the Lairig Ghru track as far as Derry Lodge. Instead of turning west in Glen Luibeg for the Lairig Ghru, keep walking northwards, over the footbridge beyond the lodge and through the pines into Glen Derry. Don't follow the new track on the east bank of the river, but stick to the footpath on the west bank. This is a popular area for deer, and I have often lain below the pines and watched herds of over a hundred move slowly past when bad weather on the tops has forced them into the glen. Continue north on the Glen Derry track, crossing the Derry Burn by the iron bridge just before the old dam. (The pool below the bridge is a fine place for a dook on a warm day.)

The glen floor now widens out and gives good views along the glen to the slopes of Beinn Mheadhoin. Follow Glen Derry for just over 2 miles (3 km) until you reach a split in the track at GR 035992, where the Ben Macdhui path forks left to the northwest. The path at this point is normally very boggy and muddy. Cross the Etchachan Burn by the old rickety bridge, and begin the long pull up and into Coire Etchachan, past the Hutchison Memorial Hut. Coire Etchachan has a most impressive quality, a vast bowl with steep craggy sidewalls, but the splendour of the scene is not yet complete. After climbing hard beside the noisy foaming burn, the gradient suddenly eases off, and in front of you, in all its splendour, lies Loch Etchachan, the highest tarn of its size in the country. Its shoreline caresses the 914-metre contour, and the loch is backed by an intricate complex of headwalls, cliffs and bulging shoulders. Snow lingers here well into the summer, and ice floats on the loch surface for almost six months of the year. The scene is totally Arctic, more reminiscent of Greenland than Scotland, and the ptarmigan, that hardy bird of the Arctic, haunts the subarctic heath which surrounds the loch. To the north, a flat col stretches towards the prominent bulk of Cairngorm, but in between, unseen from here, lies the deep recess which contains Loch Avon.

On the south side of the loch, our path climbs gradually but steadily up the slope, below the great bulge of Sron an Daimh (Promontory of the Stag). As you come out of the Etchachan bowl you reach another smaller bowl, containing a small lochan. On your left, if you care to peep over, the steep cliffs of Coire Sputain Dearg (Corrie of the Little

Red Spouts) drop away sharply to the screes below. Across the void appears the long ridge of Derry Cairngorm, and beyond it the massive whale-back of Beinn a'Bhuird.

The path to Macdhui is well cairned hereabouts, and climbs up on to the plateau over gravelly tundra. The path heads west and after a while the remains of the Sappers Bothy are reached, with the massive cairn of the summit shortly afterwards. If the weather is misty or wild, beware of the Great Grey Man. His tall, shadowy figure is said to haunt these lonely slopes and inflicts on those he encounters a feeling of dread and terror.

You can return to Linn o'Dee by the same route, but an alternative I strongly recommend heads off the summit plateau towards the small top marked on the map as 1249 metres, above the cliff edge overlooking Lochan Uaine. This Lochan Uaine of Macdhui is one of four Green Lochans in the Cairngorms, the others being in Ryvoan Pass, the eastern side of Derry Cairngorm, and across the Lairig Ghru on Cairn Toul.

From this point, descend gravelly ground and boulders to the obvious nose of the Sron Riach ridge which descends gradually to the junction of the Luibeg Burn and the Allt Carn a Mhaim. The scenery during this descent is superb. To your right, Cairn Toul and the Devil's Point stand out boldly, the great trench of the Lairig Ghru separating them from the winding ridge of Carn a Mhaim, the nearest thing to a long high-level ridge in the Cairngorms. Follow the Luibeg Burn down into Glen Luibeg and then take the Lairig Ghru track past Derry Lodge to Linn o' Dee.

Distance: 25 miles (40 km). Maps 36, 42.

Cairngorm/Macdhui Plateau and Loch Avon

This is one of the classic walks in the Cairngorms, and shows the visitor most of the great features of the range: high-level plateaux, deep glaciated corries, lonely tops, and two of the Cairngorms' finest jewels, Loch Etchachan and Loch Avon.

Cairngorm itself, although lending its name to the whole group, is seldom regarded by walkers as being a fine mountain in its own right. From the vantage points of Nethy Bridge or Dulnain Bridge on Speyside it makes a noble prospect, and its sheer enormity of splendour can be realized by viewing it from Beinn Mheadhoin or from above Loch Etchachan. Perhaps its finest aspect, and in many ways its downfall, is the row of impressive corries which form the northern ramparts of the

Central Cairngorms group; Coire Laoigh Beag, Coire Laoigh Mor, Coire na Ciste, Coire Cas, Coire an t-Sneachda, and Coire an Lochain. Coire na Ciste and Coire Cas are, of course, Scotland's major ski grounds, and the ski paraphernalia of pylons and fencing has inevitably taken away some of the grandeur of these places.

In winter though, as skiing areas, they come into their own, and offer many fine runs. Major international races are now held on Cairngorm, a fact that Scotland should be proud of. It is a mere 20 years since critics claimed that skiing would never take off in Scotland. The problem nowadays is—where to expand to? Proposals to develop Coire an t-Sneachda and Coire an Lochain are being fiercely opposed by conservationists.

One advantage of the ski development in Coire Cas is that walkers can turn hypocrite and ride the chair lift to near the summit of Cairngorm. It is of course possible to reach the summit by walking from Glenmore, up the north ridge from near Ryvoan Pass or by the Windy Hill from Clach Barraig, but in my opinion the ski areas make very sorry viewing in summer, certainly not the scenery that one associates with mountains, and I would much rather save myself two or three hours of dreary walking and reach the true splendour of the Cairngorms for the cost of a pound or so.

From the top of the chair lift, beside the Ptarmigan Restaurant, take the obvious path to the summit of Cairngorm. A huge cairn marks the top, and a weather station, run by Edinburgh University, also decorates the summit plateau. Forget the mess around you for a moment, and soak in the views. To the northeast the blue waters of the Moray Firth can be seen, with the low hills of the Black Isle beyond. Further north, the great bulk of Ben Wyvis stands out clearly. The Torridon Hills can be discerned away to the northwest, and closer at hand, in front of you, the waters of Loch Morlich with its golden sands glisten softly. The vast forests of Rothiemurchus, Glenmore and Abernethy dominate the foreground. Ben Macdhui restricts the view to the south, but to the southwest the peaks of Cairn Toul and Angels' Peak can be seen peeping over the edge of the plateau, separated of course by the Lairig Ghru. Beinn Mheadhoin with its tor-studded whale-back seems quite near, and Loch Etchachan shines like quicksilver in its high hollow.

A fine walk can be had from Cairngorm around the head of Coire an t-Sneachda (try *corrie an trecht*) and Coire an Lochain, with superb views down into the depths of the corrie floors. The view from the summit of Cairn Lochain, with its cairn perched precariously close to vertical granite cliffs, is quite remarkable, and climbers can often be seen squirming their way up the cracks. From Cairn Lochain, follow the cliff edge around and down on to Lurcher's Meadow where you can drop back to the Coire Cas car park by following Lurcher's Gully, or alternatively, take in Lurcher's Crag (Creag an Leth-choin), drop down into Chalamain Gap, and follow the obvious track back to the ski road.

From the bealach before the ascent to Cairn Lochain, a path strikes southwards, and then swings southwest across the gravelly wastes of the Cairngorm plateau. Look out for ptarmigan, dotterel and snow buntings, three birds of Arctic origin which now breed successfully here. After about 1½ miles (2 km), you will reach the lapping waters of Lochan Buidhe, The Yellow Lochan, one of the highest tarns in Britain. If you have an old map (pre-1975) you will notice that a refuge is marked beside the lochan. This was removed, along with two others, as part of the safety recommendations which came out of the Cairngorm Disaster Inquiry, the public inquiry set up after seven schoolchildren and a leader died in a blizzard in November 1971. It was generally held that these high-level bothies, the Curran bothy beside Lochan Buidhe being the one the party were making for but never found, tempted groups on to the plateau during bad weather, when they should stay on lower ground. I knew the Curran hut well and thought it an evil place—usually filthy and a dump for hill-going litter louts.

From Lochan Buidhe the path to Macdhui is well cairned, over a boulder field, up a short but steep incline, a traverse across the slopes of Macdhui's north top, and the final steady pull to the summit. The army has left abundant proof of its past presence in this area by a plethora of rude rock shelters, which should have been dismantled after use.

The views from Macdhui are stupendous, across the great An Garbh Choire of Braeriach, Cairn Toul, Devil's Point, and the Great Moss (Moine Mhor) beyond. A viewing indicator helps you to recognize familiar landmarks as far away as Caithness and the Lammermuirs.

From the summit head almost due west to reach the cairned path which leads down to Loch Etchachan. Instead of following it down into Coire Etchachan and Glen Derry, cross the western spit of land between Loch Etchachan and Little Loch Etchachan, and find another path which takes you across the col, usually very watery, and down into the deep trench which holds Loch Avon. Stop for a moment and survey the scene. Below you, with shining white sands at her head, Loch Avon lies in all her glory, like some deep-set jewel, stretching down below the steep walls of Cairngorm. At the head of the vast corrie, the enormous square-cut face of the Shelter Stone Crag frowns down upon the scene; the waters of Feith Buidhe and Garbh Uisge crash down over the slabs, and across the abyss the vertical Eagles' Crag and Hell's Lum Crag give the corrie the atmosphere of a cathedral. Follow the track down, and savour the feeling of this spot. It has a grandeur that makes one speak in hushed tones, the regality of a place wondrous wild. The noise of the crashing waters accompanies you always, and you will feel dwarfed by the size and steepness of the crags around you.

At the bottom of Shelter Stone Crag, amid a jumble of rocks, some the size of houses, lies the Shelter Stone—a howff as old as walking and rambling itself, the patriarch of mountain shelters. The Statistical Account of 1794 says 'Close by Lochavon there is a large stone called "Cladh-dhain", from Clach- a stone and Dhain- a protection or refuge . . . it has a cavity within, capable of holding 18 armed men. In times of licence or depredation, it offered a retreat for freebooters.' It is said to have been used by the notorious Wolf of Badenoch, one Alexander Stewart, the bastard son of Robert II, and has housed such celebrities as Mr Gladstone and Ramsay Macdonald. The Cairngorm Club installed a visitors' book in 1924, and the records, now kept in Aberdeen, tell its story.

From the Shelter Stone you have a choice of two routes back on to the Cairngorm plateau: by the steep path in Coire Dhomhain, or the even steeper one in Coire Raibert. The Dhomhain track will take you back to the col below Cairn Lochain, and the Raibert one to the south slopes of Cairngorm. Descend to Coire Cas by the Fiacaill Coire Cas.

Distance: 13 miles (21 km). Map: OS 36.

Braeriach and Cairn Toul

These two hills, and the great plateau of Braeriach, rival the Cairngorm/Macdhui plateau for sheer grandeur. I prefer this western area, simply because it is more remote; the effect of man (and his Vibram soles) is not so apparent here; there is a sense of spaciousness which is hard to explain, while the great drops into the corries of Braeriach and to the west into the great abyss which holds Loch Einich give one the sensation of walking on the roof of the world.

This walk is long and arduous, and an early start is necessary. It is quite likely, unless you are walking during the long daylight hours of May or June, that you will finish in the dark, so a torch is necessary.

Start from the car park which lies in the cleft of the first big bend on the Cairngorm Ski Road, GR 986075. Drop down to the footbridge which spans the Allt Mor and take the track which leads to the glacial overflow channel of Chalamain Gap. Scramble over the boulder field in the defile of the gap and drop down into the Lairig Ghru. Beyond the

Sinclair Memorial Hut a muddy track curves partly around the shoulder of Sron na Lairige. Follow it to its end, and strike south-southeast up the slope to reach the long shoulder of Sron na Lairige.

From Speyside, Braeriach doesn't warrant much more than a second glance, but up here, at close hand, the majesty of Britain's third highest mountain becomes apparent. Its summit is formed by the highest points of no less than five corries, all steep and craggy, and in midwinter the small summit plateau is encircled by cornices.

From the summit of Sron na Lairige, drop down on to the bealach between it and Braeriach, from where the route to the summit of Braeriach is westwards above the great corries of the hill's northern and southern flanks. Not many feet from the cairn the slope plunges over the sheer walls into Coire Brochain; beyond it lies a 2-mile (3-km) stretch of continuous crag which rims the neighbouring recess of An Garbh Choire.

By following this rim around, the fine peaks of Sgurr an Lochan Uaine (Angels' Peak, although the translation from Gaelic is Peak of the Green Lochan, a reference to the superb little lochan which lies in the hollow below the peaks of Angels' Peak and Cairn Toul), and Cairn Toul can be climbed over steep boulder fields, with the ever-changing view into An Garbh Choire keeping you enthralled. From Cairn Toul, follow the rim of Coire an t-Saighdeir, The Soldiers' Corrie, and drop down the slopes due south to the col before Devil's Point. Descend into Coire Odhar, and follow the track beside the burn to Corrour Bothy in the Lairig Ghru. Take the Lairig track back past the Pools of Dee to Sinclair bothy, and by way of Chalamain Gap, taking care on the boulders if it is dark, to the ski road.

Distance: 28 miles (45 km). Ascent: 2000 m. Map: OS 36.

Braeriach is the finest hill in the Cairngorms. It also has, according to the Highland Regional Council Working Party on Ski Development, the finest potential for skiing, thanks to the natural snow-holding qualities of the corries. Braeriach must remain sacrosanct. It offers a wilderness experience unequalled in Britain, but it is dearly coveted by developers.

The attitude of many mountain people is that the hill is too remote for ski development to be viable and that the cost of building access roads would be too great; but please don't be fooled by this misconception. There is already a Land-Rover track biting into the fastness of Gleann Einich. Admittedly this land is guarded jealously by the Nature Conservancy Council, and it is unlikely that they would permit such a desecration, but stranger things have happened. Before the Highland Regional Council gave outline planning consent to the Lurcher's Gully proposals, less than a hundred objections had been received from walkers, climbers, naturalists or whatever. Such is the apathy among hill lovers. Plenty shout, but few put pen to paper and do something.

These developments are not local issues but concern us all; we must act as guardians of the outdoors and do all we can to protect this great heritage which has been bestowed on us. The Cairngorms in particular have suffered badly in the past, not only from ski development but from bulldozed tracks which eat up the wilderness miles like a vile reptile.

Come and savour these hills, their solitude and vast scale, the wide skies and distant views. Then go home and imagine those corries sprouting pylons and fencing, toilets and car parks. Imagine glens like Feshie and Geldie or even the Lairig Ghru with a road running through them; then the next time you hear of disgusting proposals concerning our hills, you may feel prompted to record your disgust on paper and send it to the authorities concerned. It's the only way the hills can remain unspoilt.

Maps

The Cairngorms are covered by OS 1:50,000 sheets 36 and 43 and in part by the 1:25,000 Outdoor Leisure Map 'The High Tops of the Cairngorms'. Bartholomew's 1:100,000 sheet 51 (Aviemore and the Grampians) covers most of the area described.

Ben Macdhui

Little the map bears witness to the ground
When Beauty is the question first in mind;
Nor is the truth of Ben Macdhui found
In surveys of the hills of any kind.
Saving some contoured chart that's first and last
Etched in the biting joy of mountain days
And printed in remembrance of the past.
Where is the golden crucible whose blaze
Transmutes the melting summits one by one
And makes its western magic in a sky
Lovely with flame above Leviathan
That's red in rich efflux from that alchemy?
Thy elixir, O Lord: we seek in vain
To bring Life's image back to life again.

9
THE WESTERN HIGHLANDS
Donald Bennet

The part of Scotland described by mountaineers as the Western Highlands is bounded by the west coast, the Great Glen from Loch Linnhe to Inverness, and from there by the line of the railway to Kyle of Lochalsh. This is one of the wildest and least inhabited parts of Scotland, and vast tracts of it are quite devoid of any signs of man or his works. Few roads penetrate into this area, and nearly all the towns, villages and farms are on its perimeter, leaving the central parts as great unspoiled wildernesses. It is not surprising that this part of Scotland has a fascination for those climbers and walkers whose great joy is to get away from all signs of so-called civilization, who value more the civilizing effect of solitude and silence and find it in these remote hills and glens.

Geographically the area is characterized by the east-west line of most of the big glens, which is so pronounced that when you look at a map of Scotland the Western Highlands give the impression of having been cut into a large number of slices. This effect is emphasized along the western seaboard where many long and narrow sea lochs such as Sunart, Nevis and Hourn penetrate eastwards into the mainland. These east-west glens and lochs give a shape to the Western Highlands which is further emphasized by the parallel ridges and chains of peaks between them. One is reminded of a gnarled piece of driftwood whose grain has been scoured by sand and sea, just as the Western Highlands were scoured by ice thousands of years ago.

It is often said of Scotland that its grandest landscape is the combination of mountain, loch and sea. Nowhere is this combination seen to better effect than along the seaboard of the Western Highlands. By contrast, the eastern edge of the area from Loch Eil to Inverness is almost entirely low forested hills, giving a rather monotonous impression as you look up or down the Great Glen. It is the western half of the area that holds the greatest appeal.

There are some characteristics of the Western Highlands that climbers and walkers would do well to keep in mind. The area is one of notoriously high rainfall, and rivers and streams can be transformed into raging torrents in a few hours of heavy rain. In these conditions river crossing can become a major hazard, a situation not improved by the fact that footbridges which once existed, and may even be marked on maps, have long since disappeared. Paths, too, which in the halcyon days of stalking were well constructed, are now tending to deteriorate, become overgrown and boggy through lack of maintenance, and disappear altogether. On the other hand the work of the foresters is creating new tracks, and also new obstacles along the lower slopes of the hills in the form of fences, ditches and serried ranks of little trees which will grow to become impenetrable barriers. It is difficult for the mapmakers to keep up with these changes, so be prepared for them.

Finding places to stay when walking through the interior may be a problem unless you carry a tent. Fortunately for those who prefer not to be so burdened, there are in many of the remote corners of the Western Highlands old cottages, long since abandoned by the shepherds and keepers who once lived in them, which are now available (with the permission of the landowners) as simple unlocked and unfurnished shelters. These bothies provide nothing more than a roof and four walls, and you will need your own sleeping bag, stove and pots, but at least they give dry shelter in an area where it is often much needed. Bothies are not suitable for prolonged visits by large parties, and it is essential that those who visit and stay in them should avoid doing any damage or leaving any litter. The cardinal rule for the bothy dweller is to leave the place in better condition than you found it.

Finally, remember that you are far from help if you are unfortunate enough to have an accident in the heart of these mountains. This thought should engender caution and at the same time the confidence and pleasure of knowing that you are on your own, totally self-reliant.

Morvern

Morvern, the southernmost district of the Western Highlands, is for the most part undulating moorland and low hills whose rather featureless character is not likely to be improved by the planting activities of the Forestry Commission. The highest and most interesting hills are clustered in the northeast corner near Kingairloch: they are Creach Bheinn (853 metres, The Bare Mountain), Fuar Bheinn (765 metres, The Cold Mountain) and Beinn Mheadhoin (739 metres, The Middle Mountain).

The best day's hill walking in Morvern is the traverse of Creach Bheinn and its neighbours, the skyline of Glen Galmadale. A start can be made from the B8043 road a short distance southwest of Camasnacroise and a steep grassy ridge with granite outcrops leads to the first top, Beinn na Cille (651 metres). The ridge onwards to Fuar Bheinn and Creach Bheinn is broad and rather featureless, but on a clear day the views compensate for any lack of interest on the ridge. The prospect southwards towards the Firth of Lorne is particularly fine, and the massive stone walls on the ridge a few yards northeast of Creach Bheinn's summit may once have been a lookout post. The route continues east to Maol Odhar and then south along an undulating ridge whose eastern side drops precipitously into Loch Linnhe. The final descent brings you down to the foot of Glen Galmadale not far from your starting point.

On the opposite side of Loch a' Choire, Beinn Mheadhoin can be climbed from Kingairloch House directly up its prominent east ridge. Alternatively you can start a few kilometres further west up the glen and climb the steep point of Sgurr Shalachain before continuing to the highest point. From the summit of Beinn Mheadhoin a good continuation of this walk goes southeast for 2 miles (3 km) along an almost level ridge before dropping down to the shore of Loch a' Choire by one of the ridges which enclose Coire Reidh.

If you want to explore a completely different part of Morvern, there is a fine long-distance walk starting at Lochaline which traverses the district from the Sound of Mull to Loch Sunart. The main road out of Lochaline can be avoided by keeping to the loch-side as far as Larachbeg. Then you take the quiet (and with luck traffic-free) road past Loch Arienas to Kinlochteacuis where a deer-farming experiment is in progress and you may see deer at close quarters grazing in fields at the loch-side. The walk continues northwards across the shoulder of Beinn Ghormaig and down through the forest to Glen Cripesdale, and ends with many long miles along the Forestry Commission road on the south shore of Loch Sunart to rejoin the main road at Liddesdale—21 miles (34 km). The walk can be shortened by 4 miles (6 km) by starting at the road junction half a mile (1 km) north of Larachbeg.

Sunart and Ardgour

Sunart is sandwiched between Loch Sunart and Loch Shiel and its only feature of interest to hill walkers is Beinn Resipol (845 metres), a splendid isolated peak right in the centre of the district. Standing as it does by itself, Resipol is prominent from many distant viewpoints, and commands a superb panorama of the western seaboard. It is worth waiting for a good day to do this climb.

There are no well-defined routes to the summit, and the most convenient starting points for the ascent are on the Loch Sunart road (A861) at Resipol (where there is a pleasant camp site) or Bunalteachan. Once above the low-lying woodland, you simply head upwards across rough moorland towards the rockier cone of the summit.

Strontian, on the border between Sunart and Ardgour, is a very pleasant village with amenities for visitors. The crofting community to the north of the village in the glen of the Strontian River has an air of prosperity which is not typical of the Western Highlands. Beyond these

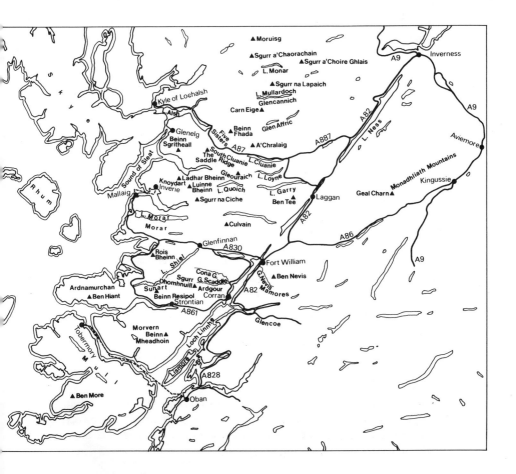

crofts a narrow road climbs past Bellsgrove Lodge to the old lead mines for which Strontian was once famous. The old miners' path from Strontian northwestwards to the disused Corrantee (Coire an t-Suidhe) mines crosses the eastern shoulder of Beinn Resipol, and you can continue down to Loch Doilet to complete the south to north traverse of Sunart. (This path, followed as far as its highest point, gives an alternative approach to Beinn Resipol from Strontian.) The return from Loch Doilet to Strontian can be made along the road past Bellsgrove Lodge and several abandoned and fenced-off mine shafts.

In Ardgour the Western Highlands begin to show their true character, for this is a region of steep and rugged mountains with wild uninhabited glens reaching into its heart. The only habitations are round the perimeter, along the shores of Loch Eil and Loch Linnhe, and at Strontian and Polloch, a remote Forestry Commission community near Loch Shiel.

The finest mountain of Ardgour is Garbh Bheinn (885 metres, The Rough Mountain), in the southeast corner of the district. Its splendid northeast face above Coire an Iubhair is a succession of great ridges and buttresses, and for rock climbers this is the Western Highlands' finest peak. Hill walkers too can explore the grandeur of Garbh Bheinn by one of two well-trodden routes. There is a good path up the Coire an Iubhair on the east side of the burn, and once you come below the steep northeast face of the mountain, continue southwestwards beside a little stream to pass to the south of the Great Ridge, the huge buttress which rises directly to the summit. Alternatively, you can climb up the long ridge on the west of Coire an Iubhair, the Sron a' Gharbh Choire Bhig, following a faint path along its crest. These two routes join at the col immediately south of the summit of Garbh Bheinn, and the last hundred metres of climbing are rocky, but not in any way difficult.

Sgurr Dhomhnuill (888 metres, Donald's Peak) is a much more remote mountain, dominating the tangle of peaks and glens in the centre of Ardgour. Although it is possible to climb it from the east, either by Glen Gour or Glen Scaddle, these are both long routes. A better approach is from Strontian up the glen of the Strontian River; the first part of this route takes you through the beautiful woodland of the Ariundle Nature Reserve. Beyond the forest you soon reach an area of old mine workings and, crossing the burn, climb gradually up a grassy hillside to the ridge, Druim Leac a' Sgiathain. The peak of Sgurr na h-Ighinn can be bypassed by a rising traverse along a broad shelf on its northwest side and the col below Sgurr Dhomhnuill is reached directly. From there the ridge rises in two steps to the summit.

There are several possibilities for long cross-country walks in Ardgour. Possibly the best choice, and one that links with public transport at both ends, is to go from Strontian north to Glenfinnan. The first section from Strontian to Kinlochan at the head of Loch Doilet is most easily done along the Bellsgrove Lodge road, and you continue northeast up Glen Hurich to Resourie near the end of the forest. (This bothy makes a good overnight stopping place if you want to do the walk in a more leisurely fashion.)

The next objective is the Bealach an Sgriodain, 1 mile (2 km) north-northeast. You can either climb steeply up the burn towards Teanga Chorrach and then traverse across the head of Coire an t-Searraich, or continue 1 mile (2 km) up Glen Hurich and climb all the way up the corrie to the bealach. Continuing northeastwards you descend into the head of the Cona Glen and make for the pass on its north side which leads to the Callop Glen. (This name does not appear on the OS map, but refers to the cottage at the foot of the glen. The path shown on the OS map as crossing the south flank of Glac Gharbh is almost non-existent.)

The remainder of the walk down the Callop Glen is delightful, as you are back on a good path. Unfortunately, once the A830 road is reached there are still 2 miles (3 km) to go to Glenfinnan Station, unless you are lucky enough to have your personal transport waiting. Done in one day this walk is a good achievement, for in addition to the distance—20 miles (32 km)—there is quite a lot of up and downhill effort. It might be more enjoyable to take two days, spending the night at Resourie bothy and possibly climbing a hill or two en route. Do not set out in or immediately after prolonged heavy rain, for the streams may be difficult to cross.

Ardnamurchan

Ardnamurchan is the westernmost peninsula of the whole British mainland. It thrusts 19 miles (31 km) westwards from the narrow neck of land between Salen and Acharacle into the Sea of the Hebrides; its tip is the Point of Ardnamurchan with its lighthouse, which is such a well-known landmark to sailors on the west coast.

It is probably true to say that the most attractive features of the Ardnamurchan landscape are round its coastline. There are beautiful sandy bays along the northern shoreline at Sanna, Port Ban and Kentra, and the sea cliffs which extend westwards beyond Kilchoan are an awe-inspiring sight to sailors battling their way round the Point. To landward Ardnamurchan is almost entirely rough moorland dotted with lochans and little hills.

The highest hill is Ben Hiant (528 metres, The Holy Mountain), and it has a fine appearance when seen from the south, for on that side it drops precipitously into the Sound of Mull. The quickest ascent can be made by leaving the B8007 road at a point 1 mile (2 km) northeast of the hill and climbing directly up the grassy ridge to the top. Beinn na Seilg (342 metres, The Mountain of Hunting), though lower than Ben Hiant, commands a better view as it is nearer the Point. It too is easily climbed from the B8007 road on the northeast side.

A fine coastal walk links Kilmory, the crofting community above Port Ban, with Arivegaig near Acharacle. At the western end of this walk, where the path climbs over the shoulder of Beinn Bhreac, you will be rewarded on a clear day by a superb view towards Eigg, Rum and Skye. A short distance further east the path drops to sea level and passes close to another delightful sandy bay at Camas na Lighe—9 miles (14 km).

Moidart

Moidart lies between Loch Shiel and the Sound of Arisaig. In the southwest, near Loch Moidart and the River Shiel, it is low-lying but surprisingly rugged country, with some beautiful stretches of woodland. Going northeast the hills become higher, so that the northern half of the district is entirely mountainous and has a rather inhospitable appearance when seen from the road near Loch Eilt.

The two highest groups of hills in Moidart are in this northern half: Rois-bheinn (882 metres, The Hill of the Showers), and its neighbours overlooking Loch Ailort, and Beinn Odhar Mhor (870 metres) and Beinn Odhar Bheag (882 metres), The Big and Little Dun Mountains, in the northeast corner near the head of Loch Shiel.

Rois-bheinn is the finest of these hills, not only for its appearance but also for the superb view of the Sea of the Hebrides; the westward panorama of sea and islands is uninterrupted. It is easily climbed by its west ridge from Roshven Farm. Alternatively you can climb up the Alisary Burn, following a steep and narrow path on the south side of the stream which leads to Coire na Cnamha. From this corrie both Rois-bheinn and its elegant neighbour An Stac (814 metres) can be climbed by steep but perfectly easy grassy slopes with rock outcrops.

Beinn Odhar Mhor is rather a shapeless hill which can be easily climbed from the hotel at Glenfinnan by Lochan na Sleubhaich. You can also start further west, leaving the A830 road near its highest point and following the headwaters of the Allt a'Ghiubhais southwards into the rough grassy corrie which forms the north side of the hill. It is worth continuing to Beinn Odhar Bheag which, despite its name, is the higher of the two peaks. It has a fine pointed summit on which you have the impression of being perched high above the long narrow fiord of Loch Shiel stretching into the distance far below.

For the walker who does not aspire to the heights there are some delightful corners in the southwest of Moidart. The gem is that little stretch of riverside and shoreline from Shiel Bridge to Loch Moidart. You should start at Shiel Bridge and walk down the narrow road on the right bank of the river, keeping to the riverside until you reach Loch Moidart and Castle Tioram on its rocky knoll, accessible across a sandy spit at low tide. Then continue along the delightful path which clings to the wooded cliff, round the point and eastwards up Loch Moidart for 1 mile (1½ km). At this point, as you approach Torr Port a' Bhata, there is a choice of routes: either back to your starting point by a tenuous path southwards over the shoulder of Beinn Bhreac, or eastwards through Ardmolich Wood to the head of the loch and the road several kilometres from your starting point.

A cross-country walk of a more arduous nature which embraces the pastoral as well as the mountainous aspects of Moidart's landscape goes from the head of Loch Moidart to Lochailort. The first few kilometres take you up Glen Moidart, past the house of that name and beyond into the treeless upper glen. At Assary (nothing but ruins) climb due north up the steep grassy hillside to the Bealach an Fhiona, from where you could climb Rois-bheinn in half an hour if you are feeling fit. The route to Lochailort drops northeastwards from the bealach into Coire a' Bhuiridh, and as you approach the foot of this corrie on the west side of the stream you will join a path which strikes off westwards through a little gap and leads down to a very unpicturesque group of buildings (some long-since abandoned military installation) near the head of Loch Ailort—10 miles (16 km).

Morar and Lochaber

The road westwards from Fort William to Glenfinnan, Lochailort and points further west is the Road to the Isles, and on its north side, extending to Loch Arkaig, Glen Dessarry and Loch Nevis are the districts of Morar and the western part of Lochaber. In the east of this area the hills above Glen Mallie and Glen Loy are rounded and rather featureless. Further west there is a much more mountainous area, including the high peaks of Gulvain, Streap and Sgurr Thuilm, and further west again the hills become lower, though no less rugged, until the land ends at the white sands of Arisaig and Morar.

The districts of Morar and Lochaber are forever associated with Prince Charles and the ill-fated rising of 1745. It was at Glenfinnan in the summer of that year that his standard was raised, and less than a year later, after the Battle of Culloden, he returned as a fugitive to those mountains. Not once but three times he traversed the wilds of Morar in his flight from the Hanoverian troops, marching over the hills with his guides by night and hiding in caves by day.

The most interesting part of this area for hill walkers is the mountainous centre, and all the high peaks can be climbed from the main road between Kinlocheil and Glenfinnan. Gulvain (987 metres) is approached by Gleann Fionnlighe, and 4 miles (6 km) up the glen, where it divides, you continue straight up the south shoulder of the mountain to its south top (961 metres) and then a further 1 mile (1½ km) to the highest point.

Streap (909 metres) is a much finer mountain, its summit being the highest point of an undulating ridge between Gleann Dubh Lighe and Glen Finnan. Gleann Dubh Lighe is the more attractive of these two glens, and the track on the west side of the river leads north through pleasant mixed woodland, with the river tumbling down through many falls and pools nearby. Beyond the end of the track, at the upper limit of the forest, you can continue northwards for 1 mile (1¼ km) into Coire an Tuim and then climb westwards up this corrie to the col at its head. You are now on the ridge which leads north-northeast over two tops to the final narrow, almost exposed edge which heralds the summit of Streap.

Glen Finnan is rather bare, though its lower reaches have recently been planted by the Forestry Commission, and in due course it will be transformed. The traverse of Sgurr Thuilm (963 metres) and Sgurr nan Coireachan (956 metres) can best be done from the glen, and there is a good high-level walk between these two peaks. The Druim Coire a' Bheithe ridge of Sgurr Thuilm is very straightforward, but the southeast ridge of Sgurr nan Coireachan over Sgurr a' Choire Riabhaich is rocky and steep-sided in places, and in misty weather its topography might be rather confusing. In such conditions it might be better to ascend this ridge and do the circuit of the two peaks in a clockwise direction.

The three cross-country walks described below have been chosen to give a view of each of the three different parts of the area. In the east there is a through route from Kinlocheil to the east end of Loch Arkaig by Gleann Fionnlighe and Glen Mallie—16 miles (26 km). There are good tracks at both ends of this walk, but a long section over the watershed is trackless. The walk from Glenfinnan to Strathan at the west end of Loch Arkaig is straightforward, but again there is a long trackless section where you cross the watershed by the steep-sided pass between Streap and Sgurr Thuilm—10 miles (16 km). Nevertheless, this is a fine route which penetrates into the heart of the mountains and gives the shortest walking access to the west end of Loch Arkaig, which is a starting point for exploration of country further north.

Finally, there is an interesting walk in Morar which will give you the chance to visit the remote and beautiful Loch Beoraid. Leave the A830 road at Arieniskill near the west end of Loch Eilt and take the path northwards over a flat boggy ridge. At its north edge the path drops steeply through birchwoods, passing close to one of Prince Charlie's many caves (in this case a hollow under some huge fallen boulders), and you come down to the west end of Loch Beoraid where there is a small private hydro-electric scheme supplying the inhabitants of Meoble. You can walk on down the road past Meoble to Loch Morar, but this is a dead end unless you are lucky enough to get a lift in a private boat. You should instead take the path along the north side of Loch Beoraid. Beyond the east end of the loch cross the river and climb southwards over the col at the head of the Allt Feith a' Chatha, and so back to the main road 6 miles (10 km) east of your starting point—8½ miles (14 km).

The Rough Bounds

Once you go north and west beyond the head of Loch Arkaig the character of the Western Highlands becomes much wilder. You are entering the Rough Bounds of Knoydart, and this area, which extends northwards to the shores of Loch Hourn, is not called rough for nothing. The mountains are steeper and rockier than anything further south (except possibly Garbh Bheinn), and there is a true feeling of wilderness about these deserted glens.

There are no roads into Knoydart, so to get there you either have to walk or go by boat. The two walking routes into the area are from the west end of Loch Arkaig up Glen Dessarry and from the road end at

Kinloch Hourn along the path on the south side of the loch to Barrisdale. The 'easy' way into Knoydart is by boat; there is a fairly regular service from Mallaig to Inverie, and it may be possible to sail right to the head of Loch Nevis, which would be a great help if you are carrying food and tents for a long stay. There is a bothy at Barrisdale beside the farm, but there is no similar accommodation at Inverie. In the interior there are bothies at A'Chuil in Glen Dessarry and at Sourlies, at the head of Loch Nevis.

In a region of so many mountains, it is possible to mention only a few. Sgurr na Ciche (1004 metres, The Pap-shaped Peak) is the highest and it stands above its neighbours like a beacon in a turbulent sea, the most prominent peak in Knoydart. If you are staying at Sourlies or near the head of Loch Nevis, the obvious route of ascent is up the long ridge, the Druim a' Ghoirtein, which rises from the loch-side direct to the summit. If you are approaching from Glen Dessarry, then follow the path up the glen for about 1½ miles (2½ km) beyond the house at Upper Glendessarry and climb north up the steep grassy corrie to the col on the west side of Sgurr nan Coireachan (953 metres, The Peak of the Corries). This peak can be climbed from the col in half an hour.

The route to Sgurr na Ciche goes west-northwest along a rough ridge where you cannot possibly lose the way, even in the worst of weather, for there is a well-built stone dyke along the crest of the ridge as far as Garbh Chioch Mhor (1013 metres, The Big Rough Pap), and down into the col below Sgurr na Ciche. The final ascent from this col calls for careful route-finding to avoid the many crags and outcrops on this side of the peak. On the return to Glen Dessarry, return to the col, descend steeply southwest until you are below the crags of Garbh Chioch Mhor and then traverse southeast until an easy descent, still southeastwards, brings you down to the watershed at the head of the glen.

To the east of Sgurr na Ciche, and not really in Knoydart, there are two more Munros on the north side of Glen Kingie; Sgurr Mor (1003 metres, The Big Peak) and Gairich (919 metres, The Peak of Yelling). Glen Kingie is long and utterly desolate, and there is a bothy at Kinbreak which provides spartan shelter and a base for climbing both peaks, provided you can get across the river. It is in fact quite possible to climb Sgurr Mor from Strathan direct, taking the northward path from Glendessarry Lodge into the head of Glen Kingie, descending as little as possible to cross the river and then climbing the steep south face of the peak by way of the Sgurr Mor-Sgurr Beag col and the path up the ridge. The simplest ascent of Gairich is from the Loch Quoich dam far to the northeast of Glen Kingie. From the dam follow a path southwards across the moor to the edge of the recently planted forest in Glen Kingie and then take the stalkers' path westwards up the Druim na Geid Salaich, the lower part of Gairich's east ridge. Continue right up this ridge, which is broad at first, but steepens and becomes quite narrow as it nears the summit.

Between Loch Nevis and Loch Hourn there are three more fine Munros: Meall Buidhe (946 metres, The Yellow Lump), Luinne Bheinn (939 metres) and Ladhar Bheinn (1020 metres, The Forked Mountain). They can all be climbed from Inverie or Barrisdale, and the first two can also be climbed from the head of Loch Nevis; possibly the best base would be a camp in Gleann an Dubh-Lochain (with the permission of the Inverie Estate factor). From there a circuit of the first two could be made by climbing the long easy-angled west ridge of Meall Buidhe, continuing round the ridge which encloses the highly glaciated Choire Odhair whose ice-scoured slabs cradle two tiny lochans. The ascent of the steep south face of Luinne Bheinn is best made by following a rising shelf westwards to reach the ridge a short distance west of the highest point, and the return to your starting point follows the ridge northwestwards down to the Mam Barrisdale and down the path into Gleann an Dubh-Lochain. To reach Ladhar Bheinn from this glen, you should climb north from Loch an Dubh-Lochain to reach the ridge above at Mam Suidheig, climb this ridge east-northeast to Aonach Sgoilte, descend northwest to the Bealach Coire Dhorrcail and finally climb Ladhar Bheinn by its southeast ridge along the headwall of the Coire Dhorrcail.

Ladhar Bheinn (pronounced Larven) is a magnificent mountain. Many would say it is the finest in the Western Highlands, and its chief glory is the Coire Dhorrcail and the line of cliffs and gullies which form its headwall. These features are best seen if you make the ascent from Barrisdale; a superb expedition is the circuit of the corrie, ascending to Stob a' Chearcaill by its northwest ridge, continuing round the corrie to the summit and descending over the little pointed peak of Stob a' Choire Odhair down to the path in the lower part of Coire Dhorrcail.

For walkers the 'trade route' from the head of Loch Arkaig through Knoydart leads up Glen Dessarry, through the narrow pass of Mam na Cloiche Airde and down to Sourlies at the head of Loch Nevis. This is a glorious walk; every step up Glen Dessarry takes you into ever grander country, and the pass is a fitting entrée to the Rough Bounds. If the tide is out at Sourlies the next kilometre is most easily taken along the foreshore, and you cross the grassy flats northwards to reach the River Carnoch near the ruins.

If your objective is Inverie, then climb up the good stalker's path northwest to the Mam Meadail and descend Gleann Meadail to Inverie—17 miles (27 km) from Strathan. If you are aiming for Barrisdale the shortest route from the Carnoch River crossing is to continue up the river for 4 miles (6 km), rough going in places but the scenery is very fine, especially at the waterfalls. Before reaching Lochan nam Breac, leave the river and climb the hillside north for a few hundred metres to join the path which goes over to Gleann Undalain and Barrisdale—17 miles (27 km) from Strathan.

If your next objective is Kinloch Hourn, there are still 6 miles (10 km) to go along the path on the south shore of Loch Hourn. If, on the other hand, you are hoping to get across Loch Hourn to Corran or Arnisdale, then you should enquire from the keeper at Barrisdale as to the possibility of a lift. (This is normally possible, Sundays excepted, weather permitting.)

The Glen Shiel Ridges

The next slice of the Western Highlands to be encountered in our progress northwards is a well-defined area bounded on the south by the road from Invergarry to Kinloch Hourn and on the north by the road from Invermoriston to Loch Duich. All the mountains in this area are very accessible, none of them being more than 2-2½ miles (3-4 km) from the nearest road. The outstanding group is the South Glen Shiel Ridge, an 8-mile (13-km) long ridge with seven distinct peaks, which gives hill walkers the most rewarding day (in terms of Munros climbed) in the Western Highlands. The western corner of this area, which forms the broad peninsula between Loch Hourn and Loch Duich, has only one mountain of note—the splendid Beinn Sgritheall—but it also has some very attractive glens and is an area well worth exploring, particularly if the weather does not favour the high tops.

Loch Quoich has been considerably enlarged and its water level raised by damming at both ends. Although this has made access to the hills at the west end of the loch much more difficult, it has not affected access to the hills on the north side. The traverse of Gleouraich (1035 metres) and Spidean Mialach (966 metres, The Pinnacle of Wild Animals) is a particularly enjoyable hill walk. The best starting point is at the bridge over the Allt Coire Peitireach, and a short way along the road southeast of this point a good path climbs diagonally across the hillside into Coire Mheil. From the end of this path at the Allt a'Mheil, continue climbing in the same direction (east-northeast) up the steep but perfectly easy slopes of Spidean Mialach. There is a considerable drop between the two peaks, but there is plenty of interest, especially looking down into the wild corries on the north side. From Gleouraich descend the ridge westwards for ⅓ mile (½ km) and look out for a stalkers' path which will give you an easy walk down to the road at your starting point.

A few kilometres to the west is the bulk of Sgurr a' Mhaoraich (1027 metres, The Peak of the Shellfish). Here again good stalkers' paths make this an easy peak. One such path goes up the ridge on the east side of the Coire nan Eiricheallach, and you traverse the peak of that name before turning west-northwest to reach Sgurr a'Mhaoraich. If you want to see more of the mountain, descend steeply northwards to a col at about 780 metres and climb the peak of Am Bathaich, from where the descent eastwards follows a zigzag stalkers' path down the ridge to Glen Quoich. On a clear day the view from Sgurr a'Mhaoraich westwards down Loch Hourn is very fine.

The South Glen Shiel Ridge is one of the best day's ridge walking in the Western Highlands, if not in the whole of Scotland. There are seven distinct peaks, but you do not have to do them all in one day as there are several places at which you can descend northwards into Glen Shiel. Possibly the most relaxing way to start the traverse (and if you are hoping to do the whole ridge you will want to conserve energy early on) is to walk up the old road which goes southeast from Cluanie Inn towards the eastern end of the ridge. From the top of the road a stalkers' path leads to the summit of Creag a' Mhaim (947 metres, The Breast Rock). Now the whole ridge stretches out to the west, leading you over peak after peak to end at Creag nan Damh (918 metres, The Rock of the Stag), 7 miles (11 km) away. The walk is superb, but not particularly strenuous as the ridge only once drops below 750 metres. The main problem of the day may well be how to get back to your starting point from the west end of the ridge, and you will want a lift or a friendly driver if you are to avoid the long walk back up the glen to Cluanie.

Possibly the finest mountain in this part of the Western Highlands is The Saddle (1010 metres), a peak of narrow ridges and deep corries. The best route up the mountain, and one that no one should miss, is the Forcan Ridge, the name given to the east ridge of The Saddle. Approach by the stalkers' path which leaves Glen Shiel ½ mile (1 km) southeast of Achnangart, and from the end of this path climb south over Meallan Odhar and then continue southwest across a grassy col to reach the foot of the Forcan Ridge. As you gain height the ridge becomes narrower and for 200-300 yards/metres it is quite rocky with some good scrambling if you keep right on the crest; however, there are no difficulties that cannot be avoided and all too soon this delightful ridge ends on the peak of Sgurr na Forcan. The continuation to The Saddle is narrow in places, but quite easy. The descent can be made either down the north ridge over Sgurr na Creige, or west and then north round the Coire Uaine. Both these descent routes give you a glimpse of the wild upper part of this corrie, and both lead eventually down the footpath in its lower part.

Sgurr na Sgine (945 metres, The Peak of the Knife), and its outlier Faochag (The Whelk), are situated 1¼ miles (2 km) southeast of The Saddle, and can be easily climbed from Glen Shiel, the most direct route being the northeast ridge of Faochag which rises direct from glen to summit without respite.

Far to the west, overlooking Loch Hourn and the Sound of Sleat, is Beinn Sgritheall (974 metres). The south face of this mountain is forbiddingly steep, rising almost a thousand metres above the sea in a distance of only 1 mile (1½ km), its upper half continuous screes and crags. The easiest routes of ascent are on this side of the mountain, though they avoid the screes just mentioned. One such route leaves the road below the wooded hillside called Coille Mhialairigh. Climb uphill through the trees until a faint path is found which leads to an old shieling on the hillside and continues in a northwesterly direction to reach the west ridge of the mountain near a tiny lochan. From there the ridge is climbed to the summit without any difficulty. Another route of ascent goes uphill behind Arnisdale village to the Bealach Arnasdail, then northwest up steep scree to a subsidiary peak and finally ½ mile (1 km) along the connecting ridge to the summit.

The peninsula between Loch Duich and Loch Hourn is full of interest for off-days. In Gleann Beag, south of Glenelg, there are two fine examples of Iron-Age brochs, the best on the mainland, and a good circular low-level walk goes up Gleann Beag and down Glen Mor. Glen Arnisdale is another attractive glen which leads into the remote area on the south side of The Saddle, although the character of the upper part of this glen has been rather spoiled by the pylons and overhead wires of the electricity transmission line to Skye. The glen divides beyond the head of the Dubh-Lochain, and the track southeastwards from this point leads to Kinloch Hourn—8 miles (13 km). Alternatively, from the junction you can continue north, following the route of an old drove road, over the pass between The Saddle and Druim na Firean, down the glen called Bealach a' Chasain for 2½ miles (4 km) and then steeply up the Allt a' Ghleannain to cross another pass at Loch Coire nan

Crogachan and so down to Shiel Bridge—13 miles (21 km). There is some fairly rough going on this walk, but it does give a link between Arnisdale and Shiel Bridge.

The Five Sisters

As you go northwards beyond Glen Shiel, the character of the Western Highlands changes yet again. This change is gradual, for the mountains on the north side of Glen Shiel—the Five Sisters of Kintail and the North Glen Shiel Ridge—are similar to those on the south side of the glen, but going further north and east, the landscape becomes quite different. The mountains are higher, but not so steep and rugged as those of Knoydart and Kintail, the glens longer and more spacious. Topographically the area is characterized by these glens which run from east to west, but there are no through roads between Glen Shiel and the Kyle railway, so the area is also very desolate in its inner regions. You could set off from Cluanie Inn, heading northwards, and walk for 25 miles (40 km) to Achnasheen, and the only sign of life on the way is the remote youth hostel at Alltbeithe in Glen Affric.

In order to describe some of the principal mountains in this area and their routes of ascent it is convenient to divide them into three groups. The first includes all those mountains in the south of the area (in Kintail and at the head of Glen Affric) which are most easily accessible from Cluanie Inn or the head of Loch Duich. Secondly there is the group in the centre of the area for which the usual approach route is from the east, up Glen Affric, Cannich or Strath Farrar. Finally, near the northwest perimeter of the Western Highlands there is another group of seven Munros which are most easily climbed from Glen Carron, where there is an excellent hostel at Craig near Achnashellach.

The mountains on the north side of Glen Shiel form an almost continuous ridge 10 miles (16 km) long which equals that on the south side of the glen. The peaks at the northwest end of this ridge are the Five Sisters of Kintail, one of the most impressive mountain groups in the Western Highlands; the western flanks of these peaks rise over a thousand metres in a single sweep from low-lying Glen Shiel to the crests of their ridges.

The traverse of the Five Sisters is one of the classic hill walks in Scotland. The best direction is from southeast to northwest, and you should leave the Glen Shiel road below the Bealach na Lapain at GR 007136. The ascent northwards to this col is steep but short, and has the merit of getting you on to the ridge quickly. From the col the ridge, which is grassy and narrow at this point, rises gradually over two minor tops to Sgurr na Ciste Duibhe (1027 metres, The Peak of the Black Chest). Continuing northwest and then north, the ridge becomes broader and stony, but there is a path so route-finding is no problem even in thick weather, and a steep climb leads to the highest of the Sisters, Sgurr Fhuaran (1068 metres). The next top, Sgurr nan Saighead (929 metres, The Peak of the Arrows), has a narrow crest and is in some respects the finest of the Five Sisters. The descent to Loch Duich can be made down Coire na Criche or down the west ridge of Sgurr nan Saighead, followed by a steep descent to Loch Shiel, where there is a footbridge over the River Shiel.

The continuation of the Five Sisters eastwards, which might be called the North Glen Shiel Ridge, gives an easy traverse between Cluanie Inn and the Bealach an Lapain, and when it is combined with the Five Sisters it adds up to quite a strenuous day. Ciste Dhubh (982 metres, The Black Chest), is a steep and isolated peak 3 miles (5 km) north of Cluanie Inn which is easily climbed by the path up An Caorann Beag to the Bealach a' Choinich, and on up the south ridge of the peak which becomes very narrow near the summit.

To the northeast of Cluanie Inn there is a group of high peaks: Sgurr nan Conbhairean (1110 metres, The Peak of the Dog-men); A'Chralaig (1120 metres, The Circular Place), and Mullach Fraoch-choire (1102 metres, The Top of the Heather Corrie). They can be climbed without any difficulty from the roadside near the west end of Loch Cluanie; the best feature of these hills is the south ridge of Mullach Fraoch-choire which is narrow and has a few rocky pinnacles which gives the ridge some character without actually causing any difficulty.

Beinn Fhada (1032 metres, The Long Mountain), has two quite distinct aspects. Seen from Glen Affric it looks unremarkable: a long grassy ridge leading from glen to summit. However, the west end of the mountain has some fine features: steep cliffs, narrow ridges and fine corries, and the most interesting route of ascent is at this end. Take the track up Strath Croe and Gleann Choinneachain below the steep north face of Sgurr a' Choire Ghairbh until you come to the zigzags near the foot of the little Coire an Sgairne, and then follow a branch path up this corrie which is climbed to its top. Finally, ½ mile (1 km) across the summit plateau leads to the highest point. The return can be varied by going out along the ridge northwards to Meall a' Bhealaich which overlooks the narrow pass from Glen Affric, the Bealach an Sgairne. The descent to the pass is steep, and some careful route-selection is called for. From the pass you can easily climb A'Ghlas-bheinn (918 metres, The Green Mountain) and descend its west ridge to join the track through the forest to Dorusduain.

Sgurr nan Ceathreamhnan (1151 metres, The Peak of the Quarters), is a magnificent mountain of many peaks and ridges at the head of Glen Affric. It is quite remote and all approaches to it are long unless you happen to be staying at Alltbeithe youth hostel which is right at the foot of the mountain. Hardy walkers would no doubt be prepared to tackle Ceathreamhnan from Cluanie Inn or the head of Loch Duich over the Bealach an Sgairne, but the best and shortest approach is from Glen Elchaig, and this route has the added advantage that you climb up past the spectacular Falls of Glomach. Once above the falls you continue up the Allt Coire-lochain and on to the ridge on the west side of Coire Lochan which leads to the summit.

Affric and Cannich

Glen Affric has the reputation of being one of Scotland's most beautiful glens. Certainly it has a richness and variety of scenery that is not excelled elsewhere: the birchwoods and pine forests of its lower reaches (best seen in autumn), the beauty of its two lochs and the spacious upper reaches surrounded by mountains.

There is a great variety of woodland and forest walks on the south side of the glen below Loch Affric, and one of the classic cross-country walks in Scotland is the route through Glen Affric to Loch Duich. The distance from the car park 1 mile (1½ km) east of Affric Lodge to Loch Duich over the Bealach an Sgairne is 19 miles (31 km). An alternative to this route on the north side of Beinn Fhada is to cross the Allt Gleann Gniomhaidh ½ mile (1 km) beyond Alltbeithe and head up the Fhionn-gleann on the south side of Beinn Fhada, past Camban bothy and down to Gleann Lichd through the gorge of the Allt Grannda. This route will give fine views of the northern corries of the Five Sisters.

The two principal mountains on the north side of Glen Affric are Mam Sodhail (1181 metres, The Rounded Hill of the Barns), and Carn Eighe (1183 metres, The Cairn of the Notch). They can both be climbed in a long day starting near the west end of Loch Beinn a' Mheadhoin, at the foot of Gleann nam Fiadh. Take the path up this glen and after 4½ miles (7 km) strike up northwest to reach the ridge between Tom a' Choinich (which can be included at this point) and Carn Eighe. This ridge continues westwards for another 2 miles (3 km);

at one point it is narrow and gives a pleasant scramble if you keep to the crest. At Carn Eighe turn south (unless you feel inspired to make the long diversion northwards to include the very remote Beinn Fhionnlaidh), and reach Mam Sodhail with its huge cairn. The return to your starting point offers two possibilities: either walk along the delightful grassy ridge to Sgurr na Lapaich (1036 metres, The Peak of the Bog), and descend to Affric Lodge; or descend direct from Mam Sodhail down the Coire Leachavie to Glen Affric and return along the path down the glen, a fitting end to a grand day's walking.

Glen Cannich does not nearly match Glen Affric's combination of forest, loch and mountain scenery. Certainly the lower part between Cannich village and Loch Mullardoch is well wooded, and the view up the loch from the huge dam towards the receding ridges in the west is attractive if you ignore the 'tidemark' round the loch; on the other hand the upper part of the glen has a feeling of sterility which is particularly noticeable at the very head of the loch where extensive mud flats are an ugly feature when the water level is low.

From the Mullardoch dam you can make a fairly easy circuit of Carn nan Gobhar (992 metres, The Cairn of the Goats), and Sgurr na Lapaich (1150 metres), returning by the south ridge of the latter peak. However, to continue the traverse to An Riabhachan (1129 metres, The Brindled Hill), and An Socach (1069 metres, The Snout), will involve you in a long return walk along the loch-side. The indication by the OS map of a path along the north side of Loch Mullardoch is rather optimistic; the going is rough.

Strathfarrar

Glen Strathfarrar is the third of the three glens which unite in Strath Glass. It is almost the equal of Glen Affric, though much less visited, probably because the gate across the road just beyond Struy is locked and you have to ask for the key at the cottage nearby. Once past the gate you can drive as far as the Loch Monar dam, a distance of almost 12 miles (19 km) through the glen, which is beautifully wooded with birch and Scots pine.

As in the case of Affric, autumn is the best time to visit Strathfarrar. The main interest for the hill walker is the group of four Munros on the north side of the glen, and their traverse is a good expedition. The path up the Allt Toll a'Mhuic gives an easy ascent as far as the loch, beyond which it disappears. It can be picked up again high up the corrie just below the first peak, Sgurr na Fearstaig (1015 metres, The Peak of the Sea Pinks). The traverse eastwards follows a well-defined ridge as far as Sgurr a' Choire Ghlais (1083 metres, The Peak of the Green Corrie), but beyond this summit the last two peaks, Carn nan Gobhar (991 metres, The Cairn of the Goats), and Sgurr na Ruaidhe (991 metres, The Peak of the Red Hind), are rounded and rather featureless. The descent from the latter takes you down to the path by the Allt Coire Mhuillidh. The Glen Cannich mountains can also be climbed from Strathfarrar by the hydro road up the Uisge Misgeach, but this approach is if anything slightly longer than that from Mullardoch.

It is quite possible to do long cross-country walks from Glen Cannich to Glen Elchaig along the shore of Loch Mullardoch, and from Strathfarrar to Glen Carron along Loch Monar and over the hills at its west end, but both these routes involve a good deal of rough going, and neither is as fine as the Glen Affric to Loch Duich route.

Glen Carron

The west end of Loch Monar is ringed by high mountains, but the approach to them from the Strathfarrar road at the east end of the loch is rather long and tedious. A shorter approach can be made from Glen Carron, and it is at Craig in this glen that we make the last stop in our tour of the Western Highlands. There are seven Munros in this area, and it will probably take you three days to climb them.

A good forestry road leads from Craig up the Allt a'Chonais, and this is a good approach. As you walk up the glen below the rocky west face of Sgurr nan Ceannaichean the mountains that confront you are Sgurr Choinnich (999 metres, The Mossy Peak), and Sgurr a' Chaorachain (1053 metres, The Peak of the Torrent), the shortest ascent goes up the corrie between them. Cross the Allt a' Chonais by a footbridge and strike south into this corrie, and from the col at its head climb the steep ridge westwards to reach the narrow level summit ridge of Sgurr Choinnich. Now retrace your steps across the col to Sgurr a'Chaorachain and along a broad stony ridge to the pointed peak of Bidean an Eoin Deirg (1046 metres, The Little Peak of the Red Bird). The flat-topped mountain to the northeast is Maoile Lunndaidh (1007 metres, The Hill of the Boggy Place), and you can include it with a bit of extra effort by descending steeply north-northeast from Bidean to a col at about 600 metres, then climbing east to Carn nam Fiaclan and walking round the broad ridge to the highest point. To return to Craig, descend north-northwest into the head of Gleann Fhiodhaig and climb over the pass beyond Glenuaig Lodge to reach the headwaters of the Allt a'Chonais.

The two remotest mountains in this area are Bidein a' Choire Sheasgaich (945 metres, The Little Peak of the Reedy Corrie), and Lurg Mhor (986 metres, The Big Shank), which rise to the southwest of Loch Monar's head. Bidein in particular is a fine peak, and worth the long walk from Craig. Follow the preceding route to the footbridge over the Allt a'Chonais, and continue up the path to the Bealach Bhearnais. From there it is more or less necessary to traverse Beinn Tharsuinn to reach the Bealach an Sgoltaidh, from where the ascent to Bidein looks impressive as the foot of the ridge appears to be barred by cliffs; however, there is a way up on the right. The ridge continues, narrow and interesting, to the summit of Bidein, but the continuation to Lurg Mhor has less character. It is probably best to return by the same route, but you might prefer to try a short cut, heading more or less due north from Lurg Mhor to Bealach Bhearnais by a long traverse across the flank of Beinn Tharsuinn.

Finally, let us visit the outposts of the Western Highlands, Moruisg (928 metres) and Sgurr nan Ceannaichean (915 metres); these two hills rise directly above Glen Carron and from their summits you look out northwestwards to a different mountain landscape—the Torridonian giants Liathach and Beinn Eighe. Follow the Allt a'Chonais track again until, ⅓ mile (½ km) beyond the tree line, you can climb fairly directly and steeply up the northwest shoulder of Sgurr nan Ceannaichean (less craggy than the OS map indicates). The upper part of the hill gives very easy walking, and you continue along the ridge to Moruisg, whose summit is very flat and mossy. After so many steep and rugged mountains further south, Moruisg is something of an anticlimax. Descend northwestwards down the long uniform hillside to cross the River Carron by the footbridge ½ mile (1 km) downstream from Loch Sgamhain.

Long Through Routes

In recent years long-distance trans-mountain walking has attracted increasing interest, and the number of climbers, walkers and backpackers setting out through the mountains on long cross-country journeys is increasing. This is a worthy extension of one-day climbs and walks, calling for fitness and self-reliance, and on a long journey through the mountains you will not only see a lot of country that is denied to car-bound travellers, but also be able to enter more completely into the spirit and solitude of the hills.

The pleasure of such expeditions lies partly in the planning, and detailed guidebook descriptions can only detract from this pleasure. However, as a starting point for further planning, the following route from south to north through the Western Highlands is suggested. It takes in many, but of course not all, of the most interesting parts of this mountain land. You may prefer to carry your own tent, but the route proposed can be done without, using bothies and (at one point) more luxurious accommodation.

Start at Strontian (which you can reach by public transport) and head north by the route already described past Resourie to the foot of the Callop Glen. Continue either by Glen Finnan (bothy at Corryhully) or by Gleann Dubh Lighe (good bothy at the upper limit of the forest) to reach Strathan and A'Chuil bothy. Press on up Glen Dessarry, over the Mam na Cloiche Airde and down to Sourlies at the head of Loch Nevis; then go up the River Carnoch to join the path to Gleann Undalain and Barrisdale. Now you have a choice; either get a passage across Loch Hourn to Corran and continue up Glen Arnisdale, or if there is no boat or you want to walk all the way, take the path to Kinloch Hourn and from there to the head of Glen Arnisdale. From there cross the Bealach a' Chasain to reach Shiel Bridge where you can replenish your food supplies and get a comfortable night's lodging.

The last two or three days of this long walk start up the Strath Croe road to Dorusduain, over the Bealach na Sroine and down to Glen Elchaig past the Falls of Glomach. Walk up Glen Elchaig to Iron Lodge and take the path north through no-man's-land to the lonely bothy at Maol-bhuidhe. Continue northwest over the shoulder of Beinn Dronaig to Bendronaig Lodge (the feasibility of this section is dependent on the River Ling not being in spate) and reach Bhearnais bothy ½ mile (1 km) north of Loch an Laoigh. Now, if you are tiring, you may decide to take the path north over the hill to Achnashellach Station. If you are still fit, however, there are still many kilometres to go over the Bealach Bhearnais and past Glenuaig Lodge to Gleann Fhiodhaig and Scardroy Lodge. Now you are on tarred roads again and it is not far down Strath Conon to the inn at Milltown; you will have earned a few pints after your week's journey through the mountains, and if you have had enough walking, the postbus will take you down the strath to Muir of Ord.

Maps

The whole stretch of the Western Highlands demands a large number of maps. OS 1:50,000 sheets 24, 25, 26, 33, 34, 35, 40, 41 and 49 cover the area described, as do Bartholomew's 1:100,000 sheets 47, 50, 51, 54 and 55.

Bibliography

Bennet, Donald, *Scottish Mountain Climbs*, Batsford
Johnstone, G. S., *The Western Highlands*, SMC District Guide, West Col Productions
Murray, W. H., *The Scottish Highlands*, SMT
Murray, W. H., *Companion Guide to the Highlands of Scotland*, Collins
Weir, Tom, *The Western Highlands*, Batsford

Glen Quoich

Doubtless the King, Kenneth, hunted the glen,
Bearing the stag, benighted, in the trees
That whisper, tempest-twisted, now as then.
The silver Chalice of the Pleiades
And bright Orion's princely sword of peace
Alike transcended the ruling custom's call
To armed expedient: should Trumpet cease
Then Truce was fit to fatten kites withal.
Nor Irish teaching nor the Tonsure's zest
Annexed a troubled Realm: these shouting days
The 'Deas gu Gath', not 'Amor Vincit' best
Winds the wild horn of passion in the Lays;
When Kenneth, idle, hunted; and his string
Vowed the red deer an arrow from the King.

(*Deas gu Gath:* ready for the fray)

10
THE FAR NORTH AND NORTHWEST HIGHLANDS
Hamish M. Brown

We take the Far North and Northwest to mean the mountain and moorland country north of the Kyle line which runs coast-to-coast across Scotland from Dingwall to Kyle of Lochalsh. This is a colossal area and it contains great, rough ranges, all with resounding names to match their characteristics: Applecross, Torridon, Fannich Forest, the Deargs, Coigach, Assynt, right up to Sutherland—which was the *south land* of the Vikings a thousand years ago.

I would hesitate to use the word *hostile* of any terrain but there is no other word suitable. If it is not hostile it crouches in an armed neutrality. Here some of the oldest rocks in the world scab the landscape; scoured and worn and peppered with thousands of lochans, it gives some of the roughest of country to climb and explore. In the whole northern half of our area there are only four Munros but this is a misleading number for the peaks of the Northwest rise virtually from sea-level moors and have a dramatic quality all too often lacking in summits above the magical Munro line. There are over 30 Munros in the southern half of the region and as they include whole *ranges* like Beinn Eighe as one Munro, this again can be a misleading simplicity. The Far North and Northwest is simply in a class of its own; the only comparison that can be made is with the Black Cuillin in Skye.

The landscape is desolate thanks to the grim history of the Clearances. Ullapool is the only real town on the whole west coast, for instance. Many of the roads are single track. Services are few and far between. It is country for those willing to do with less in order to gain more: a wilderness experience found nowhere else in Britain. Much of the country is deer forest and from mid-August into late autumn walkers should try to avoid disturbing others' sport—which is also the mainstay of the local economy. There are plenty of rights of way and areas like the Torridons are without restrictions.

The east coast is surprisingly industrialized, especially with new oil-related concerns, and the A9 is as notorious north of Inverness as it is south of the capital of the Highlands. Coastal walking is not easy and the hills tend to be lower, trackless and very wet; consequently there is not much to offer the walker when the unrivalled west coast is equally handy for walking activities. Care should be taken not to attempt too much too soon. The area cannot be judged by standards and practices which apply elsewhere. There are areas where one mile an hour is good going! Most of the routes described make use of paths, some of which are old drove ways, coffin roads or stalking paths. They are of inestimable help and should be used wherever possible.

Accommodation

As this is one area where a multi-day tramp can be made from youth hostel to youth hostel, membership of the Scottish YHA is recommended. In the midge season shelter under a roof is to be preferred to camping. The hostels are all round the seaboard: Kyle, Torridon, Craig, Carn Dearg, Ullapool, Achininver (Coigach), Achmelvich, Durness, Tongue, John o' Groats, Helmsdale, Carbisdale Castle (Invershin), Strathpeffer and Inverness. At Craig in Glencarron is a private hostel (store, drying room, baths—Gerry Howkins, Achnashellach Hostel, Craig, Strathcarron, Wester Ross, Telephone 052 06 232) which is both a good base and link in backpacking routes.

There are two club huts in the area which are available to club members applying through their secretaries: The Ling Hut (Glen Torridon GR 597563, SMC), The Smiddy (Dundonnell GR 093876, JMCS Edinburgh). Bothies are sited in some useful areas but are not generally publicized to avoid overuse which would destroy their very pleasure. Those keen enough will find them and/or join the Mountain Bothies Association.

Hotel and bed and breakfast accommodation is available along the roads but in summer tourists and fishermen may well fill hotels while in winter many close down altogether. Ullapool, being the only town of any size on the west coast and a car-ferry terminal for the Outer Hebrides, is always busy in the summer.

Transport

The Highlands and Islands Development Board produces an annual timetable of all routes by train, bus, sea and air, *Getting Around the*

Highlands and Islands, and the Post Office produces a *Scottish Postbus Timetable.* In this area the system works by radiating out from Inverness, using the Kyle and Thurso/Wick railway lines with post and other buses connecting with trains and going on to places on the west coast or up remote glens. There may only be one bus a day, but where more, the return journey and flow back towards Inverness is most likely to occur in the afternoon. I have stood more than once waiting for a bus on the wrong day of the week so check times carefully! By using such transport as there is very pleasant wanderings can be made without the necessity of always returning to a car. A cycle has much to recommend it as an aid to walking in an area where there are often long glens which may not be open to cars. Public transport does not operate on Sundays except for trains on the Wick line.

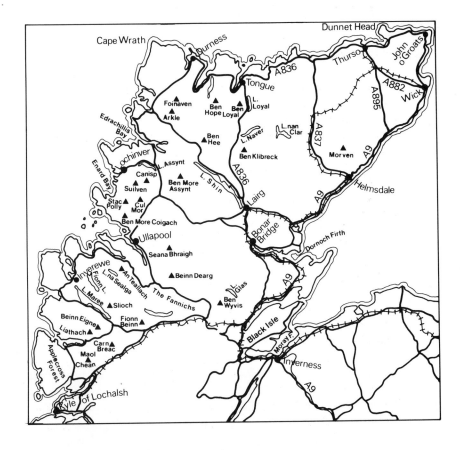

Long Multi-Day Treks

The following is just a sample of the sort of expeditions possible. Those going off on such multi-day exploits should already have considerable experience of what is involved. This is not country in which to begin one's hill-walking career. Once away it may be days before the next telephone, shop, village or pub is encountered—for example the northern half of OS sheet 20 has only two edging sections of A class road on it, 25 miles (40 km) apart as the crow flies. It is 'mountain after mountain for ever and ever'.

Start: Achnashellach Private Hostel, GR 038492 (see above) which is handy from Achnashellach Station. *Day One:* Walk back to the station and follow the path up Coire Lair to round by the Bealach Ban (GR 944517) and the Bealach na Lice (GR 933509), descending to Annat on Loch Torridon. Hotel, B&B and youth hostel accommodation are situated round the lochside. 15 miles (24 km), 700 metres of ascent. Stalking path throughout. *Day Two:* Follow the north shore road or path along Loch Torridon (shop at Fasag) to Inveralligin beyond which there is the 'easy' option of the tarred road over the pass or the demanding footpath round the rocky coast. From Lower Diabeg a path only for 3 moorland miles (5 km) to Craig Youth Hostel. 17 miles (27 km), 350 metres of ascent. *Day Three:* A couple of hours' fine coastal walking leads to Redpoint where the motor road is rejoined. Walk right round Loch Gairloch to Carn Dearg Youth Hostel (fine situation) or find accommodation in Gairloch itself. Shops there. 18-22 miles (29-35 km), 250 metres of ascent. *Day Four:* Walk to Poolewe and visit the Inverewe Gardens (NTS), particularly fine in June. A semi rest day really which can be skipped but is recommended. 9-12 miles (14-19 km), 200 metres of ascent. Accommodation and shops in Poolewe. *Day Five:* The big one but on paths most of the time. It goes through perhaps the wildest landscape in Britain. A tent to break the journey is advised if you can't face the 28 rough miles (45 km) and 1000 metres of ascent demanded! From Poolewe follow the track to Kernsary (GR 893793) and on southeast to cross the causeway (between Fionn Loch and Dubh Loch) to Carnmore. A good path rises through spectacular scenery, then drops down to Gleann na Muice Beag. The bridge near Larachantivore cannot be relied on (a crossing at about GR 052792 is usually possible). It is very boggy going across to the Sealga River and Shenavall Bothy. In spate both these rivers can be impracticable. A rough, unmade path rises from Shenavall to join the estate track down Gleann Chaorachain to the A832. Accommodation by Loch Broom:

Dundonnell Hotel, Ling Hut, Camusnagaul. The first will feel deserved, but make it in time for dinner! *Day Six:* An easy day to end with. Cross Strath Beag by the footbridge (GR 103879) and join the hill road at Eilean Darach to cross the col and drop (Land-Rover track now) to Allt na h-Airbhe (Altnaharrie) where there is an inn and passenger ferry to Ullapool. Check on its running schedule before leaving Dundonnell. (Normally four a day, May through September. Telephone Dundonnell 230.) Beinn Ghobhlach (The Forked Hill) which dominates the peninsula between the Broom Lochs is a viewpoint worth adding if there is surplus energy available. Ullapool has all tourist facilities and a youth hostel with a view up the loch of the Deargs. 7 miles (11 km), 250 metres of ascent.

This journey could be extended northwards to Achininver Youth Hostel and Lochinver or even further. It could also be aimed south to complete a circuit. From either Shenavall or Dundonnell head south up the Abhaimn Loch an Nid, then up (poor path, not on map) to the Bealach na Croise (GR 068716) to reach the end of Lochan Fada. If good, dry going, continue round and down Gleann Bianasdail to Loch Maree (option of Slioch) and Kinlochewe by Incheril. If rivers are high descend the Gleann na Muice path/road by the Heights instead. Kinlochewe has several hotels, B&B, camp site, and shop. 24 miles (39 km) and 730 metres of ascent from Dundonnell. The next day cross the historic Coulin Pass back to Achnashellach, either by following the Glen Torridon road to Loch Clair, or the path shown over the shoulder of Carn Dhomhnuill: 14 miles (23 km), 600 metres of ascent. With Gerry's hostel at Craig, the Ling Hut and a hostel in Glen Torridon, the country between (glens and summits) can be crisscrossed in comfortable days—a good introduction to this part of the country. For further ploys see Moir or my own *Hamish's Mountain Walk* in the book list. For some of the big days described later see Wilson and Gilbert: *The Big Walks*—the region is full of them!

Easy Day Walks

This is an area rich in walks of all standards. Space only permits mentioning a few. Any path shown running into glens or up hills is probably a worthwhile walk—as long as you can use a map—and any height gained invariably widens the view, a fact I have utilized in my selection.

Fionn Bheinn

The Munro north of Achnasheen, this is one of the easiest summits on that list; it can be, and is, climbed between trains! It has a fine view in all directions. Map: Bart 54, OS 20 and 25 both needed. Follow the stream up and then swing northeast by Creagan nan Laoigh to the summit—beyond is a sea of peat hags. (I think Coire Bog is a misprint for Coire Beg, but it is apt!) If more time is available descend eastwards to pick up one of the paths back down into Strath Bran: 6 miles (10 km), 800 metres of ascent.

Coulin Pass

(See above.) If transport is available at both ends this is an easy pass. Maps: Bart 54, OS 25.

Liathach Glens

Liathach is one of the most dramatic hills in Scotland but an NTS path moats it on the northern side and gives good walking with varying views. The watershed may be boggy, but mostly it is well tracked. Car parks at both ends: Coire Mhic Nobuil (GR 868575) above Loch Torridon and Coire Dubh Mor (GR 957568) in Glen Torridon: 10 miles (16 km), 400 metres of ascent. The NTS has a visitor centre by the junction at the foot of the glen (GR 905556) and runs a summer programme of guided walks like this one. Maps: Bart 54, OS 24 and 25 or better, the 1:25,000 OS Outdoor Leisure Map, *The Cuillin and Torridon Hills*.

Stac Polly

This may be only 613 metres but its serrated crest is unique in Scotland, as is the view from it. Maps: Bart 58, OS 15. A path leads to it from the car park by the roadside along Loch Lurgainn (GR 108094). This mounts to the saddle on the ridge which is not as difficult as it may appear. The whole area to the north and east is a nature reserve. On the A835 at Knockan (GR 188091) is an interpretive centre, nature trail, etc. Cul Mor and Cul Beag are fine peaks too and can be ascended, *on clear days,* from the eastern slopes without much difficulty, using the paths shown on the lower slopes.

Ben Hope and Ben Klibreck

These are the two most northerly Munros, big but easy hills. *Ben Hope.*
Maps: Bart 60, OS 9. It is most often climbed from Strath More up the
burn (2 miles (3 km) north from the broch of Dun Dornaigil) which
leads to the upper southern slopes. The western cliffs are a clear marker
on the left and the summit is reached in a couple of hours. No other
route should be attempted if an easy walk is wanted: 5 miles (8 km), 930
metres of ascent. *Ben Klibreck* (Mountain of the Fish). Maps: Bart 60,
OS 16. Follow the track along the south shore of Loch Naver from
Altnaharra (accommodation) and continue by the standing stones to a
stalking path (not on OS map) which zigzags up the north ridge leading
to the crest just west of Meall Ailein. Two miles (3 km) of ridge lead to
the summit and strong walkers could continue south to the Bealach
Easach and the path down to Crask Inn: 11 miles (18 km), 900 metres of
ascent.

Cape Wrath

Maps: Bart 58, OS 9. The northwest extremity of Britain is unspoilt and
preferable to John o' Groats. A foot ferry crosses the Kyle of Durness
from Keoldale and a mini-bus operates to the lighthouse. The highest
cliffs on mainland Britain are visible and south is uninhabited country
for many miles. (Inland, it is used as a bombing range: beware!)
Durness will probably be base for this highly recommended excursion.
A walk out along the sands and dunes to Faraid Head, and visits to the
craft village and Smoo Caves, are worthwhile.

Moderate Day Walks

Eas Coul Aluinn Waterfall

Maps: Bart 58, OS 15. This fall (GR 280276) is the highest in Britain.
Sometimes it is possible to hire a boat from Kylesku and sail up Loch
Glencoul, in which case, walk back by the access route described,
gaining the path at GR 289261 to avoid crags. A path leads round the
north end of Gainmhich, 4½ miles (7 km) south of the ferry on the
A894, to continue by Loch Bealach a' Bhuirich and down to the stream
which contains the falls. The view from above is poor (and dangerous)
and it is best to continue on to GR 289261 and descend into the glen.
Rough going: 12 miles (19 km), 750 metres of ascent. The path in
continues a straggly course round Beinn Uidhe to descend to

Inchnadamph if a long day alternative attracts. Conival and Ben More Assynt are rough summits which can be reached up Gleann Dubh from Inchnadamph. It is advisable to wait for good weather.

Beinn Alligin (The Jewelled Mountain)

Maps: Bart 54, OS 24 (or better, the 1:25,000 Outdoor Leisure Map, *The Cuillin and Torridon Hills*). Start at the car park above Loch Torridon (GR 868575) and take the path, now clear, from the west of the bridge which leads over the lower slopes to reach Coir' nan Laoigh, the (un-named on OS) south corrie of Tom na Gruagaich. From this top a dip and rise, not as difficult as the map suggests, lead to Sgurr Mhor, the Munro. The deep cleft below the summit cone can be a navigational hazard in a misty descent, otherwise the route is well beaten into a path. The ridge east from Sgurr Mhor takes in the 'Horns' and is a more serious undertaking.

Moderate Munros

Wyvis, away in the east, can be climbed from Garbat on the A835, 6 miles (10 km) north of Garve, but some playing of forest tracks is required. The eastern approaches are much more worthy and recommended—hence its inclusion here. Glen Glas has some very fine river scenery. Climb the hill now before the skiers put a railway up it! Like Wyvis, *Am Faochagach* is often done as a solitary Munro, perhaps on a day of motoring south. It is as inspiring as its name. The approach west of Glascarnoch Reservoir may mean a paddle, Strath Vaich (no cars) definitely means many miles. An Teallach's two Munros; *Bidean* and *Sgurr Fiona*, can be ascended easily by the path from Dundonnell. It continues over the gravelly plateau. The full traverse of An Teallach is a serious day—see below. *Slioch:* use the paths from Kinlochewe/ Incheril to mount the path up Gleann Bianasdail to the stream descending from Slioch. Follow it up. Twin tops. *Maol Chean-dearg* can be approached from Annat on Loch Torridon, from Coulags in Strath Carron or even via Coire Lair and Achnashellach. Ascend ultimately by the southeast ridge. (The path from the west does not reach this col, as shown on the OS, but ends on the southwest spur of Ceapairean.) Peaks like An Ruadh-stac (892 metres) or Sgurr Dubh (782 metres) may only be Corbetts but their naked grandness more than makes up for a few metres.

Long Day Walks

Before attempting these walks, you should already have considerable hill walking experience, so detailed guidance should be unnecessary. In this brief summary 'helps' are given to cover all Munros not already mentioned, plus a Sutherland day as fine as any over Munros even though not going above the magical plimsoll line. **These are summer descriptions.** In winter they are serious mountaineering expeditions.

The Coire Lair Horseshoe

Maps: Bart 54, OS 25. Start from Achnashellach (see above) and either follow the path up Coire Lair and take the western path from the 'cross roads' to reach Fuar Tholl from the Bhealach Mhoir, or start from Loch Dughaill and work up to ascend either arm of the south-east corrie, a titivating choice. There are some big crags to circuit on round for Sgurr Ruadh and the col is a complex of bumps and lochan hollows. Descend to the col at the head of Coire Lair only down slopes you can see to be clear of crags. The ascent to, and traverse along, Beinn Liath Mhor is on exposed rock, the descent off it eastwards is purgatorial. Descend again to Achnashellach.

Liathach and Beinn Eighe

Maps: Bart 54 for planning but for navigation use the 1:25,000 Cuillin/Torridon Leisure Map. For safety and satisfaction save these beautiful hills for a clear day.

Liathach is one of the grandest hills in Scotland. The easiest ways up its main top, the Spidean, are by the burn from Glen Cottage or the 'path' up the next burn east. Ascending 1000 metres in 1 mile (1½ km), both suffer a chronic steepness. In descent, care is especially needed to negotiate some of the rock bands. The Mullach can be gained by the Allt an Tuill Bhain, or the corrie up from the village. The traverse of the two Munros entails exposed scrambling (as on An Teallach) though a path has evolved on the Torridon flank below the pinnacles.

Beinn Eighe is a great sprawl of mountain with rough quartzite ridges. To do everything the following is suggested. Go up Coire Dubh Mor from the car park (GR 957568) and follow the beaten path round to Loch Coire Mhic Fhearchair, which some regard as the country's finest. Traverse round to ascend Sail Mhor's brutal north ridge. From this fine prow a col leads to a rock band (easy scrambling) to gain Coinnich Mor. The only grass of the day follows. Ruadh-stac Mor, the

Munro, is out on a limb and once collected the long switchback east follows. The hotel at Kinlochewe becomes an objective much to be desired! Descend by the Allt a' Churn.

The Big Six

A base at Shenavall cuts out several miles of approach march. The Abhainn Strath na Sealga may be unco-operative, horrible heather and awkward crags make the many tops of *Chlaidheimh* (Hill of the Sword) about enough for the beginning. Sgurr Ban should be ascended from the northeast. The big *Mullach* is rockier. A path skirts Meall Garbh on the west. *Tarsuinn* has an exuberant line of summits. There is plenty of bog on the next col and *A'Mhaighdean* (The Maiden) takes a bit of breasting. It is the remotest Munro of all. The descent to the col to *Ruadh Stac Mor* needs care. Ascend it by a left pincer movement, descend the same way and use the path from the col going northeast to join the Carnmore-Larachantivore stalking path. The bridge may not be in existence and gooey bogs lead back to Shenavall's moat. A grand round!

An Teallach Traverse

It is hard to decide on approaches. The two easiest at start and finish are the path from Dundonnell up the tame back slopes and the Shenavall track to the south. The superlative scrambling (there *are* hard places but all can be traversed lower on the west flank) deserves better. So ascend by Coire a' Ghiubhsachan with its quartz wall to gain Loch Toll an Lochain, which also claims to be the country's finest. A mainly grassy line *can* be picked up on to the Mheall Liath-Bidean ridge. Bidean to Sgurr Fiona presents no difficulty but the ridge beyond gives some fun. Lord Berkeley's Seat overhangs. Corrag Bhuidhe has four pinnacles. The way off Corrag Bhuidhe Buttress has a 'bad step' on the crest. Gobhlach lives up to its name and Sail Liath is a most welcome summit.

The Fannichs

A complete traverse will give a day of up to 30 miles (50 km). Most people take two or three visits. There are some helpful access paths, more than shown on the maps. The long glen up from the Glascarnoch Reservoir is strenuous and boggy. Gain height as soon as possible for *An Coileachan* (The Cockerel). The path west from *Meall Gorm* will take you under Sgurr Mor for *Beinn Liath Mhor*. Traverse the cone of *Sgurr Mor*, then add the outlier of *Chrasgaidh* (a path from its col runs over Creag Raineach to join the one to Braemore Junction). *Clach Geala* and *Each* lead south, then a big drop intervenes before the western pair of *Breac* and *A'Chailleach*. (This last summit *only* is on OS sheet 19, the rest are on sheet 20; so trace it on the margin at home.) Splendid walking country.

The Deargs

These are an even more demanding day for the going is not always on ridges so there is roughness and bogs in plenty. A plover-singing solitude can be guaranteed! For all-in-a-day begin at Loch Droma on the A835. A path (not shown) leads from GR 267750 to the Allt a' Gharbhrain. Cross it, and the Allt Lair, to ascend *Am Faochagach*. Descend to the outflow of Loch Prille and climb again up the east ridge of *Cona' Mheall*. A rough down-and-up follows to gain *Dearg*, then *Ceapraichean*, and an even worse rocky chaos lies on the descent northwards. *Clach Geala* then feels easy but beyond lie miles of complex bog and rock. (The gap at GR 274857 is a key!) *Seana Bhraigh* (The Old High Slopes) is my favourite remote Munro. It and Clach Geala are often done as a day (still long) from Inverlael. A good path descends from Lochan a' Chnapaich to Gleann Squaib. You can trace a straight line of 25 miles (40 km) across OS sheet 20 here without touching a tarred road!

Canisp and Suilven

Assynt has only two Munros and the horseshoe taking in Breabag, Conival and Ben More from the south is one of the best possible days. More eye-catching are the hills that stand solitary: Quinag, Cul Mor, Stac Polly, Suilven—this last upstaging its bigger neighbour Canisp. A traverse from Inchnadamph over these last two is a unique walk. Start anywhere on the A837 and the slopes will feed you up to Canisp's cone, an extensive viewpoint. Descend to the southeast until it is safe to break down to the Lochan Fada-Loch na Gainimh path. Take a rising traverse to gain the Bealach Mor, the gash of saddle on Suilven. **Climbers only** should take the eastern prow direct and once the summit, Caisteal Liath, has been reached everyone should return to the Bealach Mor. Descend south from it and exit down the River Kirkaig (falls) or north again to the path direct to Lochinver on the sea: a classic expedition.

The Arkle and Foinaven Hills

These are great heaps of quartz but several long paths crisscross the range giving demanding walks—which is all I hint at. If you have done all the rest here you will still be impressed. I hope my all too brief notes will help when you come to put feet to the dreams of the north and west.

Maps

The area described is covered by OS 1:50,000 sheets 9, 10, 15, 16, 19, 20, 21, 24, 25, 26 and 33; and by Bartholomew's 1:100,000 sheets 54, 55, 58, 59 and 60.

Bibliography

Gilbert, Richard, *Memorable Munros*, Cordee
Gordon, Seton, *Highways and Byways in the West Highlands*, Macmillan
MacInnes, Hamish, *West Highland Walks*, Hodder, 2 volumes
Mackenzie, Osgood, *A Hundred Years in the Highlands*, Bles
Murray, W. H., *Companion Guide to the West Highlands*, Collins
Prebble, John, *The Highland Clearances*, Penguin
The area is included in the books by Brown, Moir, and Gilbert/Wilson in the general list.

Multum in Parvo

It isn't that we hadn't climbed before
Each to his dazzling summit of desire,
Or watch'd high witness from some corrie's floor
Touch'd by the dawn's lean fingers tipped with fire:
For you, my friend, harsh, vaporous breath hard won
The snows of godlike Kilimanjaro knew
And I blue-framed Columbia in the sun,
Bright where the ice-axed, glittering splinters flew.
But freshness best a sense of beauty brings,
One sunlit chaffinch glinting in the wood
Is worth two mountains of remoter things;
And we would perfect keep if keep we could
The drifts, the wood smoke and the frosty air,
The hush of Bachnagairn that evening there.

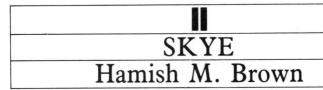

SKYE
Hamish M. Brown

Skye, oddly enough, suffers a strange neglect among walkers. I think this is partly due to its reputation as a sort of Valhalla, Mecca and Shangri La rolled into one for rock climbers, and to its reputed summer plagues of rain, midges and tourists. It sounds formidable!

Having had many heatwaves on Skye I would still not disagree with those comments. The midges are man-eaters, the rain has an uncompromising energy, the summer hordes crowd everywhere—including the famous Black Cuillin. It is still magic. May, June and September are usually better months than July and August. The Black Cuillin have no problems of access, being too barren for shooting, but much of the island is under sheep and care should be taken not to panic beasts or let dogs run wild.

I have purposely given a fair coverage of the island's walks, perhaps at the expense of the Black Cuillin, as Skye deserves to be more popular in general (the tourists don't come in droves for no reason) and the main peaks are well covered in the Bull or Slesser guides. If it rains Dunvegan and the other sites *are* worth a visit. The island is steeped in legend and history. McInnes covers much of this well.

Do not fall into the trap of keeping 'lesser' walks for off-days and wet days. Wherever you go, the view of the Black Cuillin is the most dramatic feature in sight. If it is clouded out, the loss cannot be made up for. Sample everything, even at the price of missing a Munro!

Most expeditions are not long, unless several peaks are linked together, so times and distances are seldom given. The going is often hard, however, and adequate footwear is essential. The following comments are all made with summer expeditions in mind. Skye in winter is a different game. The Cuillin under snow is to be admired—from a safe distance!

Accommodation

There are youth hostels at Kyle, Broadford, Glenbrittle, Uig and Raasay which makes it worthwhile being a member of the Scottish YHA. The camp site at Glenbrittle loses its attractions under assaults of rain or midges, both of which occur with some frequency. There is also a BMC/MCS Hut in Glenbrittle which is open to those belonging to affiliated clubs (Custodian: J. W. Simpson, 15 Banks Avenue, Chapelton, Lanarkshire. Telephone 03573 533). The only other hut is the Coruisk Hut (actually by Loch Scavaig, JMCS Glasgow) which is a quiet, pleasant base for exploring the inner Cuillin routes. Skye lacks many bothies of use to walkers and except along the main roads from ferries to Portree even bed and breakfast and hotel accommodation is limited. Broadford and Portree are the main towns. The summer brings large numbers of tourists and accommodation can be difficult. There is a shop on the popular Glenbrittle camp site. Wild camping in the glen is not allowed.

Transport

The main link to Skye is the shuttle car-ferry service from Kyle of Lochalsh. A secondary service operates from Kylerhea (Glenelg) in the summer only but there are steep passes on both sides of the sound—so cyclists beware. There is also a summer service from Mallaig to Armadale. All of these carry vehicles. Uig, in the north of Skye, has motor-steamer services to the Outer Hebrides. In summer boats cruise, or may be hired, from Mallaig to Coruisk and, on Skye, from Elgol to Coruisk—a grand approach to the Cuillin but at the mercy of fickle weather. Raasay is linked with a vehicle ferry from Sconser and in summer cruises/hiring may be possible from Portree. The bus service on Skye is limited (the major climbing base of Glenbrittle often has no public transport) and there are no Sunday services (other than the Kyle ferry). Consult *Getting Around the Highlands and Islands* and the *Scottish Postbus Timetable*. A push bike can eliminate some problems for those without private transport. You will also discover why it is called a *push* bike! It is sometimes possible to hire a boat at Glenbrittle and sail to Coruisk, then walk back.

Maps

Skye is covered on Bartholomew 1:100,000 sheet 54, useful for planning. The OS 1:50,000 needs sheets 23, 32, 33 (and 24 for Raasay). For wandering in the Black Cuillin the ground is too complex and *The Cuillin and Torridon Hills* 1:25,000 Outdoor Leisure Map is better. Also highly recommended is the 1:15,000 *Black Cuillin, Isle of Skye* map devised and drawn for the Scottish Mountaineering Trust. For non-Cuillin walks described below the 1:50,000 is perfectly adequate.

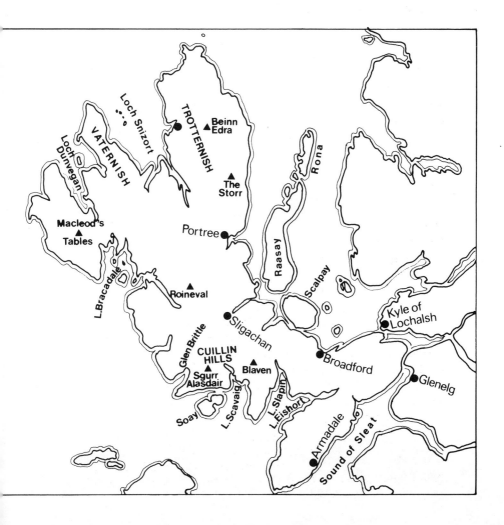

Compass

As nowhere else in Britain, a compass is affected by the magnetic nature of the rock in Skye, particularly on crests and summits where it is most likely to be needed, and can be completely useless. Much more has to be done with maps—as large scale as possible. An altimeter is handy.

Easy Day Walks

As soon as you cross to Skye there are neglected places well worth exploring. Sleat (pronounced *Slate*) is trackless paradise with good hotels at Ardvasar, Ord and Isle Ornsay and delightful coastal expeditions can be made round the Point of Sleat or on the west—perhaps rewarded by the finest views on Skye. Map: OS 32.

The Kyle Peaks

Sgurr na Coinnich (739 metres) and Beinn a' Caillich (732 metres) are almost invariably ignored. Sited as they are, moated by the Kyles and ringed by mountain ranges, they give outstanding views. The easiest approach is from the 279-metre Bealach Udal, the pass linking Kylerhea and Broadford. Map: OS 33.

Rubh' an Dunain

Rubh' an Dunain (map OS 32), or just Rhu Point, is an easy walk, from Glenbrittle out to a delightful setting with caves, cliff scrambling, a secret lochan to swim in, chambered cairns and a fine promontory fort. (Every point on Skye seems to have a ruined castle of some sort.)

MacLeod's Maidens

Map OS 23. This gives another coastal walk out to a group of legend-shrouded sea pinnacles. The MacLeod's Tables, the flat-topped summits of the Healavals, lie inland and at Waterstein Head the cliffs reach a height of nearly 300 metres—one place worth seeing on a wild day with the waterfalls flying *upward!*

Dun Caan

The 444-metre summit of Raasay makes a good day expedition, crossing from Sconser. Its flat summit once saw the irrepressible Boswell dancing a jig on it with the local chief's daughter. A path leads up the

Inverarish Burn and should be used. The going is tricky otherwise. Strong walkers can make the full path circuit—12 miles (18 km)—otherwise return the same way. A few days on Raasay would be rewarding. OS sheet 24.

Sligachan to Glenbrittle

Over the Bealach a' Mhaim, this walk has been compared to reaching Zermatt over the hills rather than by transport. It is a good walk with an easy path, yet gives views into some of the wild corries. The col is about 350 metres and 10 miles (16 km) is covered. The start is on the A863, ½ mile (¾ km) up from Sligachan, following a track towards the only building visible. Glen Sligachan has a clear path up it, leaving from the east side of the old pack bridge. A branch goes up to cross the Druim Hain ridge and descends to Loch Coruisk. The circuit of this loch is unforgettable. Return the same way: a *long* day.

A boat from Elgol may be the best way of visiting historic Loch Coruisk. As we have now moved on to more serious things, we must pause, but I hope already you find Skye an attractive proposition. It is like a good malt—try the local Talisker—too good to rush.

Moderate Day Walks

These should really include *Sligachan-Coruisk*. You can also try *Sligachan-Elgol*, or vice versa. A bothy at GR 511187 might make a good break overnight, with Blaven added (see below). Coruisk from Elgol is rough round Sgurr na Stri (a fantastic viewpoint which can be reached from the Druim Hain path) and has the notorious *Bad Step* which is an intimidating, exposed ledge across an unavoidable slab barrier. Technically it is not difficult and dignity rather than life is lost in crossing it!

The Red Hills

The Red Hills west of Broadford are pudding-bowl hills of red granite scree which I always feel are more attractive to walk round (Strath Mor/Strath Beag) and look at, rather than climb, but the summit views make up for toil. Map: OS 32.

Glamaig and Marsco

Glamaig above Sligachan and Marsco up the glen suffer the same problem but a linking traverse of the two gives a longer walker's traverse at close proximity to the Black Cuillin. Cunning route-finding can avoid the worst of the screes. Map: OS 32.

Blaven

Blaven (The Blue Mountain) can be reached from Camusunary up the corrie behind, or from there or on the A881 Elgol road using the rough track over Am Mam for Blaven's long, long south ridge. The path up the Allt na Dunaiche from near the head of Loch Slapin is the finest approach. There is a 924 metre top at GR 528215 with an awkward gap beyond. The trig point (928 metres) gives the most extensive panorama of the Cuillin array. It is the only Munro not on or near the main ridge. All other approaches to Blaven involve climbing. Some of the easy Black Cuillin peaks follow.

Bruach na Frithe

Bruach na Frithe (Brae of the Forest) is most easily approached from the Sligachan end of the Bealach a' Mhaim track. At the last burn on the right a cairned line diverts up to the Fionn Choire and it or the northwest ridge can be followed to the summit. Even after one easy Munro Skye will feel different. The Fionn Choire path leads to the Bealach na Lice, an easy pass, but the round by Harta Corrie back to Sligachan is what the French call *penible*.

Sgurr na Banachdich and Sgurr Alasdair

Sgurr na Banachdich (Smallpox Peak, 965 metres) is the easiest Munro from Glenbrittle with a well-worn approach up Coire 'an Each to gain the western slopes which run out to Sgurr nan Gobhar. Sgurr Alasdair, 993 metres, is the highest point and the easy approach to it is up the wearisome Great Stone Shoot from Coire Lagan. Every other way is barred by crags or climbing and should be left for climbers. Descend the same way.

The Storr

This extraordinary hill is easily spotted as the Old Man pinnacle can be seen from afar, but there is a whole array of sculptured forms, all against a 200-metre sheer background, while the view over the sea from Skye is magical. It is one of *the* unique places of Britain. A forestry car park is sited on the A855 about 7 miles (11 km) north of Portree and a clear path leads up to the Storr rocks. If you go north and round there is an upper corrie which leads to the summit of the Storr itself, 719 metres. The easiest ascent is from the Bealach Mor, well south. A long day can be put in to head north along the hills of the scarped backbone of Trotternish, right to the Uig-Staffin pass—16-mile (26-km) tramp, no path—from which they eye will be caught by The Quirang.

The Quirang

This is another area of extraordinary chaotic rock formations with names like the Prison, the Needle and the Table. An easy traverse along under the main scarp from the road leads to the area. A visit to it could be combined with looking at the Kilt Rock, Duntulm and other historic sites in the extreme north of Skye. Flora MacDonald is buried at Kilmuir.

Harder Hill Days

These essentially mean more Black Cuillin Munros. *Sgurr nan Eag* is a remote Munro reached by its south ridge after a flog round the boggy moors. It is worth traversing the airy ridge (easy) to *Gars-bheinn*, the most southerly top on the Skye ridge. Coire nan Laoigh is not to be used in descent. Coire a' Ghrunnda is geologically interesting and not easy to enter. *Eag* from it sets quite stern scrambling problems.

Mhaidaidh (The Foxes' Peak) and *Ghreadaidh* can be climbed with moderate scrambling from Coire a' Ghreadaidh but they are many-topped and route-finding is not easy. (*Sgurr Thuilm* is an outlier which gives a good view.) *Mhic Choinnich* is a serious scramble, exposed, and the summit rock is greasy if wet. It is climbed from the northern corner of Coire Lagan but for all these harder summits the best maps and most detailed guides should be used. *Sgurr Dubh Mor* can prove difficult to *find*, never mind climb, and is one of the less-visited tops which lure the Munroist. The whole area is a jumble of bare rock or boulders.

One abiding lure is *Sgurr nan Gillean* (Peak of the Young Men) which is so well seen from Sligachan. It is reached by a path which wends over the moors, eventually curving up on to the southeast ridge. This gives scrambling and in descent it is easy to lose the best line. It is still the easiest route up the mountain. *Am Basteir* is climbed from the east but it has an exposed crest with a nasty step and the grit on the slabs makes adhesion awkward.

Hardest of all the Munros is the *Inaccessible Pinnacle*. Sgurr Dearg, against which this blade of rock rests, is readily reached by the path up

Coire na Banachdich or from Coire Lagan or along the western ridge (some scrambling). The easiest route up the *In Pin* is its long East Ridge, a 'moderate' rock climb but very exposed. I know quite a few Munro-baggers who have done all the Munros except this one, or perhaps the last few mentioned. Do not leave them too late, and be happy to accept assistance from climbers; they are 'serious' routes in a walking sense.

There is as much enjoyment to be had exploring the corries, going round the range or crossing its easy passes, as in scaling all its rocky summits. The *Bealach Coire na Banachdich* is the easiest route over from Glenbrittle to Coruisk. Combined with walking back round the southern peaks it gives a long, demanding day. The coast is only pathed by usage, not making, and the best line runs about the 250-metre level. Approaching Loch Scavaig there are many rock bands and in spate the Mad Burn may be impassable. It is also possible to cross from Coire a' Ghrunnda down either side of the Dubhs (Coire a' Lochain or An Garbh-choire) but the going is very bouldery and demanding. From the head of Coir'-Uisg the *Bealach na Glaic Moire* can be used to gain either the Glenbrittle or Sligachan sides. On the north side there is a traverse to reach the col—the direct route is cliff. As always, be armed with a good guide book and choose a clear day if possible for any new venture.

Good combination trips can be made, such as Broadford youth hostel to Camusunary bothy; round the coast (or a pass) to Glenbrittle youth hostel; the bealach to Sligachan and bus/hitch to Portree (B&B); then traverse the Trotternish hills to Uig youth hostel. You can dream up others. Whatever you do, you soon realize that no other island in Scotland can offer such a kingdom of adventure.

Bibliography

Bull, S. P., *Black Cuillin Ridge Scramblers Guide*, SMT
Cooper, Derek, *Skye*, Routledge and Kegan Paul
Poucher, W. A., *The Magic of Skye*, Constable
Slesser, Malcolm, *The Island of Skye*, SMC District Guide, West Col Productions
Wiener, C., *Skye: A Travellers Guide*, Grasshopper Press
The area is also covered in the books by Borthwick (memorably), Brown, Weir, Wainwright and Gilbert/Wilson in the general list.

Climbing Song

Sun on the bothy, wind on the grass,
Shadow of cumulus over the pass:
Yawning and scratching and stretching of legs,
Boiling the billy and frying the eggs.

Moon on the loch, a bouldery camp,
Guy-ropes like banjo-strings, matchboxes damp:
The primus is bust, the pricker is bent,
But there's baccy and whisky galore in the tent.

An easterly wind, a bedraggling mist,
Rainwater trickling in at the wrist:
Wet to the belly, wet to the bum,
The boots are awash and the fingers are numb.

A furnace of sun, a tropical day,
Drowsy the hills across the way:
Line dangles listlessly over the edge
And the third man's asleep on a heathery ledge.

Dazzling cornice, pink cirrus or two,
Ice-crystals sparkling up in the blue:
One more Gold Flake and the bastard will go
And the fragments are dancing and tinkling below.

12
THE OUTER HEBRIDES
Roger Fleming

Between 35 and 50 miles off the northwest seaboard of Scotland, the Atlantic horizon is moulded by a tightly-knit archipelago of windswept islands stretching for over 130 miles (200 km). Often referred to as the long island or Western Isles, the Outer Hebrides form three distinct groups: the main mass of Harris and Lewis, the slender finger of the Uists and Benbecula, and the little island of Barra in the south. Geographically remote and untouched by many mainland pressures, they comprise some of the most varied and idyllic walking countryside in Scotland. Their 1100 sq miles (2850 sq km) tell of mountain and coast, wind and sky in awesome abundance. Lonely peaks contrast with white sands and acres of sweet-scented, flower-covered machair. Stark sea-racked shores give way to translucent lochs, and everywhere there is the serenity and mood that only islands can provide.

Today, the Western Isles support a population of about 30,000 and although modern technology has brought both progress and social change, the ways of the people remain unsophisticated, warm and friendly. The old 'black houses' have gone, the 'lazy beds' lie idle, but the independence of the crofting life style survives. Exploring the Hebrides on foot is therefore a fascinating experience and, despite the short summer and at times unreliable weather, the dark hills and lochs, sand and machair will always attract discerning walkers.

Access

The islands have efficient air and sea services; Loganair and British Airways operate flights to Stornoway in Lewis, Benbecula and Barra. The flying time is approximately one hour from Glasgow. The more intimate approach is by sea. The Caledonian MacBrayne company runs three separate car ferry services. RMS *Suilven* takes three hours to sail between Ullapool and Stornoway, while RMS *Hebrides* sails from Uig on Skye to Tarbert on Harris, and from there to Lochmaddy in North Uist. This crossing can take two hours in fine weather. In the south, the *Claymore* operates between Oban, Lochboisdale in South Uist and Castlebay in Barra.

Maps

The most suitable maps are the OS 1:50,000 and 1:25,000 series. The former covers all the islands in eight sheets while the larger scale of the latter is useful if a particular area is to be explored in detail. The Bartholomew 1:100,000 maps are excellent for planning purposes, sheets 57 and 53 covering the Western Isles in total. The OS 1:50,000 sheets for the area are 8, 13, 14, 18, 22 and 31.

Harris and Lewis

Harris and Lewis, although united, differ in many respects. Lewis is low and wet, and black bog blankets most of its surface. Despite this, it has a population of around 20,000, mostly scattered around the coastal fringe, and in the town of Stornoway. Divided by a range of wild hills, the landscape of Harris is quite magnificent, rock-strewn and moulded by powerful glacial action. The sea lochs are beautiful and there are many hidden corners and hollows. The principal village of Tarbert nestles at the foot of Beinn na Teanga, and is a good base from which to explore both the east and west coasts.

The east coast southwards from Tarbert is set against a hinterland of heather-clad hills and small peaty lochs. This landscape can be appreciated by following the course of the single-track roads. Perfect for the walker, and not at all like mainland highways, they harmonize with the topography, rolling and twisting over the stony surface. The road to the village of Rodel in the south is so tortuous that it was often referred to as the Golden Road on account of its construction costs. It links some of the most scattered and delightful villages of Harris.

Meavag, Drinnishader, Scadabay and Grosébay are all sheltered anchorages, standing at the head of fingers of clear green water, which thrust past rocky headlands. The walking is quite superb, with an ever-changing vista of shore, hill and loch. An excellent little camp site exists at Drinnishader, and there is a youth hostel at Stockinish.

Rodel, at the southern tip of Harris, is the site of the finest example of ecclesiastical architecture in the Western Isles. Probably built by the Macleods of Dunvegan in the sixteenth century, St Clements Church is of cruciform design and has recently been sympathetically restored. It contains several Macleod tombs, one of which has been carved from local black gneiss.

It is a short walk from the church to the picturesque harbour and pier which stand beside the Rodel Hotel. This can be extended by skirting round Loch Rodel and on to the grassy slopes of Renish Point, which projects for over a mile (1½ km) into the Sound of Harris. Roineabhal (460 metres) dominates the southeast corner of Harris, its summit providing a perfect viewpoint from which to enjoy the magnificent sight of the island-studded sound to the south, and the wild hill and loch country to the northeast.

To the west, the village of Leverburgh lies sandwiched between a tidal indent called the Obbe and the fresh water of Loch Steisevat. In the early 1920s, vast sums were expended on pier, road and jetty contracts by Lord Leverhulme, whose aim was the creation of a major fishing station. Although initial landings were excellent, the project failed with the death of its patron in 1925, and most of the port installations were sold as scrap for a mere £5000.

Two interesting walks can be started from Leverburgh. The quiet inland road past Loch Steisevat and Loch Na Moracha swings east and follows the high moorland around the southern corner of Loch Langavat, the largest loch in Harris. The track is very isolated and winds round and through some hundreds of small water-filled hollows before joining the Golden Road at Finsbay.

The coast road to the southeast of Leverburgh skirts past the fragmented Carminish Islands, a glorious sight against one of those warm Hebridean sunsets. The village of Strond, a mile (1½ km) further on, is one of the few areas in Harris where blanket peat gives way to strips of red loam.

The magnificent peninsula of Toe Head lies just 3 miles (5 km) northwest of Leverburgh and is certainly one of the most exciting walks on the islands. It is linked to the township of Northton by a low isthmus, and extends some 3 miles (5 km) into the Atlantic. Walking round the southern shoreline takes in several sandy beaches and the remains of an old chapel, now roofless and exposed to the full force of

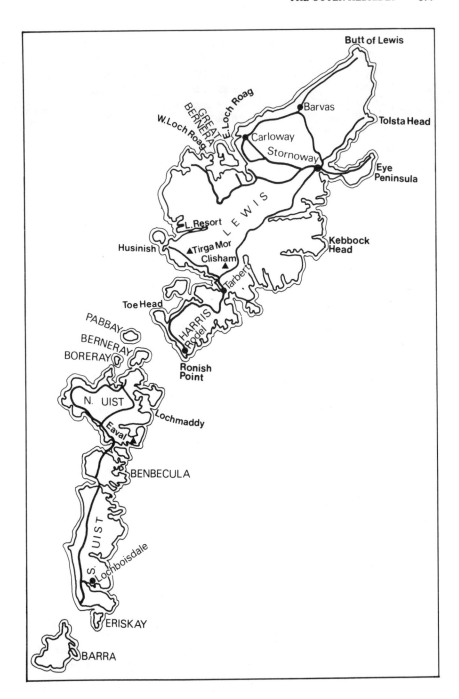

Atlantic winds. Grassy slopes rear steeply to the rocky summit of Chaipaval (365 metres) and along the way oats and potatoes are still grown in the sandy soil in the old strip fashion. Golden eagles can often be seen overhead, and gannet and fulmar glide along the fringe.

In June and July the machair is heavy with scent and ablaze with the colour of daisy, buttercup, yellow rattle, speedwell, clover and orchid. The stiff walk to the summit is worth it. On a clear day the Sound of Harris is arrayed below, with the hills of North Uist and the Cuillin of Skye in the distance. Occasionally the distant Stacs of St Kilda can be seen above the western horizon.

The Luskentyre estuary is regarded by many Harris lovers as one of the most scenic corners of the island. The walker should certainly not miss a trip down the little track which runs along this estuary from the A859. Ben Luskentyre, haven of eagle and raven, towers to the north at 436 metres, its summit affording striking views down West Loch Tarbert.

It is in North Harris that you are confronted with the most wild and rugged terrain of the Western Isles. Clisham, stark and treeless, is the highest peak of the islands at 799 metres and is surrounded by six summits over the 600-metre mark. At the base of the slope, on the north side of West Loch Tarbert, the single track B887 winds 14 tortuous miles (23 km) to the isolated village of Husinish. This particular stretch of mountain and coast offers many days of enjoyable walking and gives a true feeling of isolation. Setting out from Tarbert, the first landmark is the chimney and pier of the old whaling station at Bunavoneadar. Six thousand tons of whale meat were processed here in the 1920s by three Norwegian vessels. The venture was again instigated by Lord Leverhulme, but operations ceased in 1930 due to financial difficulties.

Several miles further on the B887 skirts around the picturesque inlet of Loch Meavaig. To the north a gravel track follows the direct descent of the Meavaig River and goes high into the towering humps of Oreval and Scourst, passing on the way Lochs Scourst and Voshimid. From Voshimid the walk can be extended by turning east and rounding the bottom of remote Loch Langavat, and through to Vigadale Bay opposite Seaforth Island on Loch Seaforth. This route is isolated so thorough preparation and good walking equipment are essential.

Several miles west of Meavaig, heather and stone suddenly give way to well-kept lawns and beds of gravel. The road at this point unexpectedly passes through the grounds of the stately Amhuinnsuidhe Castle, residence of the proprietor of the North Harris Estates. It was erected in 1868 from imported stone, and is adjacent to one of the finest salmon rivers in the Hebrides. The shoals congregate in July and August and it is a thrilling experience to watch the runs thrashing their way upstream from pool to pool.

There are several lengthy estate tracks through the wild country to the north of the castle. These give access to high-lying lochs and rivers, and to the remote habitat of herds of wild deer. All game is strictly preserved and the walker should always give notice of his movements and show consideration, especially during the stalking season.

Persevere to the end of the B887 where the village of Hushinish stands back from the white sands of the only beach on North Harris. The island of Scarp across the Sound once supported a population of over 100, complete with its own school. This westerly promontory of Harris offers a variety of first-class walks.

It is a short trip to Husinish Point, over sweet-smelling, grassy slopes. The view from the headland is of a fine coastal sweep, interrupted by the sea-pounded Taransay and Husinish Glorigs, several miles offshore. More demanding is the stony track which climbs around the lower slopes of Husival Beag, between black sea cliffs to Loch Na Cleavag. The uninhabited crofts of Scarp can be seen across the sand-fringed sound with the island of Fladday in the distance.

No visit to Harris would be complete without a walk through the prosperous and charming island of Scalpay, which lies at the entrance to East Loch Tarbert. Served by a little ferry from Kyles of Scalpay, the island supports a population of over 400 and is the main fishing centre of Harris. The Scalpay fishermen take a great pride in the appearance of their boats, which make a most photogenic sight, tied up next to the small pier. The walk from the ferry through the village to the lighthouse on the west coast, is very worthwhile as many of the characteristics of Harris are concentrated in these few square miles.

Rhenigidale is a small and extremely remote village at the mouth of Loch Seaforth. It has a youth hostel, but is entirely dependent on provisioning by the Scalpay boats. There is no adjacent road, the only access being by a 4-mile (6-km) mountain track, which begins at Laxadale Loch, and plunges steeply to sea level as it runs around the base of Loch Trollamarig. This is a first-rate walk with breathtaking views out over the rocky headlands of Lochs Seaforth and Claidh. Walkers who plan to use Rhenigidale Youth Hostel are strongly advised to carry all food supplies with them!

Leaving the hills of Harris behind and moving north into Lewis you are confronted with large tracts of bleak moorland, peppered with hundreds of shallow lochs gouged out by glacial action. Practically the whole of the interior of Lewis is covered with black peat, most of the population being located along the more fertile coastal fringe.

The most amazing road on Lewis is the seemingly never-ending B8011, which extends to the isolated parish of Uig on the west coast. It penetrates into some of the most scenic parts, and should not be omitted from your tour.

The first landmark of interest is the world-famous Grimersta River, which empties into Loch Ceann Hulvaig. Holding the record for the number of salmon caught by one angler in one day, this little river experiences phenomenal runs of fish in the summer months. It drains the long zigzagging basin of Loch Langavat, which extends right down the centre of Lewis.

Past Meavaig the road swings west through the steep glen of Valtos. A small track gives access to the 3-mile (5-km) gneiss basin of Loch Suainaval, at over 70 metres the deepest fresh-water loch in Lewis. Four hundred and twenty-nine metres above, the rugged and stark hulk of Suainaval affords panoramic views over the great bite of Loch Roag to the north, and the humps of the Lewis hills to the southwest. Suainaval discharges into one of the loveliest bays in the Hebrides at Uig Sands. It was here, in 1831, that a magnificent set of ivory chessmen was discovered in a sandbank. The road continues for another 8 miles (13 km) to the village of Brenish and gives access to some isolated hills around Loch Tamanavay and Tealasvay.

On the eastern shore of Loch Roag you can visit one of the most interesting historical features of the islands—the Standing Stones of Callanish. Second only in importance to Stonehenge, the main avenue is 980 feet (300 metres) in length, the 46 megaliths arranged in a cruciform pattern and dating from about 3000 BC. In addition there are two chambers, a dolmen and cairn. They make a wonderful sight silhouetted against the western sky.

It is a good 90-minute walk to Carloway from here. This village boasts one of the best surviving examples of an Iron-Age broch tower in Scotland. The massive dry stone walls, 13 feet (4 metres) thick and 33 feet (10 metres) high, dominate a rocky ridge, at one time overlooking the 'black houses' of the village below. The broch has been restored and the construction of the stair, galleries and wall-chambers is clearly defined.

The northwest coastline of Lewis provides some fine walking, though you will be exposed to the full force of the Atlantic wind which makes progress a battle. The Butt of Lewis, where a lighthouse over-looks awesome black cliffs, averages a gale every three days! More sheltered is the picturesque little fishing village at Port of Ness, which is tucked round the east side of the Butt.

From the isolation of northern Lewis to the busy island capital of Stornoway is only 25 miles (40 km). After walking on the remote west coast, it always seems strange jostling along crowded footpaths. In summer, the resident population of 5500 is swollen with tourist traffic, and dozens of fishing boats line the harbour. Apart from fishing, the main industries are now oil-related, although Harris Tweed is still produced in large quantities. At one time the economy depended totally on the Orb-stamped cloth, five million yards often being produced in a year.

Lewis Castle, built in 1840 and donated to the people of Stornoway by Lord Leverhulme, is worth a visit. The building is now used as a college, where navigation, textiles, building and engineering are taught. Facing the castle, across the inner harbour, is an eighteenth-century net loft house, probably the oldest surviving building in the town.

The east coast of Lewis south of Stornoway is often neglected by visitors yet it is a splendid area with which to conclude. Loch Erisort penetrates deep into the heart of the island, almost linking up with the head of Loch Seaforth. The walking is quite easy, with miles of little tracks and roads weaving through a peaceful landscape of loch, hill and shore.

North Uist

Across the Sound of Harris the 75,000 acres of North Uist comprise a landscape of real quality. When walking on this island, and indeed those to the south, I am always surprised by the tremendous contrasts.

The west coast is scalloped with huge bays of pure sand, often set under steep dunes or ridges, and against a backdrop of lush vegetation and machair. Feeding is good and cattle graze in abundance. The hills of North Uist are not high by Harris standards, but many do give comprehensive panoramas. The most amazing feature, however, is the complex network of fresh-water and tidal lochs. Loch Scadavay, for example, is quite bewildering, in that is measures merely 4 by 2 miles

(6 × 3 km) yet is so labyrinthine that its shoreline stretches for over 50 miles (80 km).

On the east coast Lochmaddy, the business centre and principal port, has a population of about 300, and is on the main route for RMS *Hebrides* from Uig and Tarbert. There are a bank, post office, hotel and several shops.

From the walking angle, the island is served by a 35-mile (56-km) circular road which links up most of the townships. Many minor roads and tracks radiate from the main route and penetrate into remote areas such as Berneray in the north or Lochportain in the northeast.

As you walk north from Lochmaddy the astonishing nature of the topography is soon apparent. The low watery basins of Lochs Fada, Strumore and Skealtar lie to the West, the blunted mounds of Maari (171 metres), Crogary (180 metres) and Blashaval (109 metres) are dead ahead and the riddled coastline of Lochmaddy is to the east. It is a 25-minute walk to the little pier at Sponish harbour, where an alginate factory processes seaweed. Two miles (3 km) further on, a side road runs for 7½ miles (12 km) to the village of Lochportain and on to remote Hoe Beg. This road weaves an incredible route between the shores of fresh- and salt-water lochs. The hilly ground to the east rises to 150 metres and is a good vantage point over the Minch.

Newtonferry is 3 miles (5 km) to the north of the A893. En route the walker passes Beinn Mhor (190 metres), a hill from which the true wilderness of North Uist can be experienced. A wrinkled plain of water and peat fans out to the south, contrasting with massive sweeps of sand right along the north coast, with the islands of Boreray, Pabbay and Berneray in the distance. The last supports a population of around 300, mostly occupied with sheep farming and lobster fishing.

The Uists are rich in machair. It is a delight to walk the peaceful grasslands in one of those long clear summer twilights, particularly the lands surrounding Tigharry and Hougharry in the extreme west. The beaches at Scalpaig and Hosta are worth seeing, Scolpaig being the nearest point to St Kilda, which can easily be seen on a clear day. Balranald, 1 mile (1½ km) to the south of Hosta, is a 1500-acre reserve run by the Royal Society for the Protection of Birds. It has a breeding population of over 40 species, including the rare red-necked phalarope. There is a resident warden to whom enquiries should be made, if time is to be spent on the reserve.

The southern part of North Uist is split by Loch Eport, the entrance to which funnels between the rocky slopes of South Lee (281 metres). The B894 skirts the southern coast, ending up at the village of Sidinish.

From the main road this walk takes a good hour each way.

The highest mountain on North Uist, Eaval (347 metres), stands to the southeast of Sidinish, but is almost totally surrounded by the 15 rock basins of Loch Obisary. Eaval is an isolated peak, and the view from the summit encompasses many of the islands and lochs between North Uist and Benbecula. Only by climbing the hills can you fully appreciate the hidden contrasts of the Uist landscape.

Benbecula

The delightful island of Benbecula lies sandwiched between the Uists and is connected to them by artificial causeways. You will be impressed by the myriads of little lochs and islands which dot the landscape, although in the whole island there is but one hill. Rueval (125 metres) is bleak and windswept, but from it you can see the Cuillins of Skye and out over the Monach Isles, 9 miles (14 km) off the west coast.

The island's 70 crofts are found on the fertile west strip of machair, the remaining land area being mostly heather and moor. Benbecula is famed for its wildlife. The lochs breed plump trout and the seashores are alive with duck, geese, waders and sea birds.

You can use the A865 which runs up the centre of the island or the more remote B892 which circles round the western shore. A complete circuit using both these roads could be achieved in about four hours' easy walking. This could be reduced by using one of the four cross-country minor roads which link the main routes.

Walking the east coast of Benbecula is a wet business. The land is all low-lying, the coastline totally shattered with dozens of irregular inlets. Uskavagh is the main tidal loch, but to reach the isolated peninsulas of Rossinish, Meanish and Rarnish involves a damp slog along footpaths, which branch from the main A865. It was from Rossinish that Prince Charlie was smuggled over to Skye after his defeat at Culloden.

In the south of the island, the island of Grimsay and the pier at Peters Port lie several miles east of the main west coast road junction. Grimsay houses a lobster compound, this form of fishing being the mainstay of the crofting pattern. The pier, 1 mile (1½ km) further east, was built in the last century, at the cost of £2000, after considerable local pressure. It was, however, located in a dangerous stretch of water, as well as in total isolation from mainland roads, so it was rarely used by skippers.

South Uist

The causeway over the South Ford gives access to South Uist, the second-largest island of the Southern Hebrides. It is 27 miles (43 km) long and 7 miles (11 km) wide, and shelters a population of about 2500, most of whom live in the south in the townships of Daliburgh and North Boisdale.

The most interesting physical feature of South Uist is the flat unbroken belt of machair which extends right down the west coast for over 20 miles (32 km). Great stretches of it are no more than 33 feet (10 metres) above sea level, the highest section being a mere 115 feet (35 metres) above the sea. The east is more hilly, with peaks over 600 metres parted by deep-cutting inlets, and only a few inland lochs. All this adds up to some superb walking countryside, easily accessible from the main A865 which runs down the west coast.

Lochboisdale, in the southeast, is a busy little port from which the car ferry operates to Oban, and to Castlebay in Barra. There are a police station, fishing hotel, bank, hospital and several shops. Walking inland from the pier, the A865 soon joins the B888, and here it is 4½ miles (7 km) to the southern tip of the island, where at Pollachar you are treated to a fine view over the Sound of Barra. Extending eastwards close to the shore, the road passes the jetty from which ferry boats cross to Eriskay and Barra. There is a scheduled service, but this can be supplemented by arrangements made with the ferryman. The road swings north to South Glen Dale, between the humps of Easaval and Maraval, whose summits afford good vantage points over the Sound of Eriskay.

Parts of the east coast are quite rugged. The four deep fiord-like indentations form the sheltered anchorages of Lochcarnan, Loch Skipport, Loch Eynort and Loch Boisdale. The hills of Triuirebheinn, Stulaval and Arnaval, the three highest of an interesting group of ten, rise to over 350 metres, and lie between Lochs Boisdale and Eynort. Between the first two hills is Bealach Chaolais (Pass of the Narrows), where stand a typical example of an earth house in a good state of preservation and the remains of several circular stone chambers.

This is idyllic upland walking terrain, the hills almost totally smothered in a coat of grass and heather. The lochs which you can see from the eastern heights are quite unusual, as in most cases they are on the west side of the fertile sandy strip, as opposed to the east, which is usually the case. The result is a most suitable habitat for brown trout which thrive well on the rich feeding afforded. The island is in fact a mecca for anglers, many of the streams and rivers having excellent runs of sea trout and salmon.

Bheinn Mhor (620 metres), just 2 miles (3 km) north of Loch Eynort, is the highest peak in South Uist. Hecla, to the north, also rises to over 600 metres, and is a well-shaped hill. Most Hebridean climbs do not disappoint as regards the view, and both these peaks are no exception, the distant hills of Ulster, 100 miles (160 km) to the south, being visible in good weather. In addition, the slopes and gorges support many alpine plants, unusual grasses, sedges and ferns.

On the west coast, opposite Bheinn Mhor, stand the stark ruins of Ormaclett Castle, an unfortified eighteenth-century house, which was once the home of the McDonalds of Clan Ranald. The building took seven years to construct, and was only inhabited for a further seven years before being accidentally burned to the ground during a celebration feast.

The short walk to the promontory of Rubha Ardvule is most worthwhile as the scenery is particularly pleasing. Isolated Ardvule Loch is right at the edge of the coast, where the remains of an Iron-Age fort are situated. This loch supports many species of wildfowl.

Flora MacDonald, whose association with the fugitive Prince Charlie is well known, was born at Milton, several miles to the south of this point, and a shieling on the nearby slopes of Sheaval was their first meeting place. Today the birthplace is marked by a monument, only the barest outline of the house remaining.

Wherever one walks in the Uists the ancient remains of cairns, wheelhouses, duns, brochs and standing stones provide a fascinating insight into the history of the first island dwellers. The wheelhouse structures are of particular interest, with thick stone piers, constructed like the spokes of a wheel, radiating from a central hub and forming eight or more compartments. The diameter of these early dwellings was about 33 feet (10 metres), and they were constructed in a dry stone manner, either free-standing or in pits excavated from the sand dunes. Wheelhouse remains are to be found at Kilpheder and Drimore, to the west of the hill of Rueval. It is here also that you will pass the slender statue of Our Lady of the Isles. Designed by Hew Lorimer, it overlooks the Ministry of Defence rocket range and the long sandy shores to the west.

One of the most pleasant walking areas of South Uist is the 4158-acre Nature Conservancy reserve at Loch Druidibeg, which was created in 1957. A full-time warden is based at Stilligarry. The islands, lochs and shores provide a haven for a rich variety of bird life including white-fronted and barnacle geese, black-throated and red-throated diver, hen harrier, golden eagle and red-necked phalarope.

Barra

The delightful little island of Barra is the largest of a chain of 15 islands which lie in a scattered line at the end of South Uist. Although it is possible to circumnavigate the entire island in an afternoon, there is much of interest to delay the walker. Barra has a long and fascinating history, there are several hills around the 200-metre mark, a great variety of wild flowers and over 150 species of birds have been recorded.

The sheltered harbour of Castlebay lies under the slopes of the highest hill, Heaval (384 metres), from which there is a splendid view of all the islands in the southern archipelago, and to the east the Knoydart and Ardnamurchan mainland.

Kissimul Castle stands on a rocky outcrop right in the centre of Castlebay. Soundly built from local stone, it was restored in 1937 by Robert Lister MacNeil, forty-fifth Chief of the Clan MacNeil, whose association with Barra stretches back to Norse times. Castlebay was also the centre of a thriving herring industry in the late nineteenth century, when over 400 boats congregated in the bay during the height of the season.

Two miles (3 km) west of Castlebay, Ben Tangaval rises to 333 metres and overlooks the narrow Sound of Vatersay. A new 40-bedroom hotel has been built at Tangusdale, 1 mile (1½ km) to the north, and nearby are the remains of a small square tower, several chambered cairns and a number of standing stones.

In the north of the island Scurrival Point penetrates 4 miles (6 km) into the Sound of Barra, its highest point being Ben Eoligarry, the northeast slope of which was the burial place of the MacNeils. There is a group of small roofless buildings here, which are made from rough stone and were at one time thatched. A little track passes this place and leads to the remains of what is thought to have been a circular galleried dun. From the ring road the walk takes a good 90 minutes each way.

Also at this end of the island is the famous Cockle Strand where a large expanse of sand allows passenger aircraft to land, depending of course on the tides.

Other beaches which you may like to visit include Borve and Allasdale in the west and Vaslane in the northeast.

Bibliography

The Islands of Scotland, (Scottish Mountaineering Club District Guide)
MacDonald, Donald, *Lewis–A History of the Island*
Murray, W. H., *The Islands of Western Scotland*
Martin, Martin, *A Description of the Western Isles of Scotland (1716)*
Thompson, Francis, *The Uists and Barra*
Thompson, Francis, *Harris Tweed–The Story of a Hebridean Industry*
The Island Blackhouse, (HMSO)

The Wind

What does the wind say on the hill
When yellow comes the daffodil
And the willow wren begins
His little song among the whins.

What does the wind say on the ben
When the roses bloom again
And in the grey ark of the gloaming
Woodcocks croak and doves are homing.

What does the wind say on the tops
When hairy forearms stook the crops
And when red the sunsets die
And skeins of wild geese cross the sky.

What does the wind say on the height
When close and rigg and park are white
When middens smoke within the yard
And tractor ruts are iron hard.

Notes: Bens, Glens, and Lochs are indexed under B, G, and L rather than the second part of the name. Names of Munros are indicated by an asterisk * before the entry. We have not attempted to index every place name in the text, but all significant points and people are included.